INDUSTRIAL GROWTH, TRADE, AND DYNAMIC PATTERNS IN THE JAPANESE ECONOMY

INDUSTRIAL GROWTH, TRADE, AND DYNAMIC PATTERNS IN THE JAPANESE ECONOMY

MIYOHEI SHINOHARA

UNIVERSITY OF TOKYO PRESS

Publication of this book was aided by a grant from The Japan Foundation.

Third printing, 1987
ISBN 4−13−047022−1

ISBN 0−86008−297−0

Printed in Japan

CONTENTS

PREFACE

In 1980, Japan, an island country inhabited by a population only half as large as that of the United States, produced almost as much steel and as many automobiles as the latter, and its products are flooding world markets. It is, therefore, no wonder that the Western industrial nations have lately become increasingly edgy over the ever-rising tide of Japanese exports into their markets. Given the serious threats the onslaught of Japanese exports pose to the employment of their workers, the United States and the European Community countries understandably are alarmed by it and have begun to take a searching look into the industrial policy of Japan, its business management, culture, and social structure to determine the sources of its economic vitality.

Until as late as the first half of the 1950s, Japan had been a struggling developing economy, but in the short span of 30 years that ensued, Japan managed to leap forward and finally forge ahead of the Western industrial nations in many important fields of industry.

This book, however, is not intended to add yet another paean to the already proliferating litany of self-eulogy. Rather, it aims at shedding a new light on the subject. In fact, most of the articles contained in this book were written originally in Japanese and published 10 to 20 years ago, although their translations have appeared in English-language magazines only since 1979.

This book is divided into three parts. Part I reviews the postwar development of an industrial structure unique to Japan, examines the industrial policies pursued by the Ministry of International Trade and Industry (MITI), and analyzes some of the peculiarities of the Japanese business community which was built on loosely-structured business groups, on the one hand, and a rigidly hierachical coalition of parent companies and subsidiaries, on the other. I have long been pointing to the critical importance of the supply side of the economy, but such an argument has until recently been dismissed as a heretical minority view—so much so that the recent chorus of scholars, here and abroad, chanting the praise of supply-side economics came as an embarrassing surprise to me.

Part II examines, from a historical perspective, the factors which contributed to sharp and sustained increases in Japan's exports and the violent changes that have occurred in the structure of its exports. "The Rise and Fall of Economic Powers" (Chapter 4) surveys the processes through which Great Britain was replaced as the world's industrial leader by the United States, whose leadership position, in turn, has come under serious challenge from Japan, with newly industrializing countries (NICs) waiting in the wings to overtake Japan. This is a situation which I describe by a new coinage as the "boomerang effect." By all tests, the concept of the boomerang effect appears to be a theorem aptly describing the historical pattern of development of capitalism since the Industrial Revolution. In this connection, it is to be kept in mind that although the systems of Joseph Schumpeter and Karl Marx have often been called the "magnificent dynamics," they failed to relate the rise and fall of economic powers to the "grand dynamics" fueled by the competition among economic powers. Particularly when applied to the reality of today's world economy, the concept of magnificent dynamics is less than adequate for explaining the recent experience the world has had.

What is more, the boomerang effect generated by local siting of industrial facilities and direct investment in Pacific basin countries by multinational corporations has already initiated a process of "intra-industry" division of labor among these countries. What is happening in these countries as a result of such direct investment may be characterized as a "horizontal" division of labor as opposed to the "vertical" division of labor which the colonizing powers had imposed on their colonies before the war.

In Chapter 7, which deals with the question of the trade friction which has recently made bad blood between Japan and its trading partners, I take a position a bit critical of textbook-type free trade advocates in general and Japan's blitz-like export drive in particular. To casual observers, the free trade advocated by the United States until a short few years ago and now by Japan may seem plausible, even fitting to their position as economic powers. But one should not forget that there is a limit to what free trade can do under the given conditions of the world economy. Indeed, the need for the economic powers to clarify what free trade can or cannot do and to explore new avenues for enlightened international cooperation has never been more urgent.

Chapter 9 (Part III) touches briefly on the process of economic development of Japan in the postwar years. Chapter 10 sheds light on the mysterious Japanese habit of saving. Despite the jolting economic dislocations caused by two oil crises and the resulting economic slowdown from a 10% to a 5% annual growth, Japanese families continued to save more than 20% of their incomes. This defies explanation in terms of any theory now in currency in the United States.

For many years now, the concepts of Juglar cycles and Kondratieff cycles have been buried in oblivion. Chapter 11 resurrects them and stresses the fact that the dynamic process of economic development Japan experienced in the postwar years cannot be adequately explained without the help of the concept of the Juglar cycle. In fact, the cycle is in operation in the United States: it has produced demonstrable ripple effects in the form of a reversed cycle on the ratio of business fixed investment to GNP at a regular interval of about ten years, as compared to the counterpart cycle in Japan. The same cycle is also in operation in South Korea and Taiwan, and I wish to direct the attention of economists of all countries to the existence of such a cycle. The experience of South Korea, Taiwan, and Japan serves to demonstrate the validity of Schumpeter's notion that the more dynamic economic expansion is, the more cyclical economic activity becomes. This reminds me of Schumpeter's remark that the "result trend" is a shadow of cycle.

Perhaps I am not the only one who recalled the Kondratieff cycle in the wake of the first oil crisis. In my view, the upswing of the Kondratieff cycle was energized by three sources of long-term motive power, namely, war, technological breakthroughs, and money supply, and topped out when it hit the ceiling of energy constraints. This is a kind of "limit cycle" theory.

The supplementary chapter entitled "Technical Progress and Production Function" contains a study I completed in 1972 (the last year of my public service as President of the Economic Research Institute of the Economic Planning Agency) on the basis of data covering the years of 1960 through 1971. In that study, I used several production function approaches based on time series and cross-sections, and sought to evaluate in depth the state of technological advance achieved by different industry groups. The findings were tested by means of measuring total factor productivity. For all the innovativeness of the approach, however, at base it was nothing more than a neo-classical approach. To be sure, it differs from the methods of analysis employed in other studies discussed earlier in the book, but I must admit that it is a second-best approach in the sense that no approach other than the neo-classical one lends itself to dealing empirically with the question of technological progress. In conducting the research embodied in this supplementary chapter, I had the benefit of the able collaboration of Mr. Kiyoshi

Asakawa, then an official of the Economic Planning Agency, but I am solely responsible for the analysis and interpretation of the findings of the research.

Admittedly, Japanese are seriously handicapped in presenting their studies in the English language, and I am not an exception to this rule. Particularly, given the press of work I have to contend with, in addition to teaching, preparation of the present volume proved to be rather demanding. Nevertheless, this represents the fifth English-language book with which I am credited, and as such, it is a source of profound personal gratification. If the present volume can be instrumental in conveying any insights to its readers, I could not hope for a better reward.

The present volume contains edited versions of articles carried in various English-language journals or papers presented at international meetings. Chapter 11 is a new paper. The original publishers of the other chapters are noted in notes attached to each chapter. I wish to express my sincere appreciation to the publishers who allowed me to use in this book the articles first carried in their journals. I am particularly grateful to Ms. Susan Schmidt of the Tokyo University Press for her valuable editorial help. My thanks also go to the members of the Asian Club and the Institute of Developing Economies and Ms. Anne Miyashiro for their translation and proofreading services.

I

INDUSTRIAL GROWTH
AND INDUSTRIAL POLICY

1

EVOLUTION OF THE
POSTWAR INDUSTRIAL STRUCTURE

Economic Growth and Industrial Structure

Until its upward climb was halted by the oil crisis of 1973, Japan's real gross national product had been growing at an average annual rate of 10% since the early 1950s. Once the postwar rehabilitation period ended around 1955, rapid economic growth wrought profound changes in the industrial structure of Japan.

First of all, the share of primary industry (agriculture, forestry, and fishing) in the net national product (at factor cost) was halved within ten years, from 23% in 1955 to 11.3% in 1965, and continued to shrink to as low as 4.7% by 1977. This sharp shrinkage in the relative importance of the primary sector was the result of the extraordinarily rapid economic growth which continued for 22 years running, during which real gross national product increased 6.3-fold and the industrial production index 9.7-fold.

According to the Labor Force Survey, 16.54 million people, or 40.2% of the nation's total labor force, were engaged in primary industry in 1955. By 1977 their numbers had decreased by 9.93 million to 6.61 million, with the result that the ratio of those engaged in primary industry dropped to 11.9% of the total labor force. Since the total number of those employed in all industries increased by 12.23 million from 1955 to 1977, if we add the 9.93 million dropped from primary-sector employment in those same years, the number of those who found jobs in other sectors amounted to 22.16 million. In terms of sectoral employment, they can be broken down as in Table 1.

As a result of these developments, the structure of employment by different sectors underwent a marked change during the period of 1955–77 (Table 2). The ratio of those employed in primary industry suffered a dramatic decline (28.3 points), while that of those employed in the tertiary sector registered the largest increase, 17.3 points (15.1 points

* This chapter was originally published as "Industrial Structure of Postwar Japan," *Journal of Enterprise Management*, Vol. 2 No. 3, 1980.

Table 1. Increase in Employment by Sector, 1955–77

Sector	Increase in no. of employed persons
	(in thousands)
Manufacturing	5,840
Construction	3,180
Transportation, communication, power and gas utilities, and city water service	1,790
Commerce, finance, insurance, and real estate	6,570
Service industry	4,470
Others	310
Total	22,160

for commerce and services plus 2.2 points for transportation, communication, and utilities).

The ratio of those employed in the construction industry itself is still low, but the fact that it more than doubled from 4.4% in 1955 to 9.2% in 1977 attests to the vigorous pace of growth in construction.

Table 2. Employment Composition by Sector

Sector	1955	1965	1977	Changes
				(points)
Agriculture, forestry, and fisheries	40.2%	23.5%	11.9%	−28.3
Manufacturing and mining	19.5	24.9	25.5	+ 6.0
Construction	4.4	7.3	9.2	+ 4.8
Transportation, communication, and utilities	4.7	6.2	6.9	+ 2.2
Commerce and services	31.2	38.4	46.3	+15.1

Source: Bureau of Statistics, Office of the Prime Minister, *The Labor Force Survey*.

Manufacturing played the role of a primary engine propelling the economy forward during the period, and it is thus perhaps to be expected that its employment ratio should have increased from 19.5% in 1955 to 25.5% in 1977. However, the rapid technological developments in manufacturing during those years make the sharpness of its rise a cause for surprise. The employment share increase for commerce and services, large as it was initially, has continued to accelerate, concomitant with the rapidly growing economy.

These changes in employment ratios notwithstanding, the mining and manufacturing sector has made unexpectedly little gain in its share of of the net national product (24.3% in 1955, 28.9% in 1965 and 26.9% in 1977). Why? As noted earlier, the volume of industrial production grew at a much faster rate than the real gross national product. Despite the increase in the GNP deflator, the prices of industrial products remained relatively stable, at least until the oil crisis of 1973. It is to be noted, therefore, that the decline in the relative prices of industrial products in the said period was responsible for the virtually unchanged share of mining and manufacturing in the net national product.

While industrial production as a whole increased 10.32-fold during the period 1955–77, the rate of increase for individual industry groups varied widely (Table 3). The automobile industry was the largest gainer, and its growth had the most far-reaching effect on other industry groups: production of passenger cars increased a whopping 297-fold for these years. While new types of consumer durables (such as refrigerators and TV sets), synthetic fibers, and other new products set the pace, the growth in conventional textiles, some of the chemicals, and coal lagged far behind the average tempo in mining and manufacturing.

Table 3. Changes in the Volume of Production by Commodities, 1955–78

Product	1955	1978	-fold
Passenger cars (thous. units)	20	5,939	296.95
Refrigerators (thous. units)	31	4,561	147.13
TV sets (thous. units)	137	13,117	88.45
Truck chassis (thous. units)	43	3,035*	69.98
Synthetic fabrics (mil. meters)	54	2,915	53.98
Polyvinyl chloride (thous. metric tons)	32	1,204	37.20
Pianos (units)	11,510	364,930	31.71
Heavy fuel oil (thous. kl)	4,081	124,270	30.45
Rolled aluminum (thous. tons)	52	1,415	27.21
Machine tools (units)	6,591	176,684	26.81
Watches and clocks (thous. units)	5,798	88,768	15.31
Steel vessels (completed) (thous. G/T)	735	10,645*	14.49
A.C. generators (thous. KVA)	1,620	22,725	14.03
Photographic film (thous. square meters)	8,006	91,046	11.37
Crude steel (thous. tons)	9,408	102,103	10.85
Standard induction motors (thous. kw)	491	5,018	10.22
Cameras (thous. units)	1,065	9,670*	9.08
Cement (thous. tons)	10,563	84,882	8.04
Electric power (mil. kwh)	54,917	431,363	7.85
Caustic soda (thous. tons)	517	2,777	5.37
Sheet glass (thous. case equiv.)	6,650	34,547	5.20
Woolen fabrics (mil. square meters)	153	336	2.19
Sulphuric acid (thous. metric tons)	3,290	6,435	1.96
Woolen yarn (thous. metric tons)	84	109	1.30
Cotton yarn (thous. metric tons)	419	448	1.07
Raw silk (thous. 60-kg. bales)	289	266	0.92
Coal (thous. metric tons)	42,423	18,991	0.45

Source: Ministry of International Trade and Industry, *Current Production Statistics Survey*.
Note: (*) is a 1977/1955 comparison.

Thus, a closer look at the growth process, rapid though it was on the whole, clearly reveals a division into growing, stagnating, and declining industry groups. Past experience suggests that dynamic growth in the industrial sector is often accompanied by uneven distribution of vigor among its segments and that growth cannot be achieved without flexible changes in its internal structure. And this is borne out by the extensive variations of changes in the 27 product categories selected at random and listed in Table 3.

While the production index of manufacturing rose 10.9-fold in 1955–78, that of the machinery industry as a whole increased 30.6-fold (17.3-fold for general machinery, 64.6-fold for electrical machinery, 28.9-fold for transportation equipment, and 23.1-fold for precision machinery). Accordingly, the share of the machinery industry in terms of value added, as shown in the Census of Manufactures, has necessarily increased significantly. Its ratio in value added gained dramatically from 18.5% in 1955 to 34.8% in 1970, and then levelled off in the 1970s (Table 4). This is largely attributable to the slowdown of the economy that began in the early 1970s, which took some of the steam out of the machinery industry. This is evident from the fact that while the production index for mining and manufacturing had increased 175.3% during the eight-year period of 1962–70, it rose only a meager 32.8% during the succeeding eight-year period of 1970–78. A similar situation occurred with respect to real gross national product: it rose 127.0% during the eight-year period of 1962–70, while it grew only 52.0%

Table 4. Relative Compositions of the Various Segments of the Machinery Industry in Terms of Value Added

(in billions of yen)

		Manu-factur-ing in-dustry	General machin-ery	Trans-portation equipment	Electrical machin-ery	Precision machin-ery	Total (%)
Firms employ-ing 4 or more	1955	2,099	133(6.3%)	111(5.3%)	120(5.7%)	26(1.2%)	18.5
	1960	4,837	498(10.3%)	500(10.3%)	444(9.2%)	74(1.5%)	31.3
All manu-fac-turers	1960	4,963	503(10.1)	501(10.1)	446 (9.0)	75(1.5)	30.7
	1965	9,665	893 (9.2)	893 (9.2)	881 (9.1)	160(1.7)	29.2
	1970	24,572	2,900(11.8)	2,925(11.9)	2,332 (9.5)	388(1.6)	34.8
	1975	42,345	4,715(11.1)	4,144 (9.8)	4,328(10.2)	777(1.8)	32.9
	1976	48,934	5,164(10.6)	5,378(11.0)	5,238(10.7)	870(1.8)	34.1
	1977	52,460	5,379(10.3)	5,858(11.2)	5,741(10.9)	1,032(2.0)	34.4
	1978	57,162	5,715(10.0)	6,516(11.4)	5,576 (9.8)	1,132(2.0)	33.2

Source: MITI, *Census of Manufactures.*

during the succeeding eight-year period of 1970–78. It is readily understandable that the relative composition of the machinery industry, which is sensitive to the nation's economic ebb and flow, should have increased in the years before 1970 but since have levelled off. During the process of sustained, rapid economic growth, the relative composition of the machinery industry increased, but as the economy slowed down, it stopped growing.

The share of key industries such as steel, non-ferrous metals, and chemicals did not increase appreciably, as we shall see in the next section. If the machinery industry had devoted itself exclusively to the production of producer goods, its weight too would have declined. Actually, however, the growing demand for passenger cars and other consumer durables (home appliances, etc.), combined with increasing export demand for machinery, fueled production growth, thus enabling the machinery industry to maintain its share at a high level.

Changes in the industrial structure, as a function of economic growth, brought about this series of changes. However, an industrial structure which is so rigid as to be unreceptive to smooth and flexible change or unconducive to switchovers of product lines would prove to be a drag on its growth potential. In this sense, maintenance of rapid growth would require what Kindleberger called the "capacity to transform" (1). It may be said that behind Japan's ability to sustain such rapid economic growth over a long period of time after the war lay the economy's capacity to transform. Thus, the causal relation between rapid economic growth and structural change of industry is not a one-way street but a reciprocal process; there was high-intensity feedback between the two.

Emphasis on Processing

Since the war, the Ministry of International Trade and Industry has devoted major efforts to fostering and developing key industries such as steel and petrochemicals. Up until the second half of the 1950s, the steel industry of Japan still lagged behind those of other industrial nations, and its unit cost of production—and, therefore, the price of its products—was substantially higher than those of its competitors. By the end of 1976, however, it had made rapid strides—so rapid, in fact, that seven of the world's ten best large-scale blast furnaces were operating in Japanese steel mills, among them Nippon Steel Corporation's steel mill at Oita (with a top furnace capacity of 5,070 m³). Today, the Japanese steel industry boasts the finest mill facilities and technological knowhow in the world. The same is true also of converters, continuous casting, and strip mill facilities (2).

In the area of petrochemicals, the industry actively sought, under the administrative guidance given by the Ministry of International Trade and Industry, to expand its capacity and upgrade its facilities and technology. Before 1964, none of the petrochemical complexes then existing in Japan had an annual capacity larger than 100,000 tons for ethylene equivalents. In the second half of the 1960s, however, a series of petrochemical plants capable of producing 100,000 tons of ethylene a year were built, and since 1969 an annual capacity of 300,000 tons has become the norm (2).

The development of such key industries did much to induce the expansion of many affiliated and processing industries such as automobiles, machinery, plastics, synthetic rubber, and synthetic fibers through the so-called forward linkage effect. And the demand-induced expansion of the processing industries and the parallel development of the key industries combined in turn to strengthen markedly the international competitive position of these sectors.

Now, this created an unforeseen situation: despite the heavy emphasis which the Ministry of International Trade and Industry had placed up to 1970 on the development of capital-intensive key industries, the less capital-intensive processing sectors, which had required little in the way of incentives and protection, outperformed the key industries.

Table 5 compares the growth of the key industries with that of the processing industries. It compares, as examples, textiles (yarns and fabrics) with apparel, lumber and wood products with furniture and furnishings, and steel and nonferrous metals with machinery—all in terms of shipments and numbers of employees.

Taken for the years from 1955 to 1978, the yen value of shipments of textiles, a basic industry, increased 6.6-fold as against 32.5-fold for apparels, a processing industry; that of lumber and wood products increased 15.6-fold as against 37.9-fold for processed furniture and furnishings; and steel and nonferrous metals increased 20.7-fold and 19.0-fold, respectively, as against 40- to 65-fold for machinery. In the case of "others" (which presumably cover sundry products), the yen value of shipments of the processing sector increased 52.9-fold during the 22-year period.

Thus, the yen value of shipments in the processing sectors is decidedly larger than that in the basic sectors. It must be noted, however, that production of basic goods is capital-intensive; their prices rose relatively slowly or even decreased, whereas, given the labor-intensiveness of the processing largely done by small-and medium-sized companies, the prices of processed goods tended to rise faster in step with rising wage and materials costs. Therefore, the great differences in the growth

Table 5. Basic vs. Processing Industries
   A: Shipments

| Industry group | In billions of yen | | | | In -fold | | |
	1955	1965	1975	1978	1965/1955	1975/1965	1978/1955
Textiles	1,096	2,602	6,457	7,236	2.38	2.48	6.60
Apparel	85	441	2,180	2,764	5.19	4.94	32.52
Lumber & wood prod.	274	1,057	3,618	4,272	3.86	3.42	15.59
Furniture & furnishings	65	402	1,974	2,465	6.18	4.91	37.92
Steel	650	2,691	11,306	13,471	4.14	4.20	20.72
Non-ferrous metals	280	1,165	3,909	5,311	4.16	3.36	18.97
General machinery	312	2,292	10,611	13,640	7.35	4.63	43.72
Electrical machinery	251	2,301	10,821	16,311	9.17	4.70	64.98
Transportation equip-ment	371	2,854	14,793	20,291	7.69	5.18	54.69
Precision machinery	56	383	1,729	2,716	6.84	4.51	48.50
Metal products	219	1,380	6,573	8,831	6.30	4.76	40.32
Others	133	976	5,060	7,039	7.34	5.18	52.92

   B: Number of Employees

| Industry group | In thousands of persons | | | | In -fold | | |
	1956	1965	1975	1978	1965/1955	1975/1965	1978/1955
Textiles	1,061	1,327	996	867	1.25	0.75	0.82
Apparel	144	311	531	547	2.16	1.71	3.80
Lumber & wood prod.	383	528	465	415	1.38	0.88	1.08
Furniture & furnishings	145	250	315	306	1.72	1.26	2.11
Steel	276	480	506	449	1.74	1.05	1.63
Non-ferrous metals	99	176	209	191	1.78	1.19	1.93
General machinery	383	902	1,102	1,055	2.36	1.23	2.75
Electrical machinery	233	851	1,214	1,240	3.65	1.43	5.32
Transportation equip-ment	322	664	945	893	2.06	1.42	2.77
Precision machinery	79	193	239	258	2.44	1.24	3.27
Metal products	358	657	855	829	1.84	1.30	2.32
Others	221	481	615	627	2.18	1.28	2.84

Source: MITI, *Census of Manufactures.*

of the yen value of shipments may largely be due to changes in the relative prices of the processed goods as against those of basic goods.

Obviously, such differences can be corrected for by deflating the yen value of the shipments by price indices compiled for each product group; but given the diversity in the quality of processed goods, a satisfactory deflation may be difficult to make. Instead of price deflation, therefore, I checked whether similar results are obtainable by comparing basic industries with processing industries also in terms of numbers of employees. During the period from 1955 to 1978, the number of workers employed in the textile industry actually decreased by 18%, while those employed in the apparel industry increased 3.8-fold, manifesting in this case too the difference between the basic and processing industries. A similar situation is found in the lumber-related (1.1-fold against 2.1-fold) and the metals-related industries (1.6 ~ 1.9-fold against 2.3 ~ 5.3-fold). These findings confirm the general tendency for the number of workers employed in the processing industries to increase faster than that in the basic industries.

It was in 1967 that I first pointed out this empirical tendency. Subsequently, the Economic Survey released by the Economic Planning Agency took note of this tendency, and *The Basic Direction of Trade and Industrial Policy in the 1970s,* a position paper released in 1971 by the Council on Industrial Structure, called it the tendency towards a "knowledge-intensive industrial structure." This, in fact, is another way of describing what I termed an "industrial structure with a higher degree of processing," for the term "knowledge-intensive industry," by definition, covers the R&D-intensive industries (as typified by computers), the assembling industries (automobiles), and the fashion goods industry.

In any event, such an empirical tendency as the processing-oriented industrial structure must be subjected to some theorizing. In my opinion, the issue can be viewed from the dual standpoints of supply and demand. From the demand side, it may be observed that as society becomes increasingly affluent, demand inevitably becomes diversified, calling for a matching diversification and sophistication of the nation's industrial structure. This necessarily increases the importance of the processing sectors relative to the basic sectors.

When viewed from the supply side, successive technological breakthroughs enable an industry to cut down the materials input required for producing a unit of output, and this, in turn, reduces the weight of the "materials" or basic industry relative to the processing industry. A case in point is in electronics, where the replacement of the electric desk-calculator by the electronic desk-computer has brought about substantial savings in materials used, and the use of integrated circuits

(IC) and large-scale integration (LSI) further cut down on raw materials requirements and, at the same time, boosted the efficiency of the calculator. What is more, the increased value-added per unit of product generated through the development of a processing-oriented industrial structure was accompanied by a gradual but perceptible shift in the mode of production from one of a manual labor- and energy-intensive nature to one of a knowledge- and information-intensive nature based on scientific and technological innovation. This, in turn, created a tendency to move from more to less material consumption, from a production system based on single-item demand to one based on systems demand. This entailed a dramatic increase in the number of component parts, from a 10^3 level to, say, a 10^4 to 10^6 level (3); witness the technological breakthroughs from vacuum tube to IC, from IC to LSI, and from LSI to hybrid integrated circuits.

Technical advances are not confined merely to electronics; similar dramatic breakthroughs were achieved in other areas of technology, and these have combined to intensify the drive toward an ever higher degree of processing. In this context, an increasing sophistication of processing is unthinkable in the absence of continual technological innovation.

However, the development toward a higher degree of processing has two important implications. One is the tendency toward the development of technology-intensive industries, which leads to the production of increasingly sophisticated goods. The other is the increasing emphasis on the "soft" aspects of products, as typified by the growing consumer preference for "fashion goods." As the consumer grows more affluent, his taste for color, design, style, and elegance in the products he consumes becomes increasingly selective and discriminating— so much so that businesses not equipped with high-level technological knowhow, imagination, and managerial acumen cannot hope to grow.

Thus, one perceives a clear tilt in the Japanese industrial structure toward higher degrees of processing. This implies an increasing diversification of consumer demands and growing pressure on the supplier for greater efficiency in the use of materials and further sophistication and fashionableness in the products.

The fact that the large-scale capital investments in the steel and petrochemical industries which fueled the rapid economic growth in the postwar years were matched by no less vigorous development in the processing sectors largely made up of small- and medium-size companies should not be overlooked in viewing the postwar structural changes in Japanese industry.

Internationalization of the Industrial Structure

I argued for many years that the yen, at ¥360 to the dollar, was undervalued in terms of purchasing power parity and therefore was extremely favorable for the promotion of Japanese exports. This argument was borne out by the subsequent appreciation of the yen under the floating rate system adopted in 1973, under which at one time it rose above the ¥200 level (4). Thanks to the competitive edge which the exchange rate of ¥360 had provided, most of Japan's major industries were able by the beginning of the 1970s to participate in the export boom. The Ministry of International Trade and Industry (MITI) was also during these years directing the major thrust of its industrial policy to strengthening the competitive position of newly developing industries across the board. As a result, a large number of modern industries became export-oriented, and the growth rate of Japanese exports has become among the highest in the world.

However, the 1971 "Nixon shock" (the jolting effects on the world monetary system of the dollar defense plan announced by then-President Richard Nixon) dampened the ebullience of Japan's export industries, reminding the Japanese government that across-the-board development of export industries had limits. Nevertheless, even with the yen revaluation, many of the growth industries have steadily increased their ratios of exports to production since the 1960s. Table 6 summarizes the changes in the export/production ratio in some of the major industries. Except for short-term changes, this points to a long-term trend (1960–1975) of increasing ratios of exports to production.

The late Kaname Akamatsu published before World War II an article substantiating his theory of the "flying geese pattern" of industrial development—the successive pattern of imports-increased domestic production-exports (5). According to Akamatsu, a newly imported industry induces the development of associated domestic demand, thus stimulating the growth of domestic production of the same goods; and once the domestic industry expands enough, it will reduce its unit production cost, thus facilitating the expansion of exports. The product cycle theory advanced by Raymond Vernon also outlines a sequential pattern of "domestic production—exports—overseas investment" (6). I shall synthesize these two theories into a pattern of "imports—domestic production—exports—overseas investment." My feeling is that the development pattern of industry in postwar Japan provides a typical example of the Akamatsu-Vernon cycle.

Table 6 shows that the ratios of exports to production in some of the industry groups have consistently risen in the years indicated

Table 6. Ratio of Exports to Production

(%)

	Passenger cars	Ordinary and rolled steel	Automotive tires	Watches and clocks	Musical instruments	Machine tools
1960	4.2	12.6	6.1	4.7	7.4	3.6
1965	14.5	27.4	12.6	15.7	12.7	12.7
1970	22.8	22.8	13.0	37.0	19.9	7.7
1975	40.0	32.8	11.9	51.3	23.9	26.7
1976	50.5	39.8	12.8	58.5	22.7	33.3
1977	54.5	39.2	13.6	61.7	18.8	37.4
1978	50.9	36.1	11.7	57.4	18.2	44.3
1979	50.2	32.3	11.9	57.2	18.8	43.4

Source: Oriental Economist, *Economic Statistical Yearbook*, 1980.

therein, and it may be observed that the more growth-oriented an industry group is, the stronger is the tendency toward an increase in its export ratio. The term "increasing export ratio" refers to a situation in which exports of an industry group grow at a pace faster than that of its total production. Vernon further visualizes a growth in overseas investments in the wake of certain increases in the export ratio. In the case of Japan, overseas investment grew at a pace (22-fold) far quicker than that of exports during the eight years from 1965 to 1973, until its forward momentum was halted by the oil crisis and export growth outstripped investment growth. However, given the growing resistance on the part of industrial nations against the rapid inroads of Japanese products, the Japanese export drive may have to be eased sooner or later in favor of direct investment in these countries.

Because exports grew at a faster pace than domestic production in many growth industries, the shares of different industry groups in the nation's total exports have drastically changed. As shown in Table 7, the export share of textiles decreased sharply from 30.2% in 1960 to 4.8% in 1979, while that of machineries (including autos and ships) rose dramatically from 25.5% in 1960 (it was as low as 13.7% in 1955) to 61.3% in 1979. In no other country have the exports of machineries

Table 7: The Shares of Different Industry Groups in the Nation's Total Exports

(%)

	Foods	Textiles	Chemicals	Metals and metal products	Machineries
1960	6.3	30.2	4.5	14.0	25.5
1970	3.4	12.5	6.4	19.6	46.3
1979	1.2	4.8	5.9	17.8	61.3

Source: MITI, *White Paper on International Trade* (General Analysis).

accounted for as much as 60% of the total value of exports. In 1977, machinery exports' share was 47.9% for West Germany, 44.0% for Sweden, 43.0% for the United States, 37.4% for the United Kingdom and France, 33.8% for Italy, and 33.2% for Switzerland. Japan's brilliant success in machinery exports was due to a great capacity to transform in the highly income-elastic automobile industry.

Figure 1 clearly shows that even though Japan had actively tried to expand its heavy and chemical industries in the 1950s, their share in the nation's total exports remained far smaller than in the Western industrial nations. In the 1960s and 1970s, however, the export shares of the heavy and chemical industries increased sharply, to the point where they accounted for as much as 85.8%. This is a very substantial increase compared with the 38% share for these industries in 1955. In such a manner, the export structure has become heavily transformed toward the heavy and chemical industries—rather, I would say, toward the machinery industry—at a pace much faster than that of the industrial structure as a whole.

True, Japanese industry has entered the phase of direct overseas investment defined by the Vernon model, but another change can be seen in the offing: a boomerang effect of overseas investment (5). There is a real possibility that the low-cost products manufactured in countries to which Japanese capital and technology have been exported may eventually find their way back to the Japanese market. In other words, the boomerang which Japanese industries threw may recoil upon them. The boomerang effect is not confined to "reversed imports" into the domestic market. The increasing export share of products from South Korea and Taiwan, the beneficiaries of Japanese technology exports, in third-country markets (e.g. the United States and Europe)—at the expense of Japan's exports—is another form of the boomerang effect in the broader sense of the term. In fact, such an effect is being felt in the area of textiles, printing and publishing, electronics, and shipbuilding. Such a boomerang effect would generate pressure on Japan for an industrial adjustment by extension of the Akamatsu-Vernon product cycle model —for example, a relinquishing of third-country markets in the affected industries in favor of the recipient countries.

This is what is meant by the "internationalization of the industrial structure." The goal of developing self-contained modern industries and strengthening their international competitive position across the board was relevant to Japan's trade and industrial structure before 1970. But now attention should be focused on how to carry out such an international industrial adjustment. I will return to this subject elsewhere in this volume (see Chapter 5).

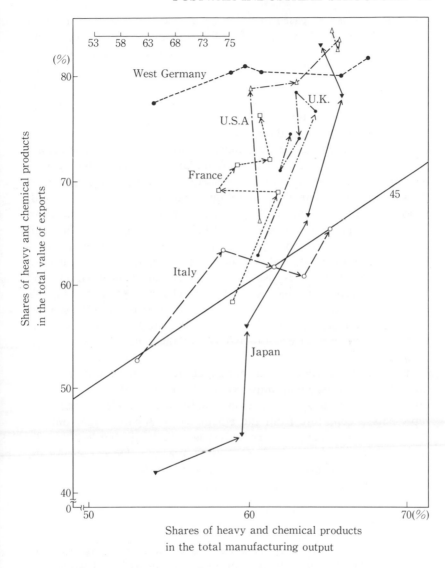

Figure 1. Heavy and chemical industries in the industrial and export structures, 1953–75.

Source: Ministry of International Trade and Industry, *White Paper on International Trade* (General Analysis), 1979.

In the eight years from 1970 to 1978, Japan's exports grew 5.1-fold, the United States's 3.3-fold, West Germany's 4.2-fold, France's 4.4-fold, and Great Britain's 4.3-fold, while those of newly industrializing countries (NICs) increased at much faster paces—15.2-fold for South Korea, 8.9-fold for Taiwan, 6.5-fold for Singapore, 5.5-fold for Spain, and 4.6-fold for Brazil. The question we must ask is whether the boomerang effect is all negative for investing countries. If the effect of the export of capital or technology is one-sidedly negative, then the boomerang effect is only a force pressing for industrial adjustment on the part of the exporters.

In actuality, however, direct investment in, and technology export to, these countries did generate increased exports of Japanese capital goods to these countries as the exported plants and technologies gained momentum. A case in point is the export of shipbuilding technology to South Korea. As Korea's shipbuilding industry began to take hold, exports of marine engines and other machinery components from Japan increased. This can be called a "positive" boomerang effect, although technology transfer to South Korea did at the same time have a "negative" boomerang effect in that exports of South Korean products to Japan and other countries rose sharply, thereby dramatically improving its current account balance with Japan. Overall, however, Japan's trade surplus with South Korea has tended to increase, and the same is true, to varying degrees, of its trade with other Asian NICs, even at the time when the current account balance of the NICs as a whole was tending to improve.

Now that it has become clear that direct investment has both negative and positive effects, Japan must recognize the inevitability of working out a scheme of horizontal division of labor with these countries. This represents a departure from the era in which Japan sought only to develop self-contained modern industries within its borders and to strengthen their international competitive position. During the 1970s, in fact, Japan has taken some steps in the direction of arriving at a viable international industrial structure.

Challenges

In addition to the problems discussed above, there are a myriad other problems related to the industrial structure. In this section, I would like to identify some of them.

(1) Stressing the Needs and Welfare of the People over an Export-Oriented Industrial Policy

One of the shortcuts for a resource-poor country to catch up with the Western advanced nations in a short period of time is to pursue an export-oriented industrial policy and set in motion a "virtuous circle" pattern of rapid economic growth through mutually reinforcing feedback between export promotion and domestic investment. However, sudden increases in exports and foreign currency reserves can accelerate an inflationary spiral. As part of the new stage of economic development, therefore, priority should be shifted from expansion of exports to widening of domestic demand, from industrial development to enchancing the welfare of the people.

It is difficult to pinpoint the concrete meaning of such a conversion. But there is no contradicting the fact that the necessity of fashioning a pluralistic and multifarious industrial structure designed to meet diversifying consumer needs, rather than the single-minded pursuit of a competitive international position for the strategic industries (steel, petrochemicals, and autos), will take on increasing importance in the coming years. Obviously, housing, mass transit, medical care, resource recycling, and the rationalization of the distribution system are the areas in need of greatest improvement. Other areas demanding attention include protection of the environment and improvement of community facilities.

(2) Building an Energy-Saving Industrial Structure
The crisis of 1973 jolted the nation into an awareness of the urgent need for creating an industrial structure which is energy-saving and less dependent on oil. In 1977, oil accounted for 73% of Japan's primary energy supply, compared with the 59% for France, 53% for West Germany, 48% for the United States, and 44% for the United Kingdom. Worse yet, Japan is dependent on imported energy for about 90% of its energy requirements. In 1977, Japan's imports of fossil fuel accounted for 44% of its total imports, as against 30% for the United States, 17% for West Germany, 21% for France, and 14% for the United Kingdom. Therefore, the pressure to reduce dependence on oil was far greater for Japan than for other industrial nations.

In the three-year period from 1970 to 1973, Japan's real gross national product grew 24.2% while its aggregate primary energy consumption increased 24.7%. Accordingly, the elasticity of energy consumption with respect to GNP was 1.02 (0.247/0.242). In the four-year period from 1973 to 1977, real GNP increased 15.5% while energy consumption increased only 0.5%. Thus, energy consumption elasticity with respect to GNP has decreased to 0.028 (0.007/0.247). This seemingly suggests that Japan has substantially conserved on its energy consumption, but its conservation is more apparent than real, for while energy consumption increased 0.7% during the four-year period, industrial production actually declined by 1.1%. So energy consumption per unit of industrial production may actually have increased a bit in the 1973–77 period. However, in the 1977–79 period, while real GNP increased by 12.1 % and industrial production by 15.0 %, primary energy consumption increased by only 6.35 %. Therefore, the elasticity of energy consumption was 0.52 with respect to real GNP, and 0.42 with respect to industrial production, for 1977–79.

(3) Is Small Beautiful?

When Japan was pursuing the development of its heavy and chemical industries, business opted for large scale and major facilities. In hindsight, however, it is possible to have second thoughts about such an approach: perhaps smaller facilities will prove more cost-efficient, less dependent on oil, more energy-saving and less destructive of the environment. That Schumacher's concept of "small is beautiful" and "intermediate technology" (7) has been capturing the imagination of business planners may not be an accident.

Although it may be necessary to heed the message contained in such a forward-looking approach, this necessity does not alter the fact that the capital-intensive mode of production still is prevalent among the important—especially among the key—industries. Nevertheless, there are many supportive processing industries in which the concept of "small is beautiful" can be brought to bear in planning. Given the broad-ranging areas in which small and medium-sized business enterprises can play an active role in the future development of Japanese industry, a modified version, if not an outright adoption, of the Schumacher concept may prove useful.

Many of the small and medium-sized companies in Japan operate as subcontractors to large corporations. Mapping out a strategy of operation for these small companies under a changed industrial structure is one of the challenges facing government and business leaders.

(4) Increasing Reliance of the Machinery Industry on Information

As noted earlier, the share of the machinery industry in the nation's total exports has exceeded 60 %, the largest in the world. Can the Japanese machinery industry maintain its relatively superior position in the world? MITI has established a Machinery Information Industry Bureau, and this suggests that the machinery industry has entered the stage where hardware and software are of equal importance. More than half of the watches and clocks being produced in Japan are electronically driven, but 15 years ago electronic watches and clocks were unknown to Japanese makers. Electronics technology became available not only to the watch industry but also to other sectors of the machinery industry.

Now the electronicization of machinery is spreading rapidly to other industry groups. Indeed, systematic sharing of advanced technologies among related industries will become a task of central importance for Japanese industry.

In the second half of the 1950s, the development of the machinery industry, particularly the automobile industry, was one of the highest priorities of MITI. With this in mind, MITI pushed through the Diet a Special Measures Law for the Promotion of the Machinery Industry (the Machinery Development Law, for short). As the 1970s advanced, the development of the computer industry has taken on growing importance, and MITI pushed through the Diet a similar law for the promotion of the computer industry known (for short) as the Machinery and Computer Promotion Law. This indicates that MITI attaches an importance to the computer industry comparable to that of the automobile industry.

In hardware, the Japanese computer industry has reached the technological level of IBM, but Japanese software is still far behind. As software takes on increasing importance, the policy objectives of MITI have become less clearly defined; consciousness within the agency of the importance of an integrated approach to the development of hardware and software for other sectors of the machinery industry has reached an unprecedented hight. In 1978 MITI persuaded the Diet to enact a Machinery Information Law (abbreviated form) enabling it to devote a determined effort to the development of software technology.

(5) Products Still Unaffected by Import Liberalization

Japan has liberalized foreign trade to a considerable degree. However, the liberalization of agricultural imports is less than adequate. Japan's grain self-sufficiency eroded from 83% in 1960 to 40% in 1977. However, Japan's total imports, excluding the rapidly swollen oil bills, have grown 7.3-fold in the 13 years from 1965 to 1978. During the same period, food imports have merely increased 7.8-fold, and herein lies the problem. On the other hand, imports of textile goods increased 93.4-fold, those of consumer durables (household goods, home appliances, automobiles, toys and musical instruments, etc.) 7.6-fold, and capital goods (including non-electrical machinery) 8.1-fold during the same period. In such a manner, imports of manufactured goods have increased dramatically, but trade barriers are still left standing in the way as far as the import of agricultural products is concerned. This has become the last problem blocking the internationalization of the Japanese industrial structure.

References

1. Kindleberger, C. P. *Foreign Trade and the National Economy*. New Haven: Yale University Press, 1962.
2. Shinohara, Miyohei. *Sangyo Kozoron* [Industrial Structure]. Tokyo: Chikuma Shobo, 1976.
3. Shinohara, Miyohei. "Evaluation of the ¥360 Exchange Rate." Chapter 1 of *The Japanese Economy and Southeast Asia: In the New International Context*. Occasional Papers Series No. 15. Tokyo: Institute of Developing Economies, 19.
4. Shinohara, Miyohei. "Japan's Strategies toward New Developments in the Economies of East and Southeast Asia." *Contemporary Southeast Asia*, May 1979.
5. Akamatsu, K. "A Theory of Unbalanced Growth in the World Economy." *Weltwirtschaftliches Archiv*, Heft 2, 1961.
6. Vernon, Raymond. *Technology Factor in International Trade*. New York: National Bureau of Economic Research, 1970.
7. Schumacher, E. F. *Small Is Beautiful: A Study of Economics As If People Mattered*. London: Blond & Briggs Ltd., 1973.

2

JAPANESE-TYPE INDUSTRIAL POLICY

Insofar as there have been consciously taken industrial policies in the industrial nations, they can only be public policies relating to "industrial organization" in each industry.

The major goal of these policies is to eliminate excessive monopoly and oligopoly and to bring about a reasonable allocation of resources by making the best use of the market mechanism. At the same time, they can be used to promote rectification, to provide aid to the weaker sectors of small and medium-sized industries, or to protect against environmental pollution.

Theoretically speaking, importance has generally been attached to the basically anti-monopolistic type of industrial organization policy. The industrial policies applied during the postwar period in Japan, however, were of a unique nature on the international scene. We can, for all intents and purposes, identify Japan's industrial policy to be described here as identical to the policies adopted by the Ministry of International Trade and Industry (MITI).

Japanese-Type Industrial Policies

These policies were designed to bring about an overall "strengthening of international competitiveness" of various modern industries. To enable a nation dependent for its basic resources on foreign countries to catch up in a relatively short time with the advanced nations, it was necessary to rapidly expand imports of raw materials, which would be accompanied by the rapid growth of the domestic economy. Rapid growth in the exports of various industrial products was, therefore, the most essential condition for maintaining the international trade balance under the circumstances.

Some protective measures were adopted toward those industries

This chapter was first presented to the International Symposium on Industrial Policies for the '80s, in Madrid, May 5–9, 1980 (sponsored by the OECD), and published as Occasional Paper A-3 by The Asian Club, Tokyo, March 1980.

which could be expected to become more powerful, although they were at that particular stage less than competitive. It has generally been considered that such methods of fostering the so-called "infant industries" should be applied to a limited number of industries, simply because to do otherwise would go against the orthodox theory of the international division of labor. However, MITI intended to protect almost all modern industries. This reasoning not only went against the theory of international division of labor, but also clashed with the theory of fostering infant industries: that the developing of infant industries should be confined to those industries whose export competitiveness can be strengthened by means of protective measures; it should not be considered applicable to various modern industries on an "all-round" basis.

This fostering of industries needed to be watched with care because it could tend to prolong the close ties between government and industry. This might easily promote institutional rigidity and weaken the flexibility of the national economy, which in turn would result in a distortion of reasonable resource allocation among various industries.

In retrospect, the above-mentioned fears concerning the fostering of infant industries in Japan were unfounded. The application of various protective measures in Japan proved indeed to be only temporary. In fact, various forms of trade liberalization, such as the lifting of import restrictions and reduction of tariff rates, were put into practice in the 1960s.

Although industrialization takes the form of import substitution in many cases, this type of industrialization has been criticized because the import substitution was believed not only to cause long-term deficits in this international trade balance, but also to create a dual structure in the domestic economy. What occurred in Japan, however, was that import substitution through the introduction of foreign technology naturally led to a linkage with "export promotion," thus avoiding a constant deficit in the balance of payments. Although some of the newly industrializing countries (NICs) are beginning to prove successful in "import substitution → export promotion," it should be pointed out that the fact that import substitution was not directly connected with export promotion in many less developed countries (LDCs) has long remained an important problem.

One of the basic factors which made export promotion easier in Japan was the huge domestic market of approximately 100 million people. If the domestic market expands in line with or ahead of export expansion, a product with a relatively higher rate of expansion would be subject to a considerable reduction in unit cost through mass production, thus allowing an increase in exports. In other words, even though the relationship between the expansion of the domestic and export markets might have been that of a trade-off on an extremely short-term basis, it proved to be highly complementary for the mid- and long-term. The existence of a feedback relationship between expansion of domestic demand and exports resulted in high growth in Japan.

Another significant point is that, beyond the boundary of "borrowed technology," rapid spontaneous development of various technologies was witnessed in various postwar Japanese industries. This was particularly so in the steel and automobile industries. The fact is that the high growth rate in Japan was not merely export-led: aided by vigorous increases in investment in plant and equipment in the domestic market, investment-led features were also marked. Growth was attributable to a combination of export- and investment-led developments, or to the parallel expansion of domestic and external markets.

Industrial policies simply forced "from above" are not necessarily long-lived. To keep these policies in long-term effect, there must be aggressive response in the private industries "from below." In Japan's case, too, the success of guidance from above was only made possible by dynamism in industrial circles.

The success achieved should be attributed to two things. On the one hand, the industrial policies of the government, which achieved the consensus of industry after negotiations, were generally acceptable. On the other hand, the reaction of private industry was developed in a highly dynamic fashion within a framework envisaged by the government.

These industrial policies, in which great importance was attached to export promotion and the strengthening of international competitiveness, had to be reevaluated in the 1970s. The first reason for this was that the balance of payments deficit on which the economy had been based became a surplus, and the second was that the continuous existence of the balance of payments surplus itself became a potential cause of inflation.

At this point MITI's industrial policies have completed their historical mission and face a major turning point. I would like, however, to discuss in a little more detail the industrial policies which were developed along with the strengthening of international competitiveness. It seems to me that these Japanese industrial policies can be a valuable source of suggestions for the NICs and LDCs of today.

Conceptual Framework

In modern economics it has been considered that in an economy of abundant labor and scarce capital, the development of labor-intensive production methods would naturally bring about a rational allocation of resources.

On the other hand, in an economy with abundant capital and a shortage of labor, it has been taken for granted that capital-intensive industries would grow by becoming export industries. It has also been assumed that any measures taken contrary to this theorem would be going against economic principles, thus distorting resource allocation.

If this reasoning is correct, the industrial policies adopted by MITI in the mid-1950s were wrong. Ironically, however, Japan's industrial policies achieved unprecedented success by going against modern economic theory. Whether it was steel, petrochemicals, or other industries, dissenting voices were raised claiming that the development of capital-intensive industries was irrational. The cost of international steel products was then comparatively high, and the industry was highly capital-intensive. In terms of classical comparative cost theory, such industries as textiles, apparel, and shipbuilding were in comparatively advantageous positions during the 1950s. However, the government tried to introduce protective measures in industries which appeared to have potential for achieving an advantageous position over the next decade, despite a comparatively disadvantageous position at the time. The policy achieved remarkable results in the case of the steel industry, which has grown into the strongest in the world.

The problem of classical thinking undeniably lies in the fact that it is essentially "static" and does not take into account the possibility of a dynamic change in the comparative advantage or disadvantage of industries over a coming 10- or 20-year period. To take the place of such a traditional theory, a new policy concept needs to be developed to deal with the possibility of intertemporal dynamic development. The two basic criteria to which the industrial structure policies adopted by MITI conformed, therefore, were an "income elasticity criterion" and a "comparative technical progress criterion." Although I do not wish to infer that MITI did not consider other domestic policy criteria at the same time, it can be said that the above two criteria had the most bearing on the policy target of strengthening international competitiveness.[1]

The "income elasticity criterion" provides a suggestion that an in-

---

[1] These two criteria were advocated by this writer (1) before they were adopted by MITI.

dustry whose elasticity of export demand with respect to world real income as a whole is comparatively high should be developed as an export industry. Under this criterion, as long as the income elasticity of textile products is higher than that of agricultural commodities, and the elasticities of automobiles and electronic products are higher than those of textile goods, automobiles are obviously preferable to textiles as export products, and textiles are more advantageous than agricultural products.

The "comparative technical progress criterion" pays more attention to the possibility of placing a particular industry in a more advantageous position in the future through a comparatively greater degree of technical progress, even if the cost of the products is relatively high at this stage. This could be termed the "dynamized comparative cost doctrine."

It must be pointed out that there are sufficient grounds for the government to foster industries which have a comparatively high growth rate on the demand side while displaying a comparatively high rate of technical progress on the supply side. In this particular regard, the industrial policy concept adopted by MITI, which tried to take into account potential intertemporal dynamic developments rather than automatically applying the ready-made static theory of international economics, proved to be a wise choice.

Another problem is that of labor (or capital) intensity. Both in Japan and Korea, the fostering of basic industries (e.g., steel and petrochemicals) which are highly capital-intensive was planned at a time when labor supply was in excess. However, this did not cause serious problems. At first glance this seems unreasonable, but according to neoclassical economic theory there should exist an inverse one-to-one relationship between factor intensities and factor prices.

No matter how capital-intensive, there are indications that many production methods could certainly become paying industries in the LDCs and NICs, provided that adoption and enforcement do not require particularly highly skilled labor. In other words, where a high standard of technology is embodied within the capital stock, thus eliminating the necessity for the labor force to be equipped with high technology and skills, the development of capital-intensive industries even in a labor-affluent economy may well be possible, insofar as it is a partial phenomenon.

However, the phrase "in parallel with development of other labor-intensive industries" should be hastily added as a necessary condition. I am not trying to totally deny the way of thinking emphasized by Schumacher, that "small is beautiful." Looking back on Japanese industrialization since the Meiji Era, we can see the parallel development of indigenous small and medium-sized enterprises and big enterprises implanted from abroad. Even in the process of postwar industrialization, while such capital-intensive industries as iron and steel and petrochemicals were gaining in competitiveness, many labor-intensive "processing" industries were also building up their technology and enjoying higher rates of growth than the basic industries.

Of course it can be said that MITI put more emphasis on capital-intensive big enterprises, which required greater protection, in order to strengthen the linkage with processing industries. The point here is the parallel development of big enterprises and small and medium-sized enterprises, as well as of the basic industries and processing industries. One should not hastily conclude that bigger or smaller is better. In the process of industrialization, it was necessary to promote the industrial linkage structure between the two sectors by means of parallel development. In particular in the case of the Japanese economy, with its huge domestic market, it is not hard to envisage that some appropriate development of basic industries with rapidity was necessary for the development of processing industries, which are situated closer to consumption.

Since the industrial policies of MITI often aimed at heavy and chemical industrialization, they tended to be misinterpreted as biased measures in favor of fostering only the capital-intensive industries such as iron and steel, chemicals, and the like. In fact, of the so-called heavy industries in Japan, the industries achieving the most outstanding growth have been the labor-intensive industries involving a high degree of processing, such as automobiles and electronics. Strengthening the automobile industry had been a cherished objective of MITI since the latter half of the 1950s.

Thus, on the one hand, MITI's industrial policies were expected to foster the industries whose demand growth and technical progress were comparatively high. At the same time, they proved successful in strengthening some key industries which took a "backward linkage" position in relation to the processing industries. From the standpoint of inter-industry structure, the "industrial block" often found in advanced countries was formed, in which such machinery-linked industries as automobiles, industrial machinery, and electrical machinery are closely related to such basic metal sectors as iron and steel and non-ferrous metals.

Achieving development up to this stage required a very large domestic market. For Japan, with a population of 100 million, it can be said that a necessary base had already been laid for making this development possible.

Policy Implementation

It is rather difficult to explain how these MITI industrial policies were implemented. But we can list some of the implementation measures used:

1) Special tax measures;
2) Low-interest loans by quasi-governmental financial institutions;
3) Import restrictions by means of duties, non-tariff barriers, etc.;
4) Coordination of investment in plant and equipment;
5) Promotion of economies of scale and improvement of production efficiency by merger and other combined production;
6) Deferment of trade and capital liberalization measures;
7) Other administrative guidance.

Let us take a look at the special taxation measures.

A special 50% increase in the depreciation allowance was allowed for a 3-year period on plant and equipment purchased after 1951. Furthermore, in 1952 special depreciation of as much as 50% in the initial year was granted for "plant and equipment which will contribute to the reconstruction of the Japanese economy." Apart from these, various other reserves such as the special revaluation of assets and special reserves for repairs (for maritime transport, iron and steel industries, etc.), and also reserves for export losses (for trading firms), were allowed. Regarding additions to such reserves as losses has been industrial policy in the field of taxation measures. These measures need to be abolished today, as their original objectives have already been accomplished. Or, alternatively, these special taxation measures should be directed toward various other fields such as pollution control, development of less developed areas, atomic energy power equipment, aircraft, and computers. The emphasis has shifted.

As to import restrictions and import duties, there are few problems as far as industrial products administered by MITI are concerned. Most of the problems remaining in this area are confined to agricultural and marine products. The high growth rate of the Japanese economy was at first cultivated in a closed system, a "hothouse" environment. But in the 1960s the nation began to move into an era of trade liberalization. The trade liberalization rate of 41% in April 1960 rose to 73% in April 1962, and continued to climb to 93% in October 1964. In October 1965, imports of completed passenger cars were finally liberalized. In April 1964, Japan accepted the obligations of an IMF Article 8 nation as well as those of a GATT Article 11 nation, pledging to forego using foreign exchange and import controls to improve its international balance of payments. The list of products subject to residual import quota restriction, which contained a total of 80 items in January of 1971, has now been reduced to 27 items. And most of these are confined to the category of agricultural products; mining and industrial products account for only 5 items.

It was agreed during the course of the Kennedy Round negotiations that import duties were to be reduced by more than 30%, with Japan being no exception. When these negotiations were completed in 1971, the average rate of Japan's import duties was reduced to about the 6% mark. These were further reduced to as low as 3.3% in 1976. Let us take the tariff rate on small cars as an example: the rate was as high as 40% in the first half of 1968, but this dropped to 6.4% in November of 1972, and at present has been reduced to zero.

As seen above, although it may be partially due to external pressure, industrial protectionism by Japan was quickly lifted, and it seems correct to say that the measures taken for the protection of infant industries were indeed "only temporary." Also, the tendency to protect industries across the board is being corrected to a considerable extent by the international transfer of industries which followed the "boomerang effect" in the 1970s.

MITI had no intention of imposing various restrictions upon investment activities; it saw its role as one of coordinating fixed investment for the highly capital-intensive iron and steel and petrochemical industries. Since it was feared that a condition of overcapacity would be created if keen interfirm competition for investment was allowed when 5000 m³-capacity blast furnaces were being built and the size of plant and equipment in general was rapidly increasing, MITI intended to play the role of coordinator so that each company could take its turn in investment on a rotation system. Although even this idea was criticizied when the desire for investment was vigorous, it was no longer an issue as soon as the market became depressed in the 1970s.

What was more significant was that MITI was aggressive in supporting the merger of Fuji and Yawata, which gave birth to Nippon Steel in 1970. This new company would control about one-third of the market for iron and steel. Despite objections by the Fair Trade Commission and many scholars, the merger was finally permitted.[2]

Looking back on the case now, this merger did not advance institutional inflexibility, nor did it bring about a stalemate in technological progress. On the contrary, technology export by Nippon Steel showed the greatest increases in the iron and steel industry, and owing to this

[2] I was one of the few who favored this merger under certain conditions (2).

merger the construction of the Oita Steel Mill, which employs a 100% continuous casting method, became possible. This made a great contribution both in unit cost reduction and in rationalization of production processes. Furthermore, as more reasonable reallocation of the kinds, standards, and sizes of products was promoted among the mills after the merger, this amalgamation between Fuji and Yawata in fact proved extremely successful.

In a separate article (see Chapter 3) I will consider the administrative guidance which was often put into effect as industrial policy. Briefly, though, this could be termed one of the methods by which the government and private industry come to a consensus, rather than a form of control. This might be one effective method for an industrially developing nation to use in catching up with the advanced nations.

During the period 1962–64, MITI presented to the Diet a measure generally referred to as DIP, for "Designated Industries Promotion Provisional Measures." In view of the coming capital (or direct investment) liberalization, this bill was aimed at strengthening the international competitiveness of Japanese enterprise, promoting reorganization of industries, and encouraging centralization, amalgamation, and specialization of enterprises on a larger scale. The goal of the promotion measures was industrial reorganization based on neither free trade nor a controlled economy but a third method of "cooperation between public and private sectors" comprised of industry, financial interests, and government.

The basic philosophy was quite similar to the crisis consciousness advocated in Le Défi Américain by J.-J. Servan-Schreiber, who urged that something be done to fight against the potential control of European industries by American corporations. However, in retrospect the drama over DIP (which failed to gain Diet approval) might well have been over-reaction by MITI. The fact is that Japanese industries, without the help of this particular program, managed to continue to grow in strength.

In the meantime, the leader in industrial development in the mid-1950s was without a doubt the machinery industry. In this respect, the Machinery Industry Promotion Provisional Measures enacted in June of 1956 (the MIP Law) and the Electronics Industry Promotion Provisional Measures enacted in June of 1957 (the EIP Law) could be considered epoch-making. These two laws divided the basic machinery, common parts, and export machinery industries into about 30 different kinds of machinery industries, and these industries, in accordance with promotion and rationalization programs, were supplied with special funds by the Development Bank and semi-governmental finance corporations specializing in small and medium-sized enterprises. The automobile and related industries achieved the most outstanding development. Production in the automotive parts industry in 1956 was only ¥58.9 billion, and more than 80% of the enterprises were small or medium in scale with capitalization at less than ¥50 million. However, aided by the promotion measures and the establishment of combined production and standardization of specifications, production by 1965 had escalated to ¥391.5 billion, or 6.6 times as high as that of 1956, while the percentage of small and medium-scale enterprises with capitalization of ¥50 million or less dropped to 55% of the total.

The MIP law was revised a second and a third time, and finally in 1971 was replaced by the Special Electronics Industry and Special Machinery Industry Provisional Measures (the ME Law). As a result, in addition to the automobile industry, computers began to attract a great deal of attention as a potential growth industry. Under the ME law the hardware side of the computer industry was greatly strengthened, and the Japanese industry achieved the same level as that of the advanced nations.

In software, however, the Japanese computer industry was far behind IBM at that time. The Special Machinery Information Industries Promotion Provisional Measures were proclaimed in July of 1978 to replace the ME Law. This legislation, usually referred to as the MI Law, suggests that serious attention be given not only to hardware but also to software development.

Microcomputers have now been widely adopted in the electronics and other machinery industries. We have moved into the "mechatronics era" —a time of combination of machinery and electronics. Electronic watches, cameras with electronically controlled devices, electronic sewing machines, electronic organs, and other such products are all contributing to the rapid electronicization of household electrical goods.

The development of electronic safety devices has brought us into the age of "automotive electronics," beginning with electronic engine control. Electronic cash registers and electronic copying machines are also on the horizon, and rapid advances in the electronicization of medical equipment are predicted. For the Japanese machinery industry, where more attention was once paid to "visible" hardware, the existence of the MI law indicates that the time has come when more serious attention must be paid to the "invisible" software side of machine development.

Changes in Industrial Policies

The goal of "building up international competitiveness," an unchanging industrial policy objective in Japan since the end of World War II, finally had to be abandoned in the 1970s.

Until that time the restrictive factor in economic growth was Japan's balance of payments ceiling. However, in the 1970s we found that a tight money policy was necessary to slow inflation even when the balance of payments showed a surplus. Thus, more attention began to be directed to the full employment ceiling, rather than to the balance of payments ceiling, as a factor which could check economic growth. The Japanese economy changed dramatically, moving from a foreign exchange shortage to a foreign exchange surplus phase.

What had been considered a virtue up to the 1960s, the maintenance of a high export growth rate by undervaluation of the yen in terms of its purchasing power parity (the rate was held at ¥360 to the dollar), became a vice in the 1970s (3). The long period when the exchange rate was fixed at ¥360 was replaced by the "managed float." During this period we even saw the dollar exchange rate break through the ¥200 mark. This could justify the judgment that "fostering almost all export industries" had only been possible because of the considerably undervalued exchange rate of ¥360.

But the ¥360 rate became a thing of the past in the 1970s. Many modern industries reached the levels of the advanced nations, both in the levels of production and technology. Therefore, it became necessary not to chase after a single visible goal of strengthening international competitiveness, but to seek various diversified national objectives.

At the end of 1970, the Minister of MITI called on the Industrial Structure Council to study "The Basic Direction of Trade and Industry in the 1970s." The interim report, issued in November of 1971, emphasized the changes in the policy attitude for the betterment of the quality of society:

> Up to now, we have continued to focus our attention on climbing a narrow, steep road, looking at clouds over the top of the hill . . . . Now, as the basic national desires have been fulfilled, attention must be paid to the "more beautiful things (in life)" and to providing a nation with clearer water and air, cities which are easier to live in, and a sense of achievement in one's work.

Specifically the report called for a shift of the fundamental attitudes concerning economic management from "growth pursuit" to "growth utilization." It mentioned the "knowledge-intensive industrial structure" as the industrial structure vision of the 1970s, and stated that it would attach importance to the industrial structure policies which emphasized such industries as:

1) Research and development-intensive industries (computer, aircraft, industrial robots, atomic power-related industries, large-scale integrated circuits, fine chemicals, ocean development, etc.);
2) High processing industries (office communication equipment, numerical counted machine tools, pollution prevention machinery, industrial housing production, high-quality printing, automated warehousing, educational equipment, etc.);
3) Fashion industries (high-quality clothing and furniture, electronic musical instruments, etc.);
4) Knowledge industries (information management services, information supplying services, education-related industries such as video, software, systems engineering, consulting, etc.).

Compared with the past slogans emphasizing economies of scale, large-scale investments, and building up of international competitiveness, the new policy puts emphasis on the necessity for diversification of industrial policies in order to enhance the welfare of citizens of the nation—creation of a better environment, expansion of education, repletion of social overhead capital, development of advanced technology, pollution prevention, promotion of social development, and systematization of industrial activities.

The development of this industrial policy has two aspects. One is the domestic aspect, which pays serious attention to the betterment of national welfare, repletion of life quality, and diversification and improvement of life environment, rather than just to the fostering and strengthening of industries. The other is that on the international level the policy of strengthening international competitiveness throughout almost all industries has been abandoned, and a shift to emphasis on industrial transfer or international industry adjustment has been confirmed. Though gradual transfers of labor-intensive light industries by means of trade have been beginning with Korea, Taiwan, and Hong Kong, the rapid advance of Japanese enterprises in overseas markets in the 1970s caused a dramatic "boomerang effect" (4). This caused not only so-called "reverse imports" of textile goods, but also a sharp decrease of Japan's share in overseas markets in various fields including shipbuilding, electronics, and general merchandise. As a whole, the policies of MITI were aimed at promoting internationalization of industrial structures, rather than adopting a policy of protectionism. In this regard, MITI presents quite a contrast with the Ministry of Agriculture,

Forestry and Fisheries, which was entirely absorbed in protection of the domestic agricultural and fisheries industries. However, as MITI had tried to foster various industries across the board for a long period of time, Japanese industries were accordingly subjected to a large repercussive industrial adjustment internationally.

It was quite natural that a democratic government could not elaborate on MITI's industrial policy statements. However, now that on a quantitative level the nation's industries have reached gigantic proportions internationally, it is inevitable that the direction of the Japanese industrial structure be decided within an international framework.

Here is an example. Let us assume that a capital goods industry such as shipbuilding continues to grow in Korea. It has inevitably become competitive with its Japanese counterpart in one way or another. However, the development of a capital goods industry in Korea will cause a sharp increase in imports of capital goods and their parts from Japan. If the former process is referred to as a "negative boomerang effect" on Japan, the latter would be a "positive boomerang effect."

If the domestic markets of the Asian NICs are not large enough to permit the overall development of capital goods industries in their own countries, an increase in imports of related capital goods becomes inevitable. As a result, an unavoidable shift in Japan's division of labor with East and Southeast Asian countries will occur.

This applies not only to the "vertical division of labor" between primary and manufacturing industries; even within manufacturing industries and capital goods industries, the emergence of a "horizontal division of labor" will become essential. Thus, the industrial structure policies of Japan from the 1970s are becoming increasingly restricted by the international environment.

MITI made public its "Trade and Industrial Policies for the 1980s" in March 1980, as a report of the Industrial Structure Council. Compared to the "Basic Direction of the Trade and Industrial Policies in the 1970s," this report covers a far wider scope. As a decidedly new view, it recognizes the 1980s as a period of preparation for energy security and of departure from an oil-oriented society in order to overcome resource limitations. At the same time, it advocates exploring ways of establishing highly sophisticated technologies, putting particular emphasis on technology based upon new-type materials, large-scale system technology, and social system technology. By so doing, MITI expects to strengthen Japan's bargaining position through research cooperation with advanced countries and transfer of appropriate technologies to the developing nations.

The following four points are considered important for the evolution of a creative industrial structure: (1) the establishment of dynamic comparative advantages, (2) the fulfillment of the needs of the people, (3) the promotion of energy and resource saving, and (4) the maintenance of security. At the same time, three S's and three F's are assumed necessary for the multi-dimensional and creative extension of knowledge-intensiveness of industries. The three S's stand for emphasis on "software," "systematization," and "specialization." The three F's stress the necessary trends for "fashionization," "feedback systems," and "flexibility."

There is no need for an explanation of "software." "Systematization" means creating new functions through linkage and combination of different industries and different technologies. It covers not only the new development of "mechatronics" but also new extensions of efficient systems which provide for social services such as medical care, education, energy supplies, disposal of waste materials and transportation.

"Specialization" is promotion of uniqueness by augmenting technology-intensiveness. For example, in coping with newly rising demands for atomic power, liquefied natural gas, oceanic and space development, new or special materials are being developed and utilized for special thermal, mechanical, chemical, optical and electronic functions.

"Fashionization" seems to be self-evident. "Feedback systems" aim at augmenting the organic linkages between the final demand sector and the intermediate products or raw materials sectors in the design of new products and technologies.

"Flexibility" means creating a higher degree of value added by developing production methods which will process and fabricate a number of products with a variety of qualities to meet multivariate needs. For instance, in apparel manufacturing new systems make possible flexible and automatic dyeing, cutting, sewing, etc., in accordance with demand for a variety of colors, shapes, designs, and materials.

In short, the aim is to promote a highly sophisticated and diversified industrial structure, but this target is to be realized within a framework which will maintain economic security as a whole, enhance the quality of life, promote local economic societies, and also develop dynamic and unique small and medium-sized enterprises.

The days when the objectives of Japanese industrial structure were straight and clear-cut are gone; it is accurate to say now that we are moving to a stage where the objectives are multiphasic and not always clear. Needless to say, this is the inevitable result which accompanies a shift to a position on a level with the advanced nations.

References

1. Shinohara, Miyohei. "Industrial Structure and Investment Allocation." *Keizei Kenkyu*, October 1957 (in Japanese).
2. Shinohara, Miyohei. "MITI's Industrial Policy and Japanese Industrial Organization—A Retrospective Evaluation." *The Developing Economies*, December 1976 (included in this book as Chapter 3).
3. Shinohara, Miyohei. "On the Evaluation of the 360-Yen Exchange Rate." *Japanese Economic Studies*, Fall 1975 (included in *The Japanese Economy and Southeast Asia* [Tokyo: Institute of Developing Economies, 1977]).
4. Shinohara, Miyohei. "Japan's New Strategies towards New Developments in the Economies of East and Southeast Asia." *Contemporary Southeast Asia*, May 1979 (included in this book as Chapter 5).

3

MITI'S INDUSTRIAL POLICY AND JAPANESE INDUSTRIAL ORGANIZATION

Many people believe that the Ministry of International Trade and Industry (MITI) should be relegated to infamy; others contend that MITI uses its "administrative guidance" (*gyosei shido*) in a constant attempt to emasculate anti-trust legislation. Still others say that MITI is in cahoots with financial and business leaders to put Japanese industry into blocked-off, closely linked, vertically organized groupings. For those who have received their training in the modern economics (price theory, industrial organization, etc.) developed particularly in the postwar United States, the actions of the Ministry are considered repugnant. Students of economics such as these are likely to decry Japanese industry and its organization, feeling that its entire direction is away from the spirit of the anti-monopoly laws.

Japan's economy has progressed in the post-World War II years in a way that makes foreign observers stand gaping in awe. One of the things achieved is that, in terms of value added per employee, big corporations in the fastest-growing industries, steel, automobiles, electrical machines, and petrochemicals, have reached a level about the same as that in America and two or three times as high as those in Europe. Another is that the export/production ratio in major industries has continued to climb. For example, the passenger car export ratio was 4.2% in 1960 but went up to 40.0% by 1975. The export ratio for steel climbed from 11.4% in 1960 to 30.3% in 1975. In addition to these increases, there was a rapid growth in foreign investment from $159 million in 1965 to $3,280 million in 1975. This more than 20-fold increase signals a new era in the internationalization of Japanese enterprises.

Some observers believe that these achievements have come from the vitality and aggressiveness of individual corporations, and have no relation either to industrial organization or to MITI's policy. However,

This chapter was first published in *The Developing Economies,* Vol. XIV No. 4, December 1976.

many foreign critics assume that Japan's industrial organization is rigidly controlled from the top by MITI; that otherwise it would have been impossible to have the kind of performance that the economy has displayed. In order to have a better idea of what has been going on, it will be necessary to look into the question of whether calling the Japanese economic framework "Japan, Incorporated" is justified.

The Image of Japan, Inc.

The economy of Japan would have to be considered very group-oriented in contrast to the model of an individually-oriented economy and society where free competition between economic units precludes the formation of groups like Mitsubishi and Mitsui and the existence of business hierarchy and subcontractor networks. Under the premises of modern economics, many people believe that the Japanese economy is far from the ideal of pure competition. The impression that Japanese industry is comprised of horizontal and vertical strata of business groups and subcontractors with MITI standing at the top of it is strong among foreign observers, who feel rather uneasy when they see the kind of exceptional growth that has been achieved. There are probably also a number of people who feel that growth will have to decline because of factors completely different from worsening environment or inflation. For the people holding the equilibrium theory view, the Japanese economy appears to be a preposterous aberration from the state of optimum resource allocation.

The publication of the 1972 U.S. Department of Commerce Report, *Japan: The Government-Business Relationship* (4), swept this odd image of the economy out the door. The report says that there is no giant group conspiracy between business and government as many harsh detractors of Japan, Inc., would have us believe. According to the report, "Japan, Incorporated is not a monolithic system in which government leads and business follows blindly"; rather there is cooperative interaction between government and business. "What makes government-business interaction in Japan different from what takes place in other countries is the extent and the scale of such interaction and a qualitative difference, a style peculiar to the Japanese, derived from Japan's history and culture with its emphasis on the consensual approach, a tradition of government leadership in industrial development, and a generally shared desire to advance the interest of the Japanese nation." In sum, the report says, "interaction between government and business is pervasive in the Japanese economy but not all-encompassing. The managers of Japan, Incorporated focus their attention mainly on the growth sectors of the Japanese economy."

During times that I participated in the Council on Industrial Structure as a public member of the Steel Industry Investment Coordination Committee, neither I nor other members ever had the feeling that MITI was forcing its will on the Council. Rather than imposing its desires, MITI was conspicuous in its position as arbitrator between, for example, Kawasaki Steel and Sumitomo Metal, which at that time were very dissatisfied and trying to influence events, and Yawata and Fuji Steel, which were on the defensive.

There may have been instances where MITI's intervention was unilateral, causing harm, but this of course depends on one's interpretation. MITI's intervention may have been too extreme when it was advocating passage of the Designated Industries Promotion Bill which was defeated in the Diet during the early 1960s. However, a look at the situation from a more realistic viewpoint and in light of the actual performances obtained shows that MITI has gone to great lengths to confer with industry; using this feedback, it sets guidelines to strengthen the growth posture of important industries. Nevertheless, some students of industrial organization have believed that MITI unilaterally forces its decisions on industry, with industry finding it difficult to change those decisions and just having to accept them.

In coordinating investment in the steel industry, it has been much more effective to have the negotiations mediated, leading to a great deal less redundant equipment than if investment were made by a disunified approach. Moreover, companies can then attempt the enormous amount of investment needed without worrying so much about future risks, since they are assured that MITI will step in if difficulties arise.

Steel is a highly capital-intensive industry. In the Fuji-Yawata merger of 1970, the tangible fixed assets (excluding construction in process) outstanding in major industries were as follows:

Industry	Number of companies	Assets (¥ billion)
Steel	6	3,431
Automobile	6	1,231
Petrochemical	5	848
Heavy electric	9	834
Synthetic fiber	6	773
Oil refining	6	501
Machine tool	8	58

Steel stands out conspicuously among these major industries. After the first part of the 1970s, technological innovation required increases in equipment size, such as, for example, an increased blast furnace capacity of 3,000 to 5,000 cubic meters. Rather than having every company competing for fixed investment and being beset by risks of overcapacity, industry leaders felt it better to have MITI act as mediator. The possibilities for steady, and yet fast, industrial growth were considered much better with occasional reliance upon MITI's coordination.

A major problem is that Japanese industrial society has a structure which makes it difficult to quickly disassemble into small atomistic firms. Given such a situation, progress would be rather difficult if MITI's industrial policy were allowed to fall behind. I am convinced that the unprecedented economic growth of the postwar period would not have been possible without the group-oriented psychology and social structure unique to Japan. This conviction may seem too farfetched for those totally steeped in the thinking of modern economics, since they would require a much more static situation with more atomistic industrial organization.

At this point in time, though, the issue is totally a thing of the past, and the historically accepted target of industrial policy based on supremacy in export and growthmanship is now something which must be relegated to antiquity. However, the important role that MITI policy played has not been adequately emphasized. For a Japan with only a partially developed economy, a late starter on the road to industrialization, the general consensus was to obtain economically advanced status as quickly as possible. To reach this goal, it was necessary for the government to take the lead in guidance and direction. It was often necessary that government be the mediator to placate the vital and active firms in the private sector. It was no mistake that government provided supportive industrial measures for those businesses with comparatively higher income elasticity and with relatively higher speed in technical progress.

Once developed economic status has been attained, however, drastic policy transformation had to be attempted. MITI's change was already apparent in about 1970.

A Peculiarity of Japanese Industrial Organization— Monopsony

The peculiar characteristics of industrial structure, part of the substructure of Japan, Inc., should be examined. In order to do this, a look has to be taken at the internal organization of individual industries; an entire range of facets must be studied, such as concentration and dispersion, oligopoly and competition, entry barriers, pricing and profit structure, cartels, subcontractors, affiliate networks, business groups, and the distribution network. In current research on industrial organization in Japan, too much emphasis has been placed on seller's monopoly; buyer's monopoly (monopsony) as a unique characteristic of the business hierarchy or subcontracting has rather been disregarded. Enterprises are linked hierarchically in this monopsony network with big corporations above and subcontractors under them. When Toyota orders auto parts from parts producers in its affiliated network, there is one buyer and several sellers, a situation that establishes a buyer's monopoly. When Toray supplies thread to weavers in its network, it also has these companies weave the yarn into cloth and pays them weaving and processing fees. Such actions establish a relationship between one buyer and several sellers. Of course, on occasion, this develops into a buyer's oligopoly, and it is also possible that the relationship will weaken when the subcontractors expand their sales channels and go outside the network.

The prevailing system of subcontracting created through buyer's monopolies is a strikingly unique part of Japanese industrial organization. However, in recent analyses by Japanese economists of their industrial organization, emulating American-type analysis, the focus is mostly on seller's monopoly or oligopoly, exactly as with the analyses in the United States. Only in special cases are medium and small enterprises ever considered, and this is an unthinkable oversight. In their research on industrial organization, the analysts never studied small and medium-sized enterprises from the angle of monopsony, rarely citing the extensive literature on Japanese small and medium firms. Of course, theories of industrial organization often take into account business groups (like Mitsui and Mitsubishi), an issue recently taken up by the Fair Trade Commission. Generally speaking, when American industrial organization analyses are applied by Japanese modern economists, they tend to forget that allowances have to be made for the uniqueness of Japan's industrial society. Thus, a simplistic imitation of American theory is evident in their analyses. Only recently have there been a few exceptions (1, 2).

Loose Structure of Business Groups

There has been a great deal of discussion about business groups such as Mitsui, Mitsubishi, Sumitomo, and Fuyo; the corporations in each of these groups are considered to have a very high degree of interdependence in terms of mutual stock holdings and a consequent high level of linkage. For instance, it is said that the rate of mutually held stocks in the Mitsubishi group was 27% in 1974. However, this refers to the percentage of "total" stock shares of Mitsubishi companies that are held by others in the same group. An examination of the percentage of stocks held on a firm-to-firm basis shows that control is not as high as it first seems. Mitsubishi Shoji, for example, holds only 2.4% of the shares of Mitsubishi Heavy Industries, 2.0% of Mitsubishi Rayon, and 1.7% of Mitsubishi Electric. This same situation holds for all business groups. In addition, the level of linkage within each group is not as high as the 27% for Mitusubishi would suggest. Since each individual firm has only from 2 to 5% of any of the other's stock, the linkage is really rather loose.

Fuji Bank, a member of the Fuyo group, is another good example. Fuji Bank does not do all financing for the Fuyo group as some commentators have suggested. In 1960, the largest loan by Fuji Bank went to Marubeni, but in 1975 it went to Mitsui Bussan, which does not belong to the Fuyo group. Loans to companies outside the Fuyo group such as Nissan Auto, Toa Fuel, and Nippon Steel have rapidly increased. Information on all business groups shows that the financing system is exceedingly flexible and has changed along with unbalanced industrial and technological development. It also clearly shows that linkage within each business group is loose.

The claim is often made that each group takes unified control over any new industry in its ranks and that group banks give priority in financing their fellow companies; thus the tendency to compete between business groups financially supported by the group network is often pointed out. But there is actually much greater flexibility than this, and the link within each group is loose enough so that each company can display great "capacity to transform" by itself. Thus, the structure of the Japanese business group is rather flexible, and there is always continual feedback between MITI and industry. The business groups as a whole have even greater flexibility, providing a cushion against rapid change in the economy.

Relative Rigidity in Vertical Networks

Large firms in the groups—such as Mitsubishi Heavy Industries or Mitsubishi Shoji—have a great number of affiliated firms tied to them in vertical hierarchy. According to a 1975 survey by Toyo Keizai Shimposha (Oriental Economist Co.), the shares of the number of affiliates, more than 70% of whose stocks are owned by the parent company, are as follows: Mitsubishi Heavy Industries, 65%; Nippon Electric, 49%; Showa Denko, 50%; Toray, 43 %; and Mitsui Bussan, 75%. For 20 large firms chosen at random, the average became 62.9%.

This is excellent evidence for the argument that ties are extremely strong between large companies and their affiliates. When the secondary and tertiary networks underpinning the affiliates and subcontracting are considered, there is a strong orientation toward buyer's monopoly or monopsony, an important characteristic probably unique to Japanese industrial organization.

In my opinion, the coexistence of flexibility and rigidity in the industrial organization offers a number of advantages. For one thing, the flexible structure of business groups provides a cushion in the rapid economic growth process. Although there may be some harmful effects in the rigid structure of affiliates, the situation differs from that of prewar affiliates and subcontractors, for they now receive technical assistance as well as assistance in sales channels and financing by receiving technicians and managers transferred from the parent firm. Moreover, through specialized concentration on certain areas of production, the affiliate derives cost reduction due to mass production, and there is greater efficiency in the specialized arrangements in sales and other areas. A first glance might lead to the conclusion that this organizational rigidity is a cause of paralysis in competition. However, the system promotes competition in various areas such as technology, pricing, and sales routes with other firms in other business groups' vertical networks.

The subcontractors of the prewar period were merely exploited by the parent company. Undeniably, some of this flavor remains in the present vertical network, but the point still is that direct linkage with the parent company and the consequent division of labor promotes efficiency.

There are those who contend that this combination of rigidity and flexibility worked to hinder growth, but in my opinion the ingeniousness of the system played an important role in providing a base to accelerate economic growth. The Japanese postwar economy's record of higher growth rates than in many other countries, a record that lasted for almost 30 years, was achieved by offering a type of economic development quite different from the static, atomistic variety described in modern economic theory. Success was achieved by harnessing the economy to a dynamic combination of flexibility and rigidity. A situation leading to an atomistic dissolution of the system would have meant the loss of dynamism. This system was of course not developed out of direct planning but came about naturally, spontaneously, producing a structure appropriate to high growth. A totally rigid system is a barrier to growth, as the experience of the socialist nations suggests. Japan's unique combination of rigidity and flexibility was very effective and highly successful.

In spite of the fact that, in comparison to the prewar period, there has been a much lower degree of exploitation in the vertical networks by means of monopsony, some exploitation, of course, still remains. According to a 1973 study by the Fair Trade Commission, 985 cartels were exempt from the stipulations of the fair trade and anti-monopoly laws, and 607, almost two-thirds, were cartels comprised of small and medium-sized firms. The utmost effort should be made to eliminate large firm cartels and ensure that they have to compete in a truly fair manner, but reservations have to be made for small and medium-sized firms. Cartels created by these smaller companies work to strengthen "countervailing power" vis-à-vis the large corporations, and this is even more so when those small companies are tied by buyer's monopoly into vertical networks. Abolition of these cartels would cause the restoration of what Joan Robinson calls monopsonistic exploitation.

There is a general tendency to assume that cartels are bad, not taking into consideration whether these cartels are composed of large companies or smaller ones. In an industrial organization where vertical networks are ubiquitous, it is doubtful that abolition of cartels would stimulate active competition as many people believe. If they were done away with, firms organized in vertical networks on the basis of monopsony would be confronted with excess competition rather than the ideal of pure free competition that advocates of total abolition envisage. Quite a number of people have been caught in this trap of thinking, among them many Japanese industrial organization scholars.

General Trading Companies and Industry

Between 1960 and 1973, 49.9 % of Japan's exports and 62.8 % of imports were handled by the 10 largest trading companies. These traders are responsible for more than 40 % of overseas investment, including that in which they are actively engaged as partners. Japan's general trading companies are unique: they have telecommunications equipment and intelligence-gathering networks that rival anything the CIA or Pentagon can come up with, enormous marketing strength in international markets, ability to procure massive capital at home and abroad, and excellent organizational capability as demonstrated in the way that they have mobilized many manufacturers to enter overseas markets. The general trading companies have been the focus of a great deal of attention in other nations.

These trading companies have played an invaluable role in import, export, and overseas investment, and in their methods of operation lies one of the secrets of Japan's high export growth. Manufacturing firms have made major contributions to progress in "hardware" technology, but to move into overseas markets most of them have neither the international experience nor the resources to effectively manage sales. The arrangement by which manufacturers give their undivided attention to technological advancement in their field while the traders concentrate on know-how and "software" technology of overseas sales is an excellent demonstration of economy of scale. The trading company is very important to Japanese industry.

The general trading company does not exist in other advanced countries, so it is not too much to say that the trading companies are a "comparative advantage" for Japan, making possible the persistence of higher rate of export growth than those in other countries. In other words, the general trading companies are one of the mainsprings of Japan's export acceleration, utilizing highly organized "soft" technology and economies of scale in an exceedingly dynamic fashion.

However, with the 1975 Fair Trade Commission report and the Lockheed payoff imbroglio and other scandalous events, the trading company became the subject of intense criticism. Whatever the position taken, one would have to consider the trading companies' conglomerate position and give close scrutiny to the way these companies exercise their influence and control over affiliated firms, whether it be through stockholdings, finance, or allocation of personnel.

The FTC report has not been influenced by the argument that the general trading companies are indispensable to the expansion of Japanese business, because it takes the position that similar organizations do not exist in the United States, Great Britain, or West Germany. However, the report's interpretation of the facts is quite misleading. If Japan were satisfied with the growth rate of other industrialized nations, then the trading company would have been unnecessary. Because the high growth rate of exports was indispensable to the Japanese economy in the past, the trading companies were likewise indispensable as an integral part of the growth structure.

The importance of their role in Japanese business cannot be ignored. If these large trading companies are disbanded, the effects on the economy can only be imagined, for manufacturers would be faced with tremendous problems in expanding international sales without the needed experience.

Industrial Policy and Large-Scale Mergers

An evaluation has to be made here of MITI's industrial policy, something which is looked on unfavorably by the vast body of Japanese economists.

These scholars seem to have thought that saying anything favorable about MITI would hurt them professionally, and for that reason alone they seem to have opposed it. One has said that "industrial policy means MITI's policy," and in Japan industrial policy has always at least partially meant this. My opinion has for a long time been in the minority, one that evaluates MITI's industrial policy by the results.

The 1970 MITI recommendation that Fuji Steel and Yawata Steel merge is a case in point. After the merger, the new company, Nippon Steel, was to control 36% of the industry's production volume. Several criticisms of the merger were made: one that MITI was emasculating the anti-monopoly laws and aiding the industry to make bigger profits, another that the merger would restrict competition and further solidify oligopolistic pricing. The social influence of the merger was another problem. I felt that, on condition that both investment coordination through the mediation of MITI and the "open sales system" be abolished, the merger should be realized.

At the time, a questionnaire was sent to 100 economists asking whether or not the merger would result in economies of scale. Two replied that the effects would be very great indeed, 36 said that there would emerge some economies of scale but they would not be of very great size, 45 stated that there would be no benefit and efficiency would drop, and seven replied in the "other" category. Since I was one of the two who selected the first category, my opinion was decidedly in the minority.

In 1970, the year of the merger, Nippon Steel's ratio of technology export to import was 2.54, but by 1974 it had increased to an amazing 20.33. The expansion of research personnel and facilities resulted immediately from the merger. In 1973, the number of employees in research departments was 2,767, or 35 out of every 1,000 employees. The rate in the steel industry as a whole was not greater than 10 in every 1,000. The number of patent applications almost doubled from 1970 to 1973: from 1,061 to 2,090. It is now generally accepted that no other firm in the industry can match Nippon Steel's technological level and progress.

Due to the merger, the Oita Mill in Kyushu was able to go on full "continuous casting." The usual process of revolving furnace, ingot, blooming, and slab was shortened by eliminating the intermediate ingot and blooming step. There are several advantages with complete continuous casting: 20% reduction of equipment costs, improvement of slab/hot metal ratio, reduction of per-unit energy requirements by one-third, and 20% labor saving. There are limitations, however, to the types of steel that can be produced by the continuous casting process. Moreover, the company is obliged to flexibly adapt to customer orders on type and size. Therefore, the operation of a steel mill doing only continuous casting, the annual production of which is 4 million tons as in the case of the Oita Mill, was only possible when the company as a whole could assure an annual production of about 40 million tons, as was the case with Nippon Steel. No other firm was able to manage a complete continuous casting plant. Because corporate scale was increased by the merger, the Oita Mill was able to fully operate the continuous casting process.

Plant input capacity increases to a great extent if a larger volume is produced of same-size items. The seven plants of Yawata and Fuji had a total number of 221 rolling molds for section steel, but this dropped to 134 after the merger because of the coordination of sizes. This raised monthly production capacity for large-scale mills in Sakai and Hirohata by 20,000 tons (before the merger each mill produced 80,000–90,000 tons a month). Thus, change in composition of input alone had the same effect as building a new rolling mill with a monthly 40,000-ton capacity. All effects of the merger cannot be listed here, but improved financial position is one of the most important. Prior to the merger, Fuji and Yawata's financial condition was worse than that of either Sumitomo Metal or Kawasaki Steel, but after the merger Nippon Steel's position was better.

At any rate, a splendid blow was dealt to the predictions of the vast majority of economists, those who said that the merger would cause technology to stagnate. The MITI's industrial policy of larger-scale merger was a success, one with very satisfactory results. Beginning in 1970 and lasting until quite recently, there has been a dramatic increase in the size of blast furnaces from 3,000 to 5,000 cubic meters, concomitant with developments in steel producing equipment, such as strip, rolling, and continuous casting mills. This process of expansion may stop in the near future. However, the generally held notion of economists at that time that "big does not mean good" was totally mistaken in view of the trends in Japanese steel technology, as far as the performances for the past several years are concerned. The idea that the concepts of a stagnant American steel industry could be applied without any modification to the dynamic Japanese steel industry was sadly mistaken.

Nurture of Infant Industries

Since steel's international competitiveness was amply demonstrated even before the merger, MITI's aim of making steel firms internationally competitive seems rather odd.

However, MITI's overall postwar industrial policy was quite effective in nurturing infant industries. MITI used administrative guidance, import restriction, coordination of investment in plant and equipment, merger and other methods of production consolidation, approval of cartels, postponing of liberalization of direct investment from outside, tax incentives for leading industries, low-interest loans, and other measures. Because of these measures, the steel and automobile industries, for example, have now acquired a leading world position, although their international competitiveness had not been high at the time when their products' prices in the world market were relatively expensive.

The government has removed trade restrictions and lowered tariffs to a dramatic degree, as we saw in Chapter 2. However, Japan's move to liberalize trade and direct investment lagged somewhat behind other developed nations. MITI's industrial policy was, in this sense, still protectionist and ostensibly aimed at protecting infant industry. Although the line that Japan followed seems similar to that taken by contemporary developing nations, in actuality it was different. In the developing nations, capital and technology were scarce and restrictions on their inflow were rather loosened to let capital and technology flow in, but, after that, objectives of "indigenization" of capital and staff were introduced. Japan, on the other hand, did not take the first major steps toward liberalization until it reached a point where domestic firms became sufficiently competitive, by developing and introducing the majority of required capital and technology by their own efforts. In that sense the purposes of the policy were preventive rather than protective towards foreign capital incursion. Viewed with the advantage of hindsight, Japanese firms did have the capability to meet those goals.

There are two characteristics peculiar to MITI's policy for infant industry. The first is that even if nurturing measures were taken, they did not work for the indefinite continuation of rigid, close relationships between government and industry. One reason for opposition to these measures was the fear that their continuation would lead to an all too close relationship between government and industry, as clearly expressed by F. A. Hayek in a newspaper interview with Saburo Okita published in 1973. Hayek stated that he was opposed to protective measures for infant industries, because once adopted, they tend to become permanent due to the extremely close affiliation developed between government and business. Yet, he added, he would have to change his thinking if Japan actually abolished the protective measures after some years of nurturing and relied thereafter on competition alone, for it would be the first time in history that this had been done. The second characteristic is that these nurturing measures covered almost all the industries under MITI's jurisdiction, although with differences according to relative importance. Strengthening international competitiveness was a goal not limited to a few designated industries.

In general, the nurturing of infant industries is limited to a certain period of time and to a certain number of industries. In Japan, however, these measures were across the board and applied to almost all industries. This Japanese-type view of infant industry may not be admissible from the generally accepted premises of international economics, for one of its fundamental concepts is international division of labor through free trade. Because of the vastly extended promotion of infant industries and across-the-board encouragement of exports, MITI's approach ran counter to the basic principles of modern international economics.

Some might think this overall nurturing of infant industries impossible without a strong centralized system of protection, but MITI's method of strengthening international competitiveness was not very high-handed. What were the conditions provided and the background that made this promotion of infant industries succeed, and why was it successful throughout the entire range of modern industry? Was this just a matter of luck or did it result from the working of an economic system which can be clearly explained?

One of the important features of this development was the maintenance of an exchange rate of ¥360 to the dollar. As I have mentioned on several other occasions (3), this undervalued exchange rate made it possible to sustain the high rate of growth in exports over the long postwar period. Here, I do not use the term "undervalued" in the sense of keeping international payments in the black, according to "balance of payments" criteria. Rather, I use the term according to "purchasing power parity," or commodity price ratio for two countries. It was this ratio that operated to increase exports more than they had been in some other countries. At the time the ¥360 exchange rate was set up, it would probably have been difficult to achieve an equilibrium in international balance of payments, but with the normalization of the world economy, and with Japanese companies beginning to operate a large network of foreign branches, the potential for excess in exports grew larger. Then, the Japanese economy did not absorb the excess by accumulating foreign exchange reserves; it was more prudent to absorb them through continuing the high domestic expansion. The rapid growth in exports rebounded, turning into a boom in domestic investment, and this boom then worked to create a boom in export by decreasing unit costs. Thus a "virtuous" circle was created between investment and exports. MITI's industrial policy might not have succeeded in another country, but its feasibility in Japan, with its undervalued currency, is one of the secrets of the nation's phenomenal economic growth.

Another point is that a resulting export expansion, together with a parallel expansion of the domestic market, accelerated mass production and lowered unit costs, leading to a greater export competitive power. Until the labor shortage trend appeared, there was no fear that this would stimulate inflation.

The Lesson of Japanese Industrial Policy

One reason why industrialization by means of import substitution has not been successful in many developing countries is that it only worked to intensify the dual structure of the domestic economy. It neither raised the level of indigenous industries having played major role in the economy nor improved the general standard of living. Another reason is that even with the introduction of modern industry, industrialization by import substitution was not necessarily directly connected with export promotion, and the products of new industries created were still relatively expensive in comparison with international price levels. This only contributed to worsened balance of payments problems.

Japan was able over time to effectively connect import substitution, by introducing foreign technology, with export promotion. This was due, first, to the fact that private industry had a high degree of capability and vitality. It was also due to the fact that MITI created a good environment in which these private firms could demonstrate those capabilities to the highest. Import restriction and postponement of capital liberalization provided a preparatory period in which firms could strengthen their competitive position through technological advance and other means. By the time the first steps were taken for capital liberalization, Japanese corporations had become strong enough that it was of little concern to them. The fact that MITI's liberalization program came too late is something which has been thoroughly discussed both in Japan and abroad. However, when a country starting late on the path to development has strong desire to catch up with industrialized nations, I do not feel that a delay of this order is something to be rued. On the contrary, I believe that such nations have every right to delay liberalization until the intermediate stages of development.

In addition to the economic conditions already mentioned, Japanese societal structure and national character are such that consensus is easily reached and cooperation is a hallmark of behavior. These psychological aspects have played an important role in making MITI's policy succeed. Because of these features, I do not believe that the same policy could be used in all countries. But, at the same time, one should not consider them useless for those nations with a fervent desire to catch up with the industrialized group. Many economists, totally weighed down by modern economic theory, believe that decentralized political systems and democratic economic policy should be applicable to all developing nations. I strongly disagree with any such notion. Because of annual population growth rates of 3 or 4% and crippling political corruption, many of the developing nations are destined to slide further into the abyss of poverty. In such a situation, it would be far more desirable to have the disorder and chaos cleared away by a strong government which would pave the way for stable development. To urge decentralized governmental forms on such nations is equivalent to ignoring their plight, or even to making it worse.

When I was a student in the United States in 1955, there was an economist belonging to the Mont Pelerin Society, a liberal economist, who urged the developing countries to establish strong, authoritative governments. This made a deep impression on me. He did not wish military dictatorships on the emerging nations; he was talking about the creation of institutions for development that are mandatory to progress in these nations. Even if the policies derived from theoretical systems dealing with atomistic competition have been beneficial to advanced countries in achieving a high economic standard, this does not mean that the same thing will have a validity in the emerging nations. On the contrary, direct application may cause great harm. In this sense, then, Japan's postwar road to industrial development is heretical compared to that of other advanced nations. But this experience does offer a lesson to the developing nations that are eager for economic progress. At the present time, several of the Southeast Asian nations have established boards of investment to coordinate and allocate the flow of incoming foreign capital and to implement tax incentives for investment that is welcome. This pattern is, in one sense, merely a matter of course. There are many points on which the policies correspond to those used by MITI.

When MITI's policy is discussed in Japan, the vast majority of economists assume a rather negative, one might even say derisive, attitude. Almost inevitably they will come out with the comment that MITI actions run counter to the spirit of the anti-monopoly laws. But in Japan, it cannot be denied that the unique industrial policy of MITI plays a very important role in the whole policy system. There are few advanced nations which have an industrial policy like that of MITI; moreover, there is no nation where the focus is on a general, wide-ranging policy of infant industry promotion. Even Friedrich List, the man who first developed the theory of infant industry protection, would be surprised at the thoroughgoing manner in which these ideas have been applied. The reason for these policies was to implement the program designed by MITI—that is, to strengthen the international competitive position. MITI's policy has, however, taken a 180-degree turn during the 1970s, shifting away from strengthening of international competitiveness towards domestic needs and welfare issues.

Now that its mission has been completed, I believe that MITI's industrial policy should be reevaluated from a much broader perspective, both by Japanese and by people from other nations. I also believe that economic historians, economists, sociologists, political scientists, anthropologists, and others in the world will sooner or later be greatly interested in the 30 postwar years of Japanese growth and be tempted to explore them, since, of all the economic policy programs that have appeared, those devised by MITI are quite unique.

I do not mean that an evaluation of these policies should be made from a narrow perspective such as that offered by industrial organization analyses developed in the United States. The study I recommend would look into such questions as the relationship between Japanese industrial society and rapid economic growth, and what sort of impact government policy had on the industrial development. If such research is not done and published for reference throughout the world, then the true picture of Japanese industrial policy will be buried under a mountain of scholarly disfavor, relegated forever to the realm of economic freakdom.

The general tendency of Japanese government policy makers is to look only to the future, and in the halls of the bureaucracy important historical documents are apt to be scattered, lost in the shuffle. The documents and records of Japan's postwar economic growth are something of value to the entire world. It is extremely important that these memoirs and statements by people involved in the actual workings of policy be collected and published as a legacy to the future.

Japan is the first nation to have successfully achieved advanced nation status from a position of backwardness. It is something unique, a nation being able to raise industrial standards the fastest in the post-World War II period. Detailed reports dealing with the realities of the situation—the role of industrial policy, industrial organization, and the societal or anthropological background supporting this postwar development—are very important.

References

1. Baba, M., Kusuda, Y., Fukubayashi, R., and Yokokura, H. "Kaite-kozo to shijo-seika" [Monopsonistic structure and market performance], *Keizai bunseki* [Economic analysis] (Economic Research Institute, Economic Planning Agency), No. 64 (February 1977).
2. Satō, Y. *Kasen-taisei to chusho-kigyo* [Oligopoly systems and small and medium enterprises]. Tokyo: Yuhikaku, 1976.
3. Shinohara, M. "Evaluation of the ¥360 Exchange Rate," in *The Japanese Economy and Southeast Asia*. Tokyo: Institute of Developing Economies, 1977.
4. United States Department of Commerce, Bureau of International Commerce. *Japan: The Government-Business Relationship*. Washington, D.C.: U.S. Government Printing Office, 1972.

II

Changes in Trade Structure

4

THE RISE AND FALL OF ECONOMIC POWERS

The Cases of Britain and the U.S.

Analyzing how capitalist economy has developed in the world as a whole to date is extremely important. In the past, the development of the world economy has often seemed to be propelled by intense competition and rivalry among nations. A certain country may achieve a globally predominant economic influence for a considerable length of time but be visited eventually by a period of relative economic decline. Nonetheless, attempts to analyze the evolution of the world economy in terms of the rise and fall of major economic powers over historical time have been until recently surprising few in number.

The growth of the American economy has lost some momentum, a slowdown occasioned by the weakening of the dollar. The dollar is still the key reserve currency, however, supporting the present international monetary system. What will happen to U.S. leadership in the world economy is an extremely important question. The Japanese economy, meanwhile, has successfully caught up with the U.S. and other industrially advanced countries and has also grown in scale. A rising force on today's world economic scene is a group of countries called the newly industrializing countries (NICs). Those located in Asia include the Republic of Korea, Taiwan, Singapore, and Hong Kong, all of which are characterized by an extremely high rate of export growth. All these phenomena are well worth analyzing in the light of the above-mentioned historical approach.

Many countries expand greatly through international competition. Some come to lead the world economy, while others falter after an initial period of growth. When a country truly achieves global economic leadership and gains the status of a major economic power, we can consider this a momentous switch in the balance of economic power—a

This chapter first appeared in *Japan Echo*, Vol. VI No. 4, 1979, as a slightly abridged translation of "Keizai taikoku no koryu to suitai," *Ekonomisuto*, Aug. 21, 1979.

"changeover of the century," as it were. But when a country's rise in economic power levels off after only 10 or, at most, 30 years, this represents only a small or medium changeover. In other words, it is useful to distinguish from the start between changeovers of major proportions in the balance of economic power and changeovers on a minor scale.

Britain and the United States provide outstanding instances of major changeovers in global economic leadership in the past. Compared with the British and American cases, the strong performances of West Germany and Japan today should be regarded as phenomena of only medium magnitude.

Pax Britannica

Britain's rise to world economic dominance started with the industrial revolution which began around the end of the eighteenth century, spearheaded by the textile industry. Britain's economic growth was also aided by its extensive colonial possessions. At the peak of its economic strength, Britain was in a position to expand exports rapidly. The growth of the British economy brought about by the industrial revolution also stimulated other parts of the world, including the British colonies, through trade.

With the phenomenal expansion of British economic power, the sterling area came into being in the field of currency. The pound sterling became the international currency. Among the common denominators of an international currency are that nations prefer it as a key currency in which they hold external assets and with which they settle international transactions and intervene in the foreign exchange market. The British economy, in its heyday, had sufficient strength to serve as the center of a sterling-dominated sphere of economic influence, and London became the most important center of international finance.

The volume of world trade grew 2.7-fold from 1850 to 1880. In the next period of about 30 years, from 1880 to 1913, it grew 1.7-fold. These are impressive figures. The volume of British exports expanded 3.4 times in the 30 years from 1850 to 1880, far surpassing the growth of world trade as a whole. Between 1880 and 1913 British exports increased 2.2-fold. Although expansion had slowed, British exports still continued to grow faster than world trade as a whole. It was this phenomenal growth during the 1850–80 period that enabled Britain to assume economic leadership of the world and usher in the age of the Pax Britannica.

All this while, the British balance of trade remained unfavorable. But a surplus of revenues in other service balances kept Britain in the black in the current account of its balance of international payments. In 1870, for instance, the British trade balance was £57.5 million in the red, but the current account balance showed a surplus of £54.6 million. Overseas investment for that year was £44.7 million, almost as great as the current account surplus. Twenty years later, in 1890, the trade balance was £86.3 million in the red and the current account balance £108.3 million in the black. An amount close to that surplus, £116.6 million, was invested abroad.

This balance of payments pattern continued into the early twentieth century. Records for the years from 1900 to 1913 show that Britain ran a total trade deficit of £736.6 million while a cumulative surplus of £568.8 million was reported in the current account. But overseas investment continued on a scale almost matching the current account surplus, with a total of £589.7 million for the same period.

In Britain's case, therefore, fairly continuous current account surpluses were cancelled out by the rapid growth of overseas investment. Put differently, the sustained current account surpluses of the British economy were translated into outward investment, instead of being held at home, during the era of British economic supremacy. In this way the world economy as a whole, including colonial areas, was supported in a feedback process.

Pax Americana

Let us now move on to the age of the Pax Americana. The growth of U.S. economic strength progressively changed the share of the American market in overall British exports. Sales to the U.S. accounted for 21% of British exports during the five years between 1851 and 1855. Between 1861 and 1895, however, the American market share declined to 10%–13%. In the 1901–35 period the share of British exports going to the U.S. dropped further to between the 5% and 7% level. This progression shows that in its early phase of economic development the U.S. relied on Britain fairly heavily for its own economic development, but that subsequently American dependence on Britain declined rapidly. Particularly after the turn of the twentieth century, the U.S. became able to continue its economic development on its own.

How did the U.S. balance of payments evolve over time? Taking a look at the developments of merchandise exports and imports (Table 1), we see that imports exceeded exports in 1850–73. From the 1870s onward, however, the U.S. economy switched to a continuing trade surplus.

Notable is the fact that the ratio of the export surplus to total exports, in terms of value, remained extremely high from the late nineteenth century through the early part of the present century. The ratio increased from 14.5% in 1874–95 to 28.8% in 1896–1914. Subsequently the export surplus grew further, to amount to nearly half the value of

Table 1. U.S. Merchandise Trade

(Unit: $1 million)

	Merchandise exports (a)	Merchandise imports (b)	Difference (a − b)	$\frac{a-b}{a}$ (%)
1850–73	6,650	8,125	−1,475	−22.2
1874–95	17,231	14,738	2,493	14.5
1896– June 30, 1914	32,128	22,866	9,262	28.8
July 1, 1914– Dec. 31, 1918	22,974	11,166	11,808	51.4
1920	8,481	5,384	3,097	36.5
1930	3,929	3,104	825	21.0
1940	4,124	2,713	1,411	34.2
1950	10,203	9,081	1,122	11.0
1960	19,650	14,758	4,892	24.9
1964	25,501	18,700	6,801	26.6
1965	26,461	2x,510	4,951	18.7
1966	29,310	25,493	3,817	13.0
1967	30,666	26,866	3,800	12.4
1968	33,626	32,991	635	1.9
1969	36,414	35,807	607	1.7
1970	42,469	39,866	2,603	6.1
1971	43,319	45,579	−2,260	−5.2
1972	49,381	55,797	−6,416	−13.0
1973	71,410	70,499	911	1.3
1974	98,306	103,649	−5,343	−5.4
1975	107,088	98,041	9,047	8.4
1976	114,745	124,054	−9,306	−8.1
1977	120,816	151,689	−30,873	−25.6
1978	142,054	175,813	−29,469	−23.8
1979	182,055	211,524	−29,469	−16.2

Sources: For 1850–1940, *Historical Statistics of the United States 1789–1945*,
U.S. Department of Commerce, 1949; for 1950–77, *Economic Report
to the President,* January 1979, and U.S. Department of Commerce
data.

exports in 1914–18. This is an export surplus of awesome proportions.
In more recent times, as in the 1920s, 1930s, and 1940s, the ratio of the
export surplus to total exports still remained at around 20% or 30%, or
even higher. This pattern was carried over into the postwar period, with
the ratio remaining 12% and 27% up to 1967.

A distinct change began to occur around 1968 as the double-digit
export surplus ratio was reduced to a single-digit figure. And since 1970
the trade balance has been in deficit every year except 1973 and 1975.
In a marked turnabout in the U.S. balance of payments pattern, a high
import surplus ratio of more than 20% was seen in 1977 and 1978.

We have limited our discussion to merchandise exports and imports, but it can still be said that in the case of the U.S. economy the export surpluses sustained through much of the nineteenth and twentieth centuries were not entirely fed back to the world in the form of foreign aid or investment. For a fairly long period gold accumulated and was "sterilized" within the U.S. An unchecked inflow of gold into banking reserves will swell the volume of currency in circulation, so action was taken to sever the link between gold inflow and currency expansion. This is what is meant by gold sterilization.

The above data reveal one condition that must be satisfied if a country is to lead the world economy for an extended period of time. The two countries that played the role of leading economic power over a long term both tended toward a surplus in the current account over a fairly extended period, and much of this surplus was invested overseas. Continuing surpluses and the manner in which these were returned to the rest of the world explain why the British pound developed into an international currency. Again, we may say that America's recurring surplus strengthened the dollar, thus elevating it to the status of an international currency.

As shown in Table 1, however, the United States experienced a reversal of its recurring trade surplus in the latter half of the 1960s and still more in the 1970s. The result was a progressive weakening of the dollar. The overall strength of the U.S. economy is still considerable, so that the reversal of its payments position in itself should not endanger the dollar's position as the key reserve currency in the immediate future. Nonetheless, it is clear that U.S. economic power has already passed its peak and is gradually diminishing.

Economic dominance and the terms of trade

In connection with the rise of an economic superstate as seen in a long-range perspective, let us examine the actual changes in the terms of trade

Table 2. Historical Changes in Terms of Trade

	Britain		Britain	U.S.	Germany
1815	134	1872	95	137	149
1816	150	1900	105	114	109
1830	118	1913	100	100	100
1840	91	1928	118	101	65(1922)
1850	96	1938	143	114	139
1864	76	1952	108	82	111

Sources: British terms of trade data for 1815–64, Werner Schlote, *British Overseas Trade from 1700 to the 1930's* (Blackwell, 1952); for other information, Charles P. Kindleberger, *The Terms of Trade* (Technology Press and Wiley, 1956).

in the case of both Britain and America. As shown in Table 2, during the period when British economic influence was expanding enormously, Britain experienced a fairly rapid deterioration in its terms of trade (the export price index divided by the import price index). The British terms of trade index was as high as 134 in 1815 and 150 in 1816, but then fell steeply, reaching a low point of 76 in 1864. The period of declining terms of trade coincided with that of a major expansion in British exports centered on the growth of cotton textiles. What happened was that domestic industrial development led to lower export prices relative to import prices because of reduced production costs.

Let us see whether a similar decline in the terms of trade index occurred in the case of the United States. The U.S. terms of trade index stood at 137 in 1872 but dropped to 100 by 1913. In other words, the American terms of trade index declined when American economic power extended worldwide. From 1872 onward the same change occurred in the U.S. trade position that had been seen earlier in Britain. But when the American economy entered this robust phase of development and a period of economic decline set in for Britain, the British terms of trade index, in contrast to that of the U.S., rose from 95 in 1872 to 118 in 1928 and to 143 in 1938.

Another interesting observation may be made about this period of history, when British economic influence was waning and two newcomers, Japan and Germany, were surging forward. The German terms of trade index dropped precipitously from 149 in 1872 to 65 in 1922. Similarly, the Japanese terms of trade index dove from 132 in 1903 to 60 in 1935. If we take 1903 as 100, the Japanese index indeed fell as low as 45. But between 1872 and 1938, Britain's terms of trade position improved by as much as 48 points. A country already in a declining phase of economic influence and being chased by newcomers tends to experience a favorable turn in its terms of trade index, while a country racing to catch up suffers a deterioration in its terms of trade index due to rapid improvement in the productivity of its export industries.

From the foregoing, we may say that the changing phases of competitition and rivalry among nations, and the rise and fall in their relative productive power, are precisely mirrored in their changing terms of trade over time. This is an adjustment process that occurs when one leading economic power is replaced by another. To sum up: Britain's terms of trade deteriorated markedly between 1815 and 1864. The U.S. experienced a decline in its terms of trade somewhat later, from 1872 to 1913. In the case of Japan, a similar development took place from around 1900 to 1935. Germany went through a similar phase from 1872 into the 1920s. It is interesting to note that long-term trends in the terms of trade reflect precisely the rise and fall in economic strength of the major economic powers. Of course neither Japan nor Germany was able to advance to a position of predominant global economic leadership. Their cases should be regarded rather as phenomena of medium magnitude.

Japan and the Newly Industrializing Countries

We must now address ourselves to contemporary issues instead of dwelling on the past. Japan's success in catching up with the industrialized West is one such issue. The emergence over the past several years of successfully industrializing countries in various parts of the world is another, and here I would like to focus primarily on NICs in Asia.

To begin with the postwar Japanese experience, the 20 years or so from 1955 onward were a period of rapid catching up with the major advanced countries. This process can be clearly explained in terms of the Akamatsu-Vernon model.[1] Indeed, I believe that this model most effectively and appropriately elucidates the catching-up process of the Japanese economy.

A tendency especially pronounced in such growth industries as steel, automobiles, and electronics is that a rapid expansion in domestic production was followed by an even more rapid expansion in exports. In other words, these industries saw their export-production ratio move upward.

This sequence, expansion of domestic production followed by export growth, as predicted in the Akamatsu-Vernon model, is seen extremely clearly in these three growth industries.

Growth of exports was followed by a sharp increase in overseas investment, a development that took shape most clearly in the 1970s. This new development was checked by the oil crisis of 1973–74. Had it

---

[1] This is a hybrid model combining the theories of economists Kaname Akamatsu of Japan and Raymond Vernon of the U.S. Akamatsu described the process of economic development in terms of three consecutive phases: import of products and industries from advanced countries; growth of domestic production due to increased domestic demand; and exportation of products and industries due to reduced costs attendant on mass production. The sequence of import—production—export, as seen in the development of Japan's cotton industry, reminded Akamatsu of formations of flying geese, and he dubbed his model the "wildgeese-flying pattern." Vernon, in a study of the life cycle of front-running industries, observed how domestic production and the subsequent export phase lead next to investment and advancement of industry overseas.

not been for the oil crisis, Japanese overseas investment probably would have grown still faster.

The upsurge in overseas investment up to 1973 had resulted in drastic changes in the percentage of total exports accounted for by various items. For example, textile exports accounted for 35% of total exports in 1957 but dropped to a mere 5% in 1978. Machinery, by contrast, which comprised 22% of total exports in 1957, grew to 64% in 1978. In no other country does machinery exceed 60% of exports. The share of machinery exports is between 40% and 50% at best in most industrialized countries. The composition of Japanese exports has thus undergone a major transformation. Especially noteworthy is the sharp rise in automobile exports. In 1957, automobiles accounted for a negligible 0.8% of annual exports, but they grew to 15.9% in 1978. The Japanese drive to catch up with the West thus found its most spectacular expression in the growth of the machinery industry.

Boomerang effect

However, there has been a still further phase of development beyond the Akamatsu-Vernon model. Export expansion was followed not only by growth in overseas investment but by a parallel rapid increase in the export of Japanese technology. With the overseas expansion of Japanese businesses and technology, the so-called boomerang effect began to make itself felt. At first it took the form of a sharp increase in textile exports from the Republic of Korea and Taiwan to Japan, spreading later to include electronics, shipbuilding, printing, and many other areas. The boomerang effect can be expected to continue to make itself felt in one way or another.

The boomerang effect is a central aspect of international competition in economic development and of the process of the rise and fall of countries' economic fortunes, and it might even be said to take precedence over the Akamatsu-Vernon model. In retrospect, it can be seen that the boomerang effect is no new phenomenon. Most probably it was powerfully at work when Germany and Japan began to challenge British economic supremacy, and also when the United States took over world economic hegemony from Britain. It is the turn of the U.S. now to feel the pain of the boomerang effect in relation to Japan. The U.S. is suffering the consequences of the know-how it itself exported. In fact, the international transfer of technology is always accompanied by the boomerang effect.

Japan for its part is confronted today with the painful need to abandon certain noncompetitive industries and adjust its industrial structure precisely because Japanese businesses are extensively involved in locally based operations abroad and have exported technology to potential competitors. What we are witnessing is an extremely dynamic process of change in the industrial structure. A truly dynamic economy is compelled to accept a major realignment of its own industries in response to new developments in its external economic relations.

Constraints on Asia's NICs
A particularly noteworthy phenomenon in connection with NICs in Asia is their high rate of export expansion. In dollar terms, South Korean exports grew at an average rate of 42.7% a year between 1970 and 1977. The average annual rate of export expansion in the same period was 21.2% for Hong Kong, 26.9% for Singapore, and 30.8% for Taiwan. To be sure, whether their exports will continue to grow at such a high rate is not certain.

The more rapidly exports and domestic investment expand, the more inevitable is the eventual advent of a slump, just as from time to time in the past the Japanese economy experienced slumps of medium duration in plant and equipment investment after a strong upsurge in investment activity. It is all but certain, nonetheless, that the Asian NICs will continue to demonstrate a higher rate of export growth than most other countries in the world. It is quite natural, however, that doubts arise over how long such a high rate of export growth will continue.

What are some of the factors likely to limit high export growth in the future? The first constraint is these countries' relatively small populations. This holds true, of course, of Singapore and Hong Kong. Even the population of South Korea, somewhat over 30 million, is only about a third of Japan's. Can such a country overcome the limits of its relatively small domestic market and continue expanding its economy? How great is its potential for further development, especially in such growth industries as automobiles? This is one major source of uncertainty over the future of the Asian NICs.

A second problem concerns industrial structure and organization. For Asian NICs to grow rapidly, it is essential that their industrial structure mature rapidly. The industrial structure of the Asian NICs remains immature, however. The automobile industry, for example, requires the manufacture of a host of products, such as engines, other steel products, and glass and rubber parts. In actuality, such parts and components are imported from foreign countries in considerable quantity, and often at a high cost. Thus the NICs do not always enjoy autonomy in their industrial structure. A certain degree of autonomy is a basic requirement for sustained industrial growth. Without this, prolonging economic growth inevitably becomes doubtful.

In the area of industrial organization, taking the example of the automobile industry again, it is necessary to have a large number of affiliated enterprises or independently established firms to carry out subcontracting work. The question is whether a supportive industrial organization of this kind will become well developed as an integral part of the economies of the NICs. If it remains underdeveloped, as at present, the future growth of these countries will suffer from a serious constraint.

Third, any attempt by NICs to accelerate economic growth is likely to run into the problem of inflation. The faster inflation develops, the sooner it can deprive them of their newly achieved competitive advantage in exports.

The fourth problem likely to be encountered by NICs concerns technology. Up to a certain point they can expand exports either by using imported technology or by making use of locally based operations of businesses from advanced countries. But the progressive expansion of exports beyond that point requires not just borrowed technology but a mature technology of their own. The failure of an indigenous technology to mature rapidly enough will act as a major constraint on further economic growth.

In considering the boomerang effect, technology transfers must be viewed together with the overseas expansion of businesses from advanced countries. Still more important, we must take into account the export of "soft" know-how as well as "hard" technology. Next, in weighing the impact of the boomerang effect on Japan, it is insufficient to think of it only in terms of the problem of "reverse imports," or increased imports of competitive products manufactured in developing countries using transferred technology. Even when these countries do not export directly to Japan, their products may come into competition with Japanese exports in third-country markets, thereby reducing the traditional Japanese share. The rising share of competitive electronic products from South Korea, Taiwan, and Hong Kong in the U.S. market at the expense of similar Japanese exports is such a manifestation of the boomerang effect.

The Future of East Asia

In any event, there is no possibility of today's newly industrializing countries taking over world economic leadership in the way that the U.S. and Britain did. For one thing, as already mentioned, the domestic markets of the NICs are too small in scale. Their industrial structure also needs further maturation. It is quite clear, however, that dynamic interaction between national economies will continue. When the boomerang effect comes into play, a temporary gap in production levels may develop among nations, with early starters leading the way in production growth for some time and other nations trailing. But even latecomers may catch up in time.

Assume, for example, that continued growth in South Korea, Taiwan, and Singapore results in an enlarged gap between them and less-developed Southeast Asian countries. This lead many well diminish in time. Industrialization in South Korea will advance to a stage where production expands strongly in the shipbuilding and other machinery manufacturing industries, for example, while in the Southeast Asian region the growth of the textile industry will pick up speed, resulting in a relative shrinking of the competing textile industries in South Korea and Taiwan. This is, as it were, a boomerang effect in reverse, and the more inflation accelerates in the NICs, the more strongly this effect will be felt. In this sense, the periods in which the economic gap among nations expands and the periods in which it diminishes reveal a most interesting process of dynamic change in relative economic development.

The most important factor in the economic future of Asia is China. A small conference on joint-venture businesses involving Japanese firms was held in 1978 in Manila. In a speech at the meeting Philippine Industry Minister Vicente Paterno stressed that as a result of the Chinese modernization policy East and Southeast Asia would probably become a major growth region. I felt that this was a bit too sanguine an outlook and, playing the role of devil's advocate, called the conference's attention to the negative aspects of the boomerang effect.

If China decides to expand not only its textile industry but also, for security reasons vis-à-vis the Soviet Union, its steel, defense, and nuclear power industries, it will have to import the necessary equipment and materials. To pay for these imports, China will probably be compelled to emphasize the development of natural resources and light industries. The growth of light industries, such as textiles, will have an adverse effect on the hard-won gains made by the NICs in Asia as well as on the prospects for the growth of light industries in the ASEAN countries. How soon such a phase of economic development in China and the rest of Asia will occur is not known. It could come 5, 10, or even 15 years from now. Nevertheless, China's emergence as an economic rival of the other Asian countries is only a matter of time.

It is equally probable, however, that other Asian countries will benefit from the increasing Chinese demand for a certain period before China emerges as a powerful competitor. If modernization does not make smooth headway in China—or if worst comes to worst and the pace of modernization remains sluggish for another 20 years or so—the other

Asian countries will reap little benefit. More likely, however, is an unexpected acceleration in China's modernization, made possible by international technology transfers. Since numerous such instances have been seen, especially since World War II, it will probably not take as long as 20 years before China's modernization benefits the other Asian countries.

Thus, the positive Chinese effect may well come into play up to a point, turning East and Southeast Asia into a growth region. At the same time, there is an equally strong likelihood that the positive effect will be overtaken eventually by the negative one, limiting economic growth in Asia. Even when we focus on the outlook for Asia alone, a highly dynamic process of economic development, marked by ups and downs in growth under the influence of China's modernization, seems to lie ahead.

Qualifications of a major economic power

Extending the line of reasoning developed thus far, an immediate issue to be considered in relation to Japan is the internationalization of the yen. We do not know whether, as Norman MacRae of the *Economist* has predicted, Japan can become a major economic power capable of replacing the U.S. in the twenty-first century. For the time being it is reasonable to consider that any modification in the world economic situation introduced by the Japanese economy will be restricted to one of medium magnitude at most and will fall short of a major changeover.

As long as the rise of Japanese economic power is limited to a phenomenon of medium magnitude, there is probably a limit to the internationalization of the yen as well. Most significant in this connection is the historical fact that both the U.S. and Britain were able to provide key currencies precisely because of their sustained current account surpluses over an extended period. In the case of Japan, the very prospect of its running a surplus as long as did the U.S. or Britain would be vehemently resisted by other countries.

Generally speaking, the role of finance is to recycle financial resources from where they are abundant to where they are scarce. The need for international financial flows only arises because some countries run export surpluses and others run export deficits. Whether the currency of an up-and-coming economic power is fully accepted as an international currency, therefore, depends on whether that country can sustain current account surpluses over a certain period of time. Maintaining current account surpluses over the long term, as was the case with the U.S. and Britain, seems to be an indispensable condition for a major change in the locus of world economic leadership.

For this reason, it is hardly likely that the yen will become the dominant international currency unless the Japanese balance of payments surplus is allowed to persist. Neither the French franc nor the German mark is the pivotal international currency today, either. The yen will remain under constraints similar to those on the mark and franc, particularly in view of the prevailing Japanence timidity in liberalizing interest rates.

Before closing, I would like to call attention to an additional problem. It is possible to describe the vicissitudes in relative economic strength among nations, as I have just attempted, but we must also remain aware of the existence of longer-term swings in economic activity, the so-called Kondratieff cycles. The first of these originated in the industrial revolution, centering on the rise of the textile industry in Britain, and extended from the 1780s to 1842. The second cycle, lasting from 1842 to 1892, was associated with the invention of the steam engine and the growth of iron and steel manufacturing. The third, beginning in 1898, was generated by the development of the electrical machinery, chemical, and automobile industries. With the fourth or latest cycle, it is difficult to pinpoint its origin and end. Most probably, however, an upsurge in technological innovation having a duration of about 50 years was touched off around 1930 and has lasted until the present.

The latest cycle is characterized by the fact that technical innovations have not been confined to a few specific industries but have taken place across the board. Its second feature is the rapid international transmission of innovations, with multinational firms, especially those based in the U.S., serving as the vehicle of transmission. As a result, the economic growth rate in every country has doubled or tripled over its prewar growth rate. Only in the U.S., where most of the technological progress was initiated, has the economy shown much the same tempo of growth after World War II as before.

To repeat, the fourth long-term cycle in the modern world economy is notable for the prevalence and rapid international transmission of technological innovations and for accelerated growth. One of the questions left unanswered is whether the long-term surge in technological innovation is related to the rise and fall in the relative economic strength of nations. I have been unable to relate the timing of the two phases quantitatively, but I suspect that further inquiry into this question would enable us to identify a significant relationship between the two.

In any event, the international economic developments I have discussed in this article are important for forecasting the future of the world economy. They also comprise an aspect of the dynamic, long-term changes in the global capitalist economic system that has been ignored in previous economic analyses. Such an analytical viewpoint is not only of urgent importance in relation to immediate problems in international economic relations but also useful to a better understanding of the longer-term dynamics of the world economy.

5

THE BOOMERANG EFFECT RECONSIDERED

This chapter discusses:

First, the boomerang effect of the rapid economic growth of Asia's newly industrializing countries (NICs), such as the Republic of Korea, Taiwan, Hong Kong, and Singapore, that has been drawing attention in the 1970s and the various factors that will limit the ongoing thrust of this high growth;

Second, the development strategy of the Association of Southeast Asian Nations (ASEAN) in terms of production of primary commodities;

Third, the significance, for Japan, of the creation of ASEAN, from the twin aspects of the stabilization of primary commodity prices following the formation of ASEAN's countervailing power and the establishment of a regional balance in Japanese investments.

Finally, the economic consequences for Japan of Asian NICs, ASEAN, and of China's recent path towards modernization and the boomerang effect which could result ten or fifteen years from now.

The Akamatsu-Vernon Process in Postwar Japan

Japan's industrial structure underwent drastic changes in the course of the high economic growth during the postwar years, but the major transformation took place in the export sector. From the 1960s onwards, exports grew at a faster rate than domestic production in the growing industries, resulting in a startling rise in the ratio of exports to the quantity of domestic production. For instance, in the automotive industry, the export ratio for passenger cars stood at only 4.2% in 1960, grew to 22.8% in 1970, and rose rapidly to 40% in 1975, to reach 54.5% in 1977. Similarly, the proportion of machinery in Japan's total exports reached 61.8% in 1977, a ratio that is without parallel among industrially developed nations, none of which has reached a 50% ratio.

This chapter was originally published as "Japan's Strategies towards New Developments in the Economics of East and Southeast Asia," in *Contemporary Southeast Asia*, Vol. 1 No. 1, May 1979.

Such growing dependence on exports can also be seen in the steel industry. A survey of the export-to-production ratio for ordinary and rolled steel shows that in 1960 it stood at only 13.0%, rising to 23.3% in 1970 and 33.3% in 1975, and reaching 37.6% in 1977. These are examples of only two industries, but generally speaking the same marked trend can be seen in all expanding industries.

This trend shows that a sharp swell in exports followed the trends in domestic production during the period 1960–70. This, in turn, was followed by the rapid overseas expansion of Japanese enterprises, which was for a few years impeded by the effects of the oil crisis. Authorized overseas investment grew 2.3-fold between 1964 and 1967 and 3.3-fold between 1967 and 1970, and then accelerated at the rate of 3.9-fold from 1970 to 1973. This pace, needless to say, was far more rapid than that of the increase in exports. Since 1974, however, overseas investments have been sluggish. This clearly shows that the long-range trend towards the internationalization of the Japanese industrial structure in the postwar years developed along the lines of Raymond Vernon's hypothesis of:

domestic production → exports → overseas expansion.

This important point must be clearly recognized in observing the linkage between the economic development of East and Southeast Asia and Japan's economic strategy. And it appears that it was in Japan that the Akamatsu-Vernon process has been most evident in the postwar period.

To the process as described above (see Chapter 4), I should like to add as a hypothesis another important phenomenon. This is the "boomerang effect" that I first referred to in my Japanese-language book *Industrial Structure* (Tokyo: Chikuma Shobo, 1976). The phenomenon I dealt with referred to the "imports in reverse" into Japan that follow the overseas expansion of Japanese enterprises and the subsequent need to make adjustments in domestic industry. My hypothesis is that this effect follows in the wake of overseas expansion.

The Boomerang Effect

Japanese textile imports from 1972 to 1973 registered a sharp 3.1-fold increase, with the result that Japan's textile industry, which had long maintained an export surplus, suddenly registered an import surplus, thus seriously aggravating the prevailing recession in the industry at that time. However, this import surplus situation lasted only one year as Japanese textile exports, spurred by the export drive caused by the general economic recession from 1974 onwards, resumed a steady growth. Nevertheless, textile imports between 1972 and 1973 increased 3.1-fold in one year from US$547,380,000 to US$1,714,780,000. Compared to the US$161,270,000 worth of textile imports in 1968, the amount in 1973 represented a 10.6-fold increase. Despite the recession, these textile imports in 1977 remained at about the same level as in 1973, amounting to US$1,732,300,000.

This process spread from textiles to sundry goods, and its proliferation was first expected to halt at electronics. However, as is generally known, it is also visible today in the printing industry, following the sharp increase in the preparation of block copy by the use of cheap labor in Korea and Taiwan.

Moreover, in the shipbuilding industry it is obvious that South Korea, which used to be looked upon as a possible eventual substitute for Japan for the construction of small vessels, is now building large ships. For instance, the Hyundai Shipbuilding Yard at Ulsan recently had orders on hand that were comparable to those for the largest Japanese yards. While in Japan the backlog for shipbuilding orders was decreasing, the Korean shipbuilding industry was growing rapidly.

The boomerang is a throwing club used by Australian aborigines and is so designed that it will return to the thrower after describing a large arc. The term "boomerang effect" may be appropriately applied to the phenomenon in which goods cheaply produced by Japanese enterprises in factories abroad are imported into Japan.

Although these "imports in reverse" are only natural, they provoke a rearrangement of the domestic industrial structure, rendering an industrial adjustment unavoidable. Of course, when this phenomenon occurs during a period of high economic growth, industries that are on the wane as a result of industrial adjustment could be replaced by new industries so that the resulting boomerang does not bring about a decrease in the economic growth rate. However, the world economy as a whole has entered a period of slower growth since the oil crisis. Under such circumstances, it is extremely difficult to avoid a deceleration of growth as a result of industrial adjustment.

However, it seems that a reformulation of my 1976 explanation of the phenomenon is now called for.

Redefinition of the Boomerang Effect

I originally sought to describe the boomerang effect as a phenomenon that brought about industrial adjustments in Japan as a consequence of "imports in reverse," arising from the overseas expansion of Japanese enterprises. However, it seems to me that this definition needs to be broadened.

The boomerang effect is not solely caused by the overseas expansion of enterprises. It can also be created by exports of technologies that are not always linked to joint ventures. For instance, there was no question of joint ventures when Japan exported steelmaking and shipbuilding technologies to South Korea.

Japanese *sogo shosha* (trading conglomerates) have played an extremely dynamic role in exporting locally manufactured products. Therefore, even without the overseas expansion of manufacturing firms or technological exports, the overseas expansion of these trading conglomerates, with their extremely powerful marketing capacity, can effectively subject Japan to a boomerang effect through the application of their know-how and "soft technology." Thus an NIC can conceivably apply Japanese management and marketing techniques in its export drives into the Japanese market.

So far I have only emphasized the "imports in reverse" arising from the overseas expansion of Japanese enterprises. But the boomerang effect, taken in a broader sense, should also include the intensification of competition in third markets and a reduction of the Japanese market share. For instance, in 1970, Japanese exports of television sets held an 80.9% share in the American market, but by 1975 this share dropped to 59.7%. In contrast, the share of exports in the same market from Asian NICs (Korea, Singapore, Hong Kong, and Taiwan) grew during the same period from 12.6% to 39.5%.

If this phenomenon of the replacement of Japan by Asia's NICs in third markets is taken into consideration, it can be said that the effect has been slowly growing over the long postwar period. With a labor shortage and the rise in wages in Japan, the export share of Hong Kong, Taiwan, and Korea for textiles and sundry goods has shown an increase since the latter part of the 1950s while Japan's share dwindled. It goes without saying that this trend has been accelerated by the establishment of joint ventures and export of technology by Japanese enterprises as well as investment in the NICs by other industrially advanced nations.

If we redefine the phenomenon in this manner, the area of application becomes extremely wide. For example, with the rapid growth of Japanese textile exports in all the world markets in the 1920s and 1930s, Britain's world export share was reduced. The global shift from Pax Britannica to Pax Americana was also effectively, in a sense, an economic boomerang effect on a grand scale. In essence, it meant a change-over in leadership in the world economy.

Taken in this context, the effect can be applied as a principle in explaining the ebb and flow and the rise and fall of nations that assume economic leadership by controlling the development process of the world economy. Marx's theory of capitalism was centered on domestic economy, and his theory of imperialism was just an appendage. It is exactly the same, insofar as these points are concerned, in the "magnificent dynamics" of Schumpeter's "business cycles." However, the real dynamism of the world economy should be grasped in the light of the competition among nations to acquire economic leadership.

There is today sufficient data to substantiate the dynamic changes that are taking place in the comparative advantage between nations arising from competition in exports, the overseas expansion of enterprises, and export of technology. Is there, however, a possibility that a Pax Japonica will replace the Pax Americana? There are those who believe so. I am not quite certain. The prime question here is whether Asia's NICs will succeed in catching up with Japan.

Asia's NICs and Their Future Direction

A survey on the recent economic growth of Korea, Hong Kong, Singapore, and Taiwan, which are called Asia's NICs, shows that the average real GNP growth rate between 1968 and 1977 was 11.2% for South Korea, 8.2% for Hong Kong, 10.4% for Singapore, and 9.0% for Taiwan—an overall average of about 10%. Their export growth rate from 1970 to 1977 in U.S. dollars, however, was 42.7% for South Korea, 21.2% for Hong Kong, 26.9% for Singapore, and 30.8% for Taiwan, averaging about 30% and ranging from 20 to 40% according to the country.

A future projection of South Korea's export growth rate made on this basis produces some startling figures. Supposing that Korean exports grow by 40% each year, the US $10.047 million in exports in 1977 will grow to US $105.9 billion by 1984, exceeding the US $80.5 billion level of Japanese exports in 1977. Even assuming a slower growth rate of 20%, Korean exports will amount to US $89.6 billion by 1989. To sum up, this means that, at either rate, the amount of South Korea's exports in the next decade will match that of Japan today.

The amount of exports in 1977 ranging from Singapore's US $8,241 million, Taiwan's US $9,349 million, and Hong Kong's US $9,626 million showed little variation from the US $10,047 million figure achieved by South Korea. This means that, if they can achieve a 20% growth rate, each of Asia's NICs can be expected to match the present amount of Japan's exports in about fifteen years. However, it should be noted that many of Singapore's exports are actually re-exports of primary commodities produced in the surrounding region.

It therefore becomes necessary to examine closely the factors that will restrain the potential for growth in exports, as well as the capacity for growth in the domestic economy. It is difficult to designate for each country in definite quantitative terms the factors that will restrain the maintenance of their common high rate of export growth. It is nevertheless possible to make a qualitative examination of various problems involved.

Among these Asian NICs, South Korea has a population of 36.4 million, but Hong Kong has only 4.5 million and Singapore about 2.3 million. It will probably be difficult for the latter two, in seeking export-led high economic growth, to develop mass-production machinery industries, such as, for example, an automotive industry. It appears impossible for Hong Kong or Singapore to develop an automotive industry without relying on a system of division of labor involving other countries. Even in South Korea and Taiwan, an automotive industry that could become a powerful export industry would not be viable unless domestic demand expands to the point where costs can be reduced through mass production. Japan's postwar experience shows that the rapid expansion of the automotive industry in the late 1950s paved the way for possible development of ancillary industries in order that high industrial development could be achieved.

In this context, it seems that the development of a continuous high rate of growth in exports, particularly in the machinery sector, requires an expanded domestic market. Such a market would make possible the essential linkage in the Akamatsu-Vernon process involving the expansion of domestic production that leads to cost reduction which, in turn, results in the growth of exports. In the case of South Korea however, the development of an automotive industry may be possible, given sufficient time, if consideration is given to the fact that its population is more than one-third as large as Japan's. Nevertheless, the process will not be as easy as in Japan, inasmuch as the manufacturing cost of a car in Korea today is about double the international price level for such a vehicle. Attention should also be paid to the fact that the smallness of its domestic market may constitute a barrier to the expansion of a mass-production industry.

Should NICs seek rapid expansion, they will find that inflation will be aggravated, with a resultant rise in wages that is likely to adversely affect the export competitiveness of the very labor-intensive industries they have developed. In such an event, labor-intensive industries there will face the possibility of losing ground to Asia's less developed countries (LDCs). This in itself may be considered a favorable development in the sense that it will narrow the income level gap between NICs and LDCs. But, on the other hand, it could as well jeopardize the continuity of the NICs' efforts to catch up with industrially developed nations. In this context, it appears necessary for NICs to avoid as much as possible falling into the vortex of inflation if they are to maintain the continuity of their development.

As we look at the industrial structure in terms of the input-output tables of most industrially developed countries, we find that few or no gaps can be found in the boxes of their inter-industry tables. But we do not find this same characteristic in the LDCs. For instance, even though automobiles may be produced by the assembly method, many essential parts must be imported. And when domestic production of intermediate products such as steel proves insufficient, there will be an absence of an interrelated structure, such as that which can be seen in industrially advanced nations, forming a closeknit industrial block taking in the automotive industry and its ancillary industries. This results in inter-industry gaps in the LDCs.

In the case of the NICs, the inter-industry characteristics are halfway between the industrially-developed nation type and the LDC type. Consequently, should the NICs seek to expand a key export industry and, in particular, various machinery industries, it becomes essential for them to carry out a parallel expansion of ancillary industries. However, should they lay emphasis on speed, they will find that the more they do so the larger becomes the imbalance between sectors. This can well become a restraining factor both on their development and on their efforts to catch up with the industrialized nations. In this manner, factors that do not have a restraining effect during gradual development could well become restraining factors in an attempt to achieve rapid development.

In Japan, the subcontracting system had already been developed before the Second World War. It is true that this system led to abuses by large enterprises who exploited their subcontractors or shifted cost-reduction burdens onto them. However, in the postwar years close technological cooperation, financial assistance, and an interflow of personnel have developed between the major "parent" enterprise and its medium or small subcontractors to the point where the latter have come to be known as "cooperating firms" or affiliates.

In the automotive industry, about 60% of the total manufacturing cost consists of parts ordered from these outside subcontracting manufacturers. Had these subcontractors been unable to lower costs by increasing productivity and improving the quality of their products, it is doubtful whether the Japanese automotive industry could have acquired its present strong international competitiveness. In Asia's NICs we find that the automotive industries have not properly nurtured these enterprises manufacturing component parts. It is true that the American practice shows that these parts manufacturers need not be affiliate companies. But, unfortunately, the preparations made by the NICs in setting up an industrial organization that will permit smooth manufacturing operations at the parent company's plant are insufficient. If various industries with relatively high technological progress and with a high income elasticity can be developed into export industries it may be possible for the NICs, which have aimed for the growth of export-oriented economies, to catch up with the industrialized nations. The question is how fast they can develop an industrial organization like the one I have described for such growth industries.

The last point deals with the nature of technological progress. In order to give continuity to the catching-up process, it will be necessary to advance from the stage where borrowed technology and low wages are combined to that where the adopted technology will become more sophisticated and raised to a higher level. Unless this task is accomplished, it will be impossible to catch up. That is why continuity requires a cumulative uplift of technological levels. Japan's perseverance in this helped to bring about its continuous high growth in the postwar years.

Japan has now reached a new stage in which the penetration of invisible soft technologies that are interchangeable among industries has become a more important objective than the adoption of hard technology or the establishment of a visible leading industry. In this new situation, machinery hardware and information software are generally losing their separate identities and becoming the obverse and reverse of the same thing.

In the light of these experiences, the key to forecasting the cumulative and continuous character of the catching-up efforts of Asia's NICs can be said to lie in whether or not such technological evolution can be continued. It is possible for them for the time being to quicken the pace in industrial and export growth simply by importing technology. However, the secret for longer-term growth at high speed may decidedly lie in the evolutionary process described here.

Development Strategies in Resource-Rich Countries

Exports of primary commodities from ASEAN countries to Japan, excepting Singapore, represent a minimal fraction of Japan's total imports. In 1977, this ratio was 1.3% for the Philippines, 1.1% for Thailand, 7.1% for Indonesia, and 2.2% for Malaysia. Nevertheless, these exports to Japan constitute a substantial proportion of the total exports of these nations. In 1977, the ratio to total exports was 29.0% for the Philippines, 21.4% for Thailand, 60.6% for Indonesia, and 25.7% for Malaysia. A large proportion of these exports consists of primary commodities such as foodstuffs, raw materials, and mineral fuels. Principal among them are lumber from the Philippines, Indonesia, and Malaysia; copper ore from the Philippines; raw rubber and tin from Malaysia and Thailand; and sugar from the Philippines and Thailand. Exports of processed goods constitute a negligible amount of their exports to Japan. While the importance of exports of processed goods relative to total exports is growing, the output share of such goods in these countries remains extremely low.

This shows that, unlike the case of Asia's NICs, primary commodities constitute an overwhelming proportion in the exports of these four nations—Thailand, the Philippines, Indonesia, and Malaysia. In order to raise the living standards of the people in general, it will be necessary to raise the productivity of primary industries. However, the growth rate in primary industries is relatively low and the terms of trade may be unstable. Moreover, if the terms of trade deteriorate, the advantage gained by increased productivity might disappear. In addition, primary commodities with lower income elasticity will be handicapped in technological progress.

It is only natural that, in order to solve this problem, emphasis should be laid on the processing of primary commodities and the export of their resulting products. This forms the background for the emphasis on agro-industries and on the resource-based industries for local natural resources. Inasmuch as import substitution leads to the aggravation of a dual industrial structure, thus perpetuating the deficit in the balance of payments, stress should be laid on the export of processed goods, that is, on realizing "export substitution."

However, these countries, rich in resources, in contrast to the resource-poor Asian NICs, find it less urgent to emphasize exports. As a result, their export growth rate tends to be lower than that of the NICs. Nevertheless, their export growth rate in the 1970s, calculated on a dollar base, is high. Between 1970 and 1977, the annual rate of growth in exports was 29.2% for Indonesia, 25.6% for Thailand, 19.9%

for Malaysia, and 16.9% for the Philippines. However, the real growth rate is actually lower as the prices of primary commodities have moved upwards considerably.

Attention should also be given to the fact that the export dependency ratio on industrial products with a relatively high export growth rate rose in all these countries. Moreover, even when the demand growth rate for most primary commodities remains low, exports of varieties with a relatively high demand growth rate may automatically raise the export growth rate. For instance, a high export growth rate could be attained for good-quality tropical hardwood among forest resources and lobsters and tuna in maritime resources. Oil constituted a very large proportion in the composition of Indonesia's exports following the extraordinary rise in oil prices after the oil crisis. The fact that Indonesia has petroleum resources in this age of energy restriction seems to form the basis for the rise of that country's overall export growth rate to 29.2%.

In any case, the economic strategies of those ASEAN countries that produce primary commodities should never be one-sided, but plural. Thus emphasis should be placed on labor-intensive industries, in order to absorb excess labor resources. However, the following points have also to be borne in mind.

Welcoming only small and medium industries from abroad will give rise to conflict with existing indigenous industries. For this reason, necessary "big projects" and nurturing of big enterprises should not be ignored in attracting resource development and modern industries.

While the expansion of the domestic market is necessary to raise the national income level and to absorb unemployment, equally important is the expansion of export markets to secure funds to pay for the import of essential capital goods.

In countries like Indonesia where the export of oil is important, the development of the oil industry should be undertaken by major enterprises. Funds obtained from oil exports should be used for developing labor-intensive medium-sized and small industries that would absorb the excess manpower in Java. It is sensible to stress parallel development of major enterprises and these medium and small industries, as advocated by Sumitro Djojohadiksumo.

In addition, while it is sensible to give weight to primary industries, industrialization—regardless of whether it is aimed at import subsitution, export orientation, or resource development—is also very important. A strategy tending to lean towards either option would be short-sighted, especially in the case of resource-rich countries.

Japanese enterprises expanding abroad have been criticized for neglecting "upstream" investments. The parallel development of both the "upstream" and "downstream" aspects is, however, necessary.

Taking all these into consideration, it is evident that it would be harmful for these resource-rich countries, in adopting a development strategy, to tilt towards any of the various available options, namely, major enterprises versus medium and small enterprises; exports versus domestic markets; import substitution versus export orientation; or "upstream" versus "downstream" investments. Each country should decide which course to follow on a case-by-case basis, depending on the prevailing circumstances, while giving full thought to the cost-benefit aspect. Japanese economic cooperation should also be determined by taking into consideration the peculiar conditions existing in each country.

ASEAN versus Japan

The formation of ASEAN should be appreciated by Japan in terms of economic development. This is primarily because the creation of a countervailing power in this area against the advanced countries carries great significance in that it helps rationalize the price formation of primary commodities whose prices by nature tend to be unstable and to settle at a low level. At present, there is not a single advanced country that does not provide domestic price supports for its agricultural produce. By the same token, such action should be equally appropriate when applied on an international scale. The question arises, however, whether this should be implemented by the Common Fund or by some other mechanism.

At a time when worldwide market prices of primary commodities are fluctuating, it will be necessary to make a further study of the particular consequences of price stabilization applicable only to ASEAN primary commodities. It is even more important to establish standards for the price levels at which this stabilization will be carried out. Moreover, the levels which will serve as standards will have to change in the medium and long terms. Although "cyclical price flexibility" may be sacrificed to some extent in the short run, "structural price flexibility" in the medium and long term must not be sacrificed. For should this happen, not only will a rational allocation of world resources be impeded but international stagflation could be aggravated.

In this context, while the objective of avoiding short-term instability of primary commodity prices and of preventing them from being set at a low level may be proper, it will be necessary at the same time to carry out a dialogue on the maintenance of structural price flexibility in order to arrive at applicable uniform standards from time to time.

The second reason the creation of ASEAN is important for, and welcomed by, Japan is that the existence of such a regional entity may help further rationalize the regional balance of Japanese aid and overseas investments. If ASEAN did not exist, Japanese investments in Southeast Asia might have been geographically biased, following only the Japanese entrepreneurial spirit. While this may not necessarily destroy the regional balance of such investments, it could well upset this balance in the short and medium terms. In order to avoid such a development, at least in respect to big capital-intensive projects, it will be necessary for ASEAN to formulate rational and reasonable regional industrial projects so that Japanese and other investments may be carried out in a rational manner by maintaining a balance within the ASEAN region itself.

However, among the ASEAN industrial projects agreed upon at the ASEAN Economic Ministers' Conference in Kuala Lumpur in 1976, the Singapore diesel engine project seems to have collapsed because of demands by Indonesia and other nations to have their own facilities for the manufacture of relatively large diesel engines. Moreover, according to articles by H.W. Arndt and Lim Chong Yah in the autumn of 1978 issue of *Asian Pacific Community*, the urea projects in Indonesia and Malaysia, the Philippine project for superphosphate fertilizer, and the soda ash project in Thailand appear to be encountering some difficulties. Although such difficulties may indeed exist, it has been recognized, since the publication of the Robinson Report in 1974, that a regional unity of this type is necessary insofar as big industrial projects are concerned.

The first criticism directed at Japan when it invested in ASEAN was that of Japanese "over-presence." Since this criticism seems to have disappeared today, it is to be assumed that a steady flow of Japanese investments continues to be welcomed. Nevertheless, a violent increase in investments of the so-called torrential flood variety and the alternating "on-off" type of impulsive investments are still looked upon with disapproval. Instability and violent fluctuations of Japanese investments can be attributed to the instability of the world economy and the inappropriate handling of domestic economic policies in Japan, as well as to the specific variations of policies concerning foreign capital investment in the host countries. In this respect, there seems to be room for adjustments by both sides.

If up to now Japanese investments have given rise to criticism of the Japanese over-presence, it will be necessary for the ASEAN nations

as host countries to formulate a consistent plan to induce such investments so as to avoid another kind of criticism, namely, that of a re-
gionally biased presence, which is bound to arise in the future. The
longer the establishment and implementation of this plan is delayed, the
more confused will Japanese economic cooperation with ASEAN become. In this "Age of Uncertainty," the implementation of big industrial
projects requiring huge amounts of capital calls for complete understanding based on rational perception and a spirit of mutual concession. A
regional division of labor based on understanding should be looked
upon as a shortcut for today's LDCs which are seeking to catch up
with the advanced countries, starting from a low level.

In order to avoid future uncertainties associated with big projects,
Japan as an investor frequently provides funds from semi-governmental
organizations such as the Overseas Economic Cooperation Fund and the
Japan Export-Import Bank. This participation of semigovernmental
organizations in consortiums of enterprises expanding overseas should
be welcomed so long as the importance of the big projects is internationally recognized. However, should the construction of a mammoth
project be agreed upon at the political level and then forced upon industry, it will run the risk of developing into a "political boomerang."
For instance, if no country agreed to buy the products for such a huge
industry, Japan would have to buy them. The result would be that the
relevant Japanese industry would have to make sacrifices for political
reasons. It is therefore necessary to pay close attention to this matter in
order to avoid having Japanese overseas investment projects influenced
by politics and by the irresponsible statements of Japanese politicians.

China, the NICs, and ASEAN

Finally, two issues, namely, the relation of the NICs to ASEAN, and
that of China to the NICs and the ASEAN, should be examined. The
development of Asian NICs could well create a favorable economic
environment for the ASEAN nations that produce primary commodities. From a worldwide viewpoint, Southeast Asian nations have
so far registered a comparatively high rate of economic growth, probably due, in part, to Japan's high growth rate. The same may be said of the
effects of the future development of the NICs. Should the NICs face a
shortage of labor or rising wage costs in the future, the Southeast Asian
nations that produce primary commodities will also find that their
light industries will benefit from an expanded export demand in addition to the present domestic demand. Consequently, the per-capita

income gap between the NICs and the LDCs, which may have been widening to that point, may possibly begin to shrink.

On the one hand, the development of the NICs will directly stimulate the LDCs' development by stimulating imports from the LDCs; while, on the other, the LDCs' development will have a boomerang effect on the NICs. However, these positive effects on the LDCs may eventually be replaced by a larger negative effect on them as the continued high growth of the NICs will widen the per-captia income gap between the LDCs and the NICs.

Should the new modernization line adopted by China in 1978 prove to be sustained, it will give rise to another issue. Faced with the Soviet threat, China may well engage in modernizing its defense establishment and expand its military and basic industries. To achieve this, it is evident that China will seek to import technology, management know-how, and capital for its steel and other basic industries from Japan and the United States. However, should China—where wages are said to be one-fifth of those in Korea—seek to develop its light industries, for example the textile industry, this would contribute to the improvement of its people's livelihood. But it may also trigger a startling expansion in exports based on low labor costs. Such may be the negative impact of China's economic modernization on Asia's NICs and LDCs in the next decade.

However, should the fear of such a development lead to a refusal on the part of Japan and the United States to cooperate in China's modernization, China will naturally turn to other industrially-developed nations, such as West Germany, France, and Britain, for the import of capital and technology. Under these circumstances, neither Japan nor the United States can avoid actively cooperating with China in the development of its latent economic power. Until the anticipated Chinese boomerang effect takes place, Japan, the NICs, and the LDCs will compete to garner their respective advantages from the fruits of China's economic modernization and concentrate on transforming their respective areas into growth regions. (Early in the 1980s, the speed of Chinese modernization centered on the investment industries seems to have been intentionally slowed. However, I feel that since a socialist country like China may follow a zig-zag dynamic course, the suppression of growth may not continue long, say for more than five years).

Japan's strategies to meet these expected changes are yet to be formulated. For the time being, Japanese industry will benefit from the trade with China, and the Japanese government will probably seek to promote this trend. How long this tendency will continue remains unknown. It will depend on whether there is a positive response from

Chinese industry to economic cooperation with Japan and other countries and, if there is one, on how fast this response materializes.

As time goes by, Japan, ASEAN, and Asia's NICs may gradually show a growing enthusiasm for the elaboration of programs, plans, and policies that cut across borders to meet the competition that may develop in the future. It will also be necessary for the ASEAN nations to take concerted action on economic projects and raise their income levels.

On the Japanese side, it will be necessary for politicians, businessmen, and intellectuals, who at last have awakened to the need for internationalization, to carry out reforms in the country's administrative and business structures. Above all, the Japanese people will first have to be liberated from their recluse-like outlook so that they can begin to engage in dialogues with the peoples of Asia, with a new sense of international values. In this context, Japan's strategies today should not be confined to minimal measures for individual problems. What Japan needs now is the emergence of a new vision and the development of sympathy towards its Asian neighbors who have so long been neglected. The more such attitudes become widespread, the more rapidly will economic relations between Japan and its Asian neighbors, including Southeast Asia, improve.

6

TRADE AND INDUSTRIAL ADJUSTMENTS IN THE ASIA–PACIFIC REGION

Issues

During the period of high-pitched growth after World War II, Japan's trade and industrial structure underwent striking changes. In fact, due to Japan's impact, the economies of its neighboring nations may also have undergone unprecedentedly rapid structural changes. Speaking broadly, when the economy of a major country gathers strength at a rapid pace, its achievements often bring about significant repercussions in its neighboring nations. Cases in point are Great Britain from the end of the nineteenth century onward and the United States in the first half of the twentieth century. Japan's rapid economic growth after World War II, which lasted for more than 30 years, also had an impact on the economies of the Asia-Pacific region in one way or another. It has been prophesied over and over again that East and Southeast Asia will be one of the world's "growth regions" in the twenty years before the end of this century. This projection sounds even more convincing when the postwar growth performance of Japan and other nations in the Asia-Pacific region is taken into account. In this performance, foreign trade and overseas investment were instrumental in spreading the growth from one country to others. However, the repercussions are not necessarily a one-way street. It is a matter of course that the acceleration of growth in peripheral nations should be fed back, contributing to the further growth of a major economic power. Through such mutual influence, significant changes emerge in the trade and industrial structures.

The design and scope of this study are meant to be flexible. For one thing, the author has no alternative but to put forth his analysis without an established definition of what is decribed here as the Asia-Pacific region. For the sake of the analysis here, the Asia-Pacific region will be mainly restricted to the five ASEAN member nations, the Republic of

This paper was submitted to the Conference on United States–Asia Economic Relations, April 16–18, 1981, at Rutgers–The State University of New Jersey. It appeared, in slightly different form, in *Asian Economics* (Seoul), December 1981.

Korea and Taiwan, and, at times, Hong Kong and Australia. Admittedly, it is only natural that the United States, Canada, Mexico, China, and other Pacific nations should be included for a more scrupulous analysis.

The author wishes to mainly focus his analysis on changes in the "trade" structure of the Asia-Pacific region and thereby touch upon the direction of the international division of labor in the region. However, the role of overseas investments in these changes will not be discussed.

This paper, albeit limited in analytical perspective, will attempt to visualize how the international division of labor in the Asia-Pacific region will look in the future, while taking structural changes in the region into account.

Changes in Trade Structure

Before East and Southeast Asia are taken up, it is of importance to review the changes that have emerged in Japan's trade structure in the last twenty-five years. For Japan, a lesser power insofar as resources are concerned, imports of raw materials and energy are exceedingly high, whereas imports of finished products are low. As can be seen from Table 1, the change in Japan's export structure was drastic; change of this kind might ordinarily be expected to occur over the course of one century, but in this case structural change took place over the short span of 25 years. For example, the share of machinery and equipment, including industrial, electric, transport, and precision machinery, in total exports stood at a mere 13.7% in 1955 but zoomed to an astonishing 61.3% in

Table 1. Japan's Export Structure, 1955–79

	1955	1960	1965	1970	1975	1979
Total (million US $)	2,011	4,055	8,452	19,318	55,753	103,032
Metals	19.2	13.8	20.3	19.7	22.5	17.8
Iron & steel	12.9	9.6	15.3	14.7	18.3	13.7
Machinery and equipment	13.7	25.3	35.2	46.3	53.8	61.3
Industrial	—	—	—	10.4	12.1	14.4
Electrical	—	—	—	14.8	12.4	16.9
Transport	—	—	—	17.8	26.1	25.0
Precision	—	—	—	3.3	3.3	5.0
Chemicals	5.1	4.5	6.5	6.4	7.0	5.9
Textiles	37.3	30.0	18.7	12.5	6.7	4.8
Nonmetallic mineral ores	4.9	4.4	3.1	1.9	1.3	1.5
Food	3.3	6.3	4.1	3.4	1.4	1.2

Percentage compositions

Source: Ministry of International Trade and Industry, *White Paper on International Trade,* annual.

1979. Meanwhile, the share of textile products in exports plunged sharply from 37.3% to 4.8%. The adjustment of the industrial structure during Japan's high growth period was naturally sustained by its high capacity to transform, but the changes in trade structure were far more profound.

Table 2 provides an overview of how four NICs in Asia—Taiwan, the Republic of Korea, Hong Kong, and Singapore—changed their export structures during the 1960s and 1970s.

Table 2. Commodity Composition of Exports in Asian NICs
A. Taiwan

SITC (Standard International Trade Classification)	Values of exports (f.o.b.) (million N.T. dollars)			Percentage composition of exports			1978/1961
	1961	1971	1978	1961	1971	1978	
							-fold
Total	7,812.2	79,906.4	468,509.3	100.0	100.0	100.0	60.0
0,1 Food, beverages, and tobacco	4,388.7	13,319.3	47,859.2	56.2	16.7	10.2	10.9
2,3 Crude materials and mineral fuels	558.5	2,715.8	18,910.6	7.1	3.4	4.0	33.9
4,5 Chemicals, oils, and fats	449.0	1,468.0	8,852.0	5.7	1.8	1.9	19.7
65 Yarn, fabrics, etc.	987.5	9,471.6	43,043.2⎫	15.2	31.2	23.0	90.5
84 Clothing	203.0	15,401.9	64,692.9⎭				
7 Machinery and transp. equipment	102.3	13,803.4	109,356.5⎫	1.4	17.7	25.6	1,124.1
86 Precision instruments	4.7	323.9	10,924.3⎭				

B. Korea

SITC	Value of exports (f.o.b.) (million US dollars)			Percentage composition of exports			1978/1961
	1961	1971	1978	1961	1971	1978	
							-fold
Total	38.6	1,067.6	12,710.6	100.0	100.0	100.0	329.3
0,1 Food, beverages, and tobacco	9.1	85.0	1,052.6	23.7	7.9	8.2	115.7
2,3 Crude materials and mineral fuels	23.2	106.2	369.3	60.1	9.9	2.9	15.9
4,5 Chemicals, oils, and fats	0.7	15.0	352.1	0.2	1.4	2.8	503.0
65 Yarn, fabrics, etc.	1.0	137.8	1,533.3⎫	2.6	41.4	32.4	4,108.0
84 Clothing	—	304.3	2,574.7⎭				
7 Machinery and transp. equipment	0.9	87.4	2,587.1⎫	0.3	8.6	21.9	3,088.9
86 Precision instruments	—	4.5	192.9⎭				

(continued on next page)

C. Hong Kong

SITC		Value of exports (f.o.b.) (million HK dollars)			Percentage composition of exports			1977/1960
		1960	1970	1977	1960	1970	1977	
								-fold
	Total	2,867.2	12,346.5	35,003.9	100.0	100.0	100.0	12.2
0,1	Food, beverages, and tobacco	143.5	243.1	682.1	5.0	2.0	1.9	4.8
2,3	Crude materials and mineral fuels	137.9	233.2	379.9	4.8	1.9	1.1	2.8
4,5	Chemicals, oils, and fats	54.7	108.4	299.0	1.9	0.9	0.9	5.5
65	Yarn, fabrics, etc.	554.2	1,276.7	2,648.9 ⎫	54.5	45.4	47.3	10.6
84	Clothing	1,010.4	4,336.6	13,908.5 ⎭				
7	Machinery and transp. equipment	76.8	1,454.7	5,614.5 ⎫	3.3	13.5	22.2	84.2
86	Precision instruments	15.8	215.8	2,181.5 ⎭				

D. Singapore

SITC		Value of exports (f.o.b.) —million S'pore dollars—			Percentage composition of exports (%)			1978/1957
		1957	1965	1978	1957	1965	1978	
								-fold
	Total	3,478.1	3,004.1	22,985.5	100.0	100.0	100.0	6.6
0,1	Food, beverages, and tobacco	583.2	472.8	1,587.9	16.8	15.7	6.9	2.7
2,3	Crude materials and mineral fuels	1,824.8	1,249.4	8,812.1	52.5	41.6	38.3	4.8
4,5	Chemicals, oils, and fats	130.2	167.7	1,384.0	3.7	5.6	6.0	10.6
65	Yarn, fabrics, etc.	136.4	140.5	606.3 ⎫	4.6	6.4	5.5	8.0
84	Clothing	23.3	50.4	672.2 ⎭				
7	Machinery and transp. equipment	173.4	312.5	5,715.1 ⎫	5.4	11.0	26.7	32.9
86	Precision instruments	13.3	19.0	423.7 ⎭				

Source: Summarized from Institute of Developing Economies, *Rapid Industrialization in Asian Countries and its Influences upon Japan* (in Japanese), NIRA, Dec. 1980, pp. 87–92.

First, an inspection of fluctuations in the shares of machinery exports reveals that Taiwan rapidly grew from 1.4% to 25.6%, the Republic of Korea from 0.3% to 21.9%, Hong Kong from 3.3% to 22.2%, and Singapore from 5.4% to 26.7% during that period. Second, in the exports of textile goods, Hong Kong constantly maintained a high share of 40–50%, whereas Taiwan and the Republic of Korea registered high shares in the first half which fell off in the second half. These fluctuations suggest that the latter two nations have shifted to the phase where their shares in machinery exports are now on the rise, although they once enjoyed rises in their shares of textile exports. Third, from the beginning, Singapore had a low share in the export of textile goods, and there were no significant changes throughout that period, with its share hovering between 4% and 6%. In this respect, Singapore differs markedly from Hong Kong.

One significant feature common to the four Asian NICs is that the growth rate for machinery exports was surprisingly high during the period.

These characteristic changes in the composition of exports in terms of commodities can be taken as an indication of the "graduation" of these Asian NICs from the status of LDCs. In another sense, however, the fact remains that they have continued to import significant percentages of capital goods in response to their high economic growth. These four nations' imports from Japan are enumerated by commodity in Table 3. First, the share of textile goods from Japan sharply fell off in the 1965–79 period: from 11.1% to 4.3% for Taiwan, 20.2% to 5.3% for the Republic of Korea, 34.7% to 16.2% for Hong Kong, and 28.1% to 6.8% for Singapore. These changes suggest that there was great progress in the adjustment of Japan's industrial structure, primarily in its textile industry.

However, another sign discernible from Table 3 is that there have been rapid rises in the import by the Asian NICs of capital goods from Japan. The imports of metals and machineries per se cannot be described as representing capital goods, since some of the machinery imports are durable consumer goods. Some of the steel products may be intermediate in nature, but when they are used as materials for construction, they are capital goods. A check of the percentage gained by dividing the imports of metals plus machineries, including other than capital goods, by the total value of imports reveals that the percentage rose from 66.9% to 72.4% for Taiwan, 43.0% to 65.2% for the Republic of Korea, 37.5% to 60.6% for Hong Kong, and 48.1% to 75.6% for Singapore in the 1965–79 period. It is evident that their imports from Japan were heavy in capital goods and that their domestic growth was sustained by imports.

The NICs aside, a table similar to Table 3 was prepared in 1979 for LDCs in Southeast Asia, two nations in Oceania, and Mexico and is given here as Table 4. A look at the imports of metals and machinery from Japan by commodity indicates that Thailand imported 75.0%, Malaysia 81.7%, the Philippines 72.6%, Indonesia 68.3%, Australia 74.2%, New Zealand 74.6%, and Mexico 91.0%. Imports of capital

Table 3. Imports from Japan and Their Commodity Compositions for Asian NICs

Taiwan	1965	1975	1979
Total (1000 US dollars)	217,916	1,821,669	4,366,850
Textiles	11.1%	8.5%	4.3%
Metals	23.7	20.2	22.3
Machinery and equipment	43.2	39.4	50.1
Korea	1965	1975	1979
Total (1000 US dollars)	180,304	2,247,723	6,246,890
Textiles	20.2%	10.8%	5.3%
Metals	15.8	15.5	18.1
Machinery and equipment	27.2	39.9	47.1
Hong Kong	1965	1975	1979
Total (1000 US dollars)	287,851	1,378,155	3,678,751
Textiles	34.7%	23.9%	16.2%
Metals	14.5	11.2	11.7
Machinery and equipment	23.0	34.6	48.9
Singapore	1965	1975	1979
Total (1000 US dollars)	123,964	1,523,711	2,679,139
Textiles	28.1%	7.3%	6.8%
Metals	22.7	25.5	19.1
Machinery and equipment	25.4	52.3	56.5

Source: Japan Trade Association, *The Summary Report, Trade of Japan,* Dec. 1979.

goods were overwhelmingly great for all these nations. Since the machinery and equipment item includes the imports of passenger cars and electronics, the imports of capital goods and durable consumer goods were naturally conspicuous. However, because these percentages are significantly high, it can be safely assumed that imports from Japan take on the character of capital goods, so that now, even if durable consumer goods are excluded from the imports, the remaining capital goods have an extremely high share.

It can be argued, from the demand side, that Japan's high economic growth has provided impetus to exports to Japan from neighboring countries, thus augmenting their effective demand and also diversifying their export structure to an appreciable degree. It can also be argued, from the supply side, that the process of boosting the exports to these nations from Japan at a rapid pace has at the same time encouraged capital formation in NICs and LDCs. In other words, the channel through which the effects of Japan's high economic growth are transmitted to its surrounding nations through the medium of trade is a two-way, not just a one-way, street. It might be said that the impact came in the form of not only stimulating import demand by Japan from neighboring nations but also encouraging growth in the supply of capital goods to them (i.e., import of capital goods from Japan).

Table 4. Imports from Japan and Their Commodity Compositions for
Some Asia-Pacific Countries, 1979

Thailand (1000 US dollars)	1,713,697
Textiles	3.1%
Metals	24.6
Machinery and equipment	50.4
Malaysia (1000 US dollars)	1,506,952
Textiles	3.5%
Metals	19.4
Machinery and equipment	62.3
Philippines (1000 US dollars)	1,622,029
Textiles	6.7%
Metals	25.1
Machinery and equipment	47.5
Indonesia (1000 US dollars)	2,123,798
Textiles	6.0%
Metals	22.0
Machinery and equipment	46.3
Australia (1000 US dollars)	2,606,641
Textiles	6.9%
Metals	9.8
Machinery and equipment	64.4
New Zealand (1000 US dollars)	584,487
Textiles	13.5%
Metals	27.3
Machinery and equipment	47.3
Mexico (1000 US dollars)	841,012
Textiles	1.2%
Metals	30.8
Machinery and equipment	60.2

Source: Japan Trade Association, *The Summary Report, Trade of Japan,* Dec.
1979.

In the preceding, an attempt has been made to visualize changes in
the trade structure for NICs and ASEAN. It is of significance now to
invite your attention also to the dramatic changes that have taken place
in the compositions of Australia's exports and imports by country in the
last 30 years. This is because, as indicated in Table 5, Japan's share in
Australia's total exports has sharply soared from 4.5% to 28.9% for the
1950–79 period, in sharp contrast to Britain's share, which has plum-
meted from 36.6% to a mere 4.0%. On the other hand, Japan's share in
Australia's total imports has risen from 1.5% to 17.6% during the
period, as against Britain's share, which has plunged from 50.7% to
10.8%. The rapid economic growth of an Asian nation and the economic stagnation of a European country have brought about this impressive change in the trade structure of Australia. This fact *per se*

Table 5. Export and Import Shares by Country in Australia, 1950–79

	1950	1955	1960	1965	1970	1974	1978–79
Relative to Australian total exports (%):							
Japan's share	4.5	9.2	15.2	16.4	26.4	28.8	28.9
U.K. share	36.6	34.7	27.0	17.4	11.4	5.9	4.0
U.S. share	8.6	7.0	6.6	10.9	12.8	9.3	12.5
Relative to Australian total imports (%):							
Japan's share	1.5	2.8	5.8	9.7	12.7	18.4	17.6
U.K. share	50.7	44.0	33.4	26.4	21.2	13.5	10.8
U.S. share	8.3	11.9	18.3	23.3	25.5	20.8	23.5

Sources: 1950–74: John Crawford and Saburo Okita, eds., *Australia, Japan and Western Pacific Economic Relations, A Report to the Governments of Australia and Japan*, pp. 35–36.
1978–79: Ministry of International Trade and Industry, *White Paper on International Trade*, 1980.

inevitably leads us to the conviction that 'should nations in the Asia-Pacific region continue to enjoy relatively higher economic growth, the relations of trade interdependence among the various nations of this region will undoubtedly be even more notably transformed. Incidentally, Australia's share in exports to Japan is appreciably higher than its share in imports from Japan, reflecting Japan's high dependence on Australia's resources.

The share of the United States in exports and imports started leveling off around 1970 or so. Until then, the U.S. share had been on the rise.

Some Observations in Terms of Causation

Exports by NICs in Asia began to grow at a rapid pace with the advent of the 1970s. Whereas the exports of advanced industrial nations were 4.8 times higher in U.S. dollars during the 1970–79 period (4.3 times for the United States, 5.1 times for the European Community nations, and 5.3 times for Japan), the Republic of Korea registered 18.0 times higher exports, Singapore 8.1 times, and Taiwan 10.9. The percentage of exports to GNP for the Republic of Korea soared from 14.3% to 29.9% in the 1970–79 period. Taiwan's percentage rose from 29.7% to 53.3%.

The ASEAN member nations also showed exceedingly high export growth in that period. If we look at the values of merchandise exports enumerated in the International Monetary Fund (IMF)'s International Financial Statistics (expressed in terms of the currency of the member nations except for Indonesia) converted into U.S. dollars, increases in exports during the 1970–79 period can be clearly seen. The rise was

14.1 times for Indonesia, 7.5 times for Thailand, 6.6 times for Malaysia, and 4.3 times for the Philippines. The rise of 14.1 times in Indonesia's exports can be attributed to the rises in crude oil prices. As a result, the percentage of exports to GNP for Indonesia rose from 12.8% to 20.8% in the 1970–78 period. The percentage increased from 16.7% to 22.7% for Thailand and from 46.1% to 58.0% for Malaysia. In the case of the Philippines, almost no changes were observed in its dependence on exports; the percentage barely changed from 19.1% to 19.0%.

Therefore, it might be said in broad terms that the ASEAN nations and other nations of Southeast Asia experienced a growth of the "export-oriented" type in the 1970s. However, it would be misleading simply to define it in those terms. A look at changes in the percentage of gross fixed investment to gross domestic product (GDP) in ASEAN and East Asia, as enumerated in Table 6, suggests that the investment ratio in the 1960s was higher than in the 1950s, and that in the 1970s was much higher than that in the 1960s. Judged at least from this angle, it must be said that these Asian economies fall into the category of the "investment-oriented" type.

Table 6. Gross Fixed Investment as Ratio to Gross Domestic Product (%)

	Indonesia*	Thailand	Philippines	Malaysia*	Singapore	Korea	Taiwan
1955	—	11.9	11.6	9.5	—	10.4	11.4
1960	—	14.4	13.5	12.8	9.5	10.9	16.7
1965	8.3	18.2	17.6	15.7	21.1	14.9	17.1
1970	13.6	24.1	15.8	20.3	32.5	24.5	21.8
1975	20.3	22.1	24.3	25.0	35.1	25.6	31.5
1979	21.6	25.9	26.1	26.6	34.5	31.4	28.6

Source: IMF, *International Financial Statistics*, Yearbook 1980.
Note : * Gross capital formation/GDP ratio.

However, East and Southeast Asia have enjoyed a higher economic growth rate than some other parts of the Third World and are now considered to be in a future growth region of the world. This is presumably because a virtuous-circular pattern of cumulative expansion has made its appearance between exports and investment; while the export-oriented type of growth has been tied in with the investment-oriented type, exports and investments provide mutual feedback. Should the export-oriented type alone be sustained, skepticism would arise about its continuity. Inevitably, it would give rise to an investment boom at home, thereby reinforcing the competitive power of the export industries. A boom in investment would lead to a boom in exports, which in turn would naturally ignite another investment boom at home.

If a domestic investment boom is generated in one country, there may be a sharp rise in its imports of capital goods. We have seen in Table 4 that imports of Japanese capital goods by the surrounding nations registered exceedingly high rates. This constitutes significant momentum in the process of feedback between export and investment; economic growth of the investment-oriented type cannot be assured unless there is a rise in the import of capital goods. It is necessary for us to note as a link in the process of the causational evolution a rise in the "supply of imports," which will come after an increase in the "demand for exports" from Japan and other advanced industrial countries.

Granted that such a growth process, including foreign trade, starts with the input of export demand from Japan, a growth pole, the demand will once again revert to Japan eventually through the process in which captial goods are imported to surrounding countries. In this context, there is a need to take account of the mechanism whereby growth spreads among these nations through the medium of foreign trade. At the same time, it is necessary at this point to refer to an important factor for which quantitative analysis has not been performed in this study. The factor is that in parallel to the exports of capital goods, the transfer of technology and know-how due to the overseas investment of enterprises has played an important role. Examination of Japan's overseas investment (on an authorized basis) suggests that there was a sharp rise of about 30 times in the 1964–73 period (1). The overseas investment continued topping out for four years after the oil crisis, but soared above the level of 1973 ($3,494 million) by 31.6% to $4,598 million in 1978, and further to $4,995 million in 1979, up 43.0% from the 1973 level. Thus, to check mutual repercussions between nations, it is necessary to observe the role of foreign investments and the transfer of technology. This is not the place to dwell further on this subject.

As stated earlier, however, an unprecedentedly significant structural change has taken place in the trade sector. Such structural change will not take place immediately in the industrial structure as a matter of course. A sudden drastic change in relative industrial composition, particularly in the primary goods-producing countries, is inconceivable. Nevertheless, a check of the industrial composition for GDP reveals, as shown in Table 7, that the speed with which structural changes in GDP took place in the period 1960–78 was very rapid, as the percentage of manufacturing industry rose from 7.2% to 19.1% for Malaysia, 16.4% to 24.6% for the Philippines, and 12.5% to 19.1% for Thailand; in the case of NICs in Asia, it rose from 11.6% to 26.3% for Singapore, 22.3% to 35.9% for Taiwan, and 13.8% to 26.9% for the Republic of Korea. In the case of Indonesia, the percentage rose only from 6.3% to

Table 7. Industrial Origin of GDP in ASEAN, Taiwan, and Korea

	Indoneisa				Malaysia				Philippines				Thailand			
	1963	1970	1975	1978	1960	1970	1975*	1978*	1960	1970	1975	1978	1960	1970	1975	1978
GDP	100.0	100.0	100.0	100.0	100.0	100.0	100.0	100.0	100.0	100.0	100.0	100.0	100.0	100.0	100.0	100.0
Agricul-ture	59.4	47.2	31.7	31.1	33.8	28.8	27.7	24.8	27.3	27.8	28.8	27.3	39.8	28.3	31.6	27.1
Mining	3.1	5.2	19.7	17.8	5.1	7.7	4.6	4.9	1.0	2.8	1.7	1.9	1.0	2.0	1.4	2.2
Manu-facturing	6.3	9.3	8.9	9.3	7.2	14.7	16.4	19.1	16.4	22.6	24.9	24.6	12.5	16.0	18.3	19.1
Others	31.2	38.3	39.7	41.8	53.9	48.8	51.3	51.2	55.3	46.8	44.6	46.2	46.7	53.7	48.7	51.6

	Singapore				Taiwan**				Korea			
	1960	1970	1975	1978	1960	1970	1975	1978	1960	1970	1975	1978
GDP	100.0	100.0	100.0	100.0	100.0	100.0	100.0	100.0	100.0	100.0	100.0	100.0
Agricul-ture	3.4	2.3	1.9	1.5	32.4	17.6	14.4	11.0	36.7	26.9	24.5	21.8
Mining	0.3	0.3	0.4	0.2	2.3	1.4	1.4	2.2	2.1	1.5	1.5	1.4
Manu-facturing	11.6	20.4	24.1	26.3	22.3	27.3	30.5	35.9	13.8	20.9	26.0	26.9
Others	84.7	77.0	73.6	72.0	43.0	53.7	53.7	50.9	47.4	50.7	48.0	49.9

Sources: UN, *Yearbook of National Accounts Statistics*, 1979; Directorate-General of Budget, Executive Yuan, *National Income of the Republic of China*, 1979.

Notes: 1) Percentage industrial origin of GDP in producers' values at current prices.
2) * in 1970 constant prices.
3) ** GDP at factor cost.

9.3%, but structural changes seem to have been conspicuous, for when manufacturing and mining (including oil) are combined, the 1978 percentage is as high as 27.1%.

In any case, it has long been lamented that industrialization through "import substitution" in the LDCs has not been well linked so far with "export promotion," but the NICs in Asia have now solved this problem and embarked upon industrialization of the export-oriented type. It is inconceivable, however, that "graduates" from the status of the LDCs will be limited to the present NICs. It has already been observed that Thailand, the Philippines, Malaysia, and Indonesia, enjoying the stauts of quasi-NICs, are approaching the time when they can advance to full NIC status.

It is indisputable that these nations are bothered with widespread poverty and inequity. Their situation is quite similar to that of Japan until twenty years ago: Japan had not yet been considered an advanced economic nation, its economy being of a dual structure difficult to come to grips with. However quickly industrialization progresses, a long span of time is required for the elimination of poverty and inequity. A similar observation can also be made about East and Southeast Asia. However, it is high time we took special account of the unprecedentedly conspicuous changes in the trade and industrial structures due to the export and inflow of foreign investment.

Orientation toward Horizontal Division of Labor

Assuming that the statistical data that have thus far been enumerated are correct, and that this is the basic trend which will govern the next twenty years, it is possible to make some projections of the international division of labor in the Asia-Pacific region. This is not the place to make a future projection of the basic statistical data or to come out with a realistic scenario. Admittedly, this is an important task. But what the author wishes to do here is point out the possibility that a "horizontal division of labor" or "intra-industry division of labor," which is heterogenous to the so-called vertical division of labor that prevailed between agrarian and industrial nations in the prewar years, might make much progress in the Asia-Pacific region.

To avoid possible confusion about the definition of vertical and horizontal divisions of labor, the author hastens to draw a line, parenthetically. The index of revealed comparative advantage (RCA) presented by Balassa in 1965 or the intra-industry trade index used by Gruble and Lloyd in 1975 is such that the more the trade classification of commodities is subdivided, the lower is the index of horizontal division of labor thus computed but the higher is the index of vertical division of labor (2).

In plainer language, let us simply define as the vertical division of labor the kind of international division of labor which may materialize between the production of primary products and industrial production. We then look upon the kind of international division of labor which may come into existence between industrial products simply as a horizontal division of labor. Therefore, even if a vertical division of labor may be considered as having come into existence in the textile and machinery industries respectively between nations A and B, and even if it eventually turns out that specialization toward the production of trucks and passenger cars in the automotive industry is vertical between the two nations, let us define it as a horizontal division of labor for the sake of our discussion. In this paper, too, the author wishes to quote the computed values of the above indices later, but simply by defining the intra-manufacturing division of labor as the horizontal division of labor, let us focus our attention on an analysis of the historical transformation of the international division of labor. For this purpose, the author wishes to define as vertical division of labor the prewar, colonial, and monoculture type division of labor which relegates counterpart countries to the status of primary product-producing nations, and to regard as an important historical transformation the latest signs that the intra-manufacturing division of labor has also made its appearance in both NICs and LDCs (a shift to the horizontal division of labor). In this context, it is useful to stick to the old definitions as they stand for the time being.

The emergence of a horizontal division of labor in the aforementioned context in the Asia-Pacific region is demonstrated first by the data that have thus far been enumerated. However, the author wishes to present a graph which consolidates these facts and brings into relief the basic trend that has emerged up to now. Figure 1 shows the changes in the shares of manufactures in total exports for the Republic of Korea, Taiwan, and some of the ASEAN nations over about twenty years.

In enumerating data of this kind, it is extremely important to know which items in the trade classification are used. If polished rice in Thailand and block tin in Malaysia are classified as part of their manufacturing products, the export share of manufactures may reach the level of 50% for Thailand and 30% for Malaysia. For this reason, an attempt had deliberately been made to exclude such commodities from the category of manufacturing products. Instead, the commodities assigned to sections 5, 6, 7, and 8 of the Standard International Trade Classification (SITC) are taken to be manufacturing products They are

Figure 1. Percentage shares of manufactures in total exports of ASEAN and Asian NICs, 1960–79.

5 (chemical goods), 61–64 (leather and leather goods, fur, rubber goods, wooden goods, cork and paper products), 65 (yarns and fabrics), 66 (nonmetallic mineral goods), 67–69 (metallic goods), 7 (general machinery, electric machinery and transport machinery), 81–83 and 86–89 (musical instruments, toys, sporting goods, and various miscellaneous goods), 841 (clothing), 842 (fur products), and 85 (footwear). In the case

of Malaysia, however, 266 (synthetic fibers) is included, whereas 68 (nonferrous metals) is excluded. The 266 (synthetic fibers) group was not excluded for Taiwan from 1970 onward, for the Republic of Korea in the 1968–70 period, and for Malaysia in the 1960–78 period, even though the values were small. A discontinuity more or less remains in terms of classification, but this discontinuity is not important enough to change the overall picture. Incidentally, as processed foods are excluded in advance so as to avoid the inclusion of polished rice and other similar products, the figures are all underestimates to some extent.

The graph does not cover Indonesia because a consistent classification of manufacturing exports was not available for this period. However, exports of manufacturing products, including 266 (synthetic fibers), were 5.3% of Indonesia's total exports in 1979. Since exports of manufacturing products had been practically nil before 1967, it might be concluded that Indonesia began to export manufacturing products in or around 1970, accounting for 5% or so of all exports in 1979.

Figure 1 presents some fascinating data. One example is that the exports of manufactures by the Republic of Korea and Taiwan stood somewhere between 20% and 30% early in the 1960s but have now reached 85–90%. Another is that the percentages of manufacturing product exports by Thailand, the Philippines, and Malaysia in 1978 reached the level of those the Republic of Korea and Taiwan 20 years ago. There have also been signs of increase in the percentages of nanufacturing exports from Thailand, the Philippines, and Malaysia.

The question is, will these nations continue to increase their manufacturing exports at the pace set by the Republic of Korea and Taiwan? Thailand, the Philippines, Malaysia, and Indonesia probably will not do so, because unlike the Republic of Korea and Taiwan they have abundant rescources and are not in an environment where they must boost their manufacturing exports that much. However, they have attained the same percentages of manufacturing exports as realized by the Republic of Korea and Taiwan 20 years ago, and even if they do not attain 85–90%, which is the percentage range registered at present by the Republic of Korea and Taiwan for their exports of manufactures, it should be possible for them to reach at least the level of 50–60%. In other words, these nations have also begun to shift from industrialization with import substitution to export promotion. If that is the case, it follows that these LDCs in Southeast Asia are beginning to approach a horizontal division of labor with Japan and the NICs in Asia, although a vertical division of labor still predominates.

However, manufactured products are already 85–90% of exports for the Republic of Korea and Taiwan. Thus it might be said that a horizontal division of labor is already in effect between Japan and the Republic of Korea and Taiwan. It is well known that imports of textile goods from the latter nations and competition with them in the world market have forced the Japanese textile industry to undergo downward industrial adjustment to some extent. This boomerang effect, however, has not been confined to such light industries as the textile industry: it has also spread to the electronic and shipbuilding industries.

If the effect of the Republic of Korea, Taiwan, and other NICs chasing after Japan were confined to the related industries in Japan, the boomerang effect would prove only to be negative. As the electronic and shipbuilding industries in the Republic of Korea make progress, however, parts and engines will naturally be imported from Japan. The faster the pace at which such capital goods are exported from Japan, the more the negative boomerang effect is offset. Therefore, let us designate the effect of a rise in the exports of capital goods from Japan induced by the first boomerang effect as the "positive boomerang effect." As is discernible from Table 8, the excess of imports over exports in the Republic of Korea, Taiwan, Singapore, and Hong Kong in their relation to Japan has increased year by year, and this amply suggests how great the positive boomerang effect has been in the past. Worthy of note is that even in the capital goods industry, a horizontal division of labor is being created between Japan and these four nations. Judging from the fact that these NICs are lesser economic powers, the evolution of a horizontal division of labor between them and Japan is inevitable.

Table 8. Japan's Exports, Imports, and Trade Balances vis-à-vis Asian NICs

Unit: million US dollars

	Korea				Taiwan			
	Exports (a)	Imports (b)	Balance (c)	$\frac{c}{a}$	Exports (a)	Imports (b)	Balance (c)	$\frac{c}{a}$
1965	180.3	41.3	139.0	77.1	217.9	157.3	60.6	27.8
1970	818.2	229.0	589.2	72.0	700.4	250.8	449.5	64.2
1975	2,247.7	1,308.0	939.7	41.8	1,821.7	811.6	1,010.1	55.4
1979	6,246.9	3,359.4	2,887.5	46.2	4,336.9	2,475.9	1,861.0	42.9
	Singapore				Hong Kong			
	Exports (a)	Imports (b)	Balance (c)	$\frac{c}{a}$	Exports (a)	Imports (b)	Balance (c)	$\frac{c}{a}$
1965	124.0	32.7	91.2	73.6	287.9	35.3	252.6	87.8
1970	423.0	86.9	336.1	79.4	700.3	91.8	608.5	86.9
1975	1,523.7	399.0	1,124.8	73.8	1,378.2	245.5	1,132.7	82.2
1979	2,679.1	1,473.4	1,205.7	45.0	3,678.8	663.5	3,015.3	82.0

Source: Japan Trade Association, *The Summary Report, Trade of Japan*, Dec. 1979.

For this reason, unbalanced trade may be required for the time being. The surplus of imports over exports in these nations will increase in terms of absolute value, while eventually dropping in terms of the ratio of exports to imports (c/a). There are already conspicuous signs of a drop in c/a for three of these countries.

Moreover, the ASEAN nations are tending to raise their ratios of manufactured products, to be sure, but it appears that they are boosting exports of textile goods and other products in light industries, rather than depending upon so-called "export substitution" (exports of basic resources after processing). Table 9 indicates the trend for the export values in U.S. dollars of textile goods (yarns, fabrics, and clothing). It is true that exports of textile goods are great in value for the Republic of Korea and Taiwan. However, Thailand in 1978 reached the levels attained by Taiwan in 1970 and the Republic of Korea in 1971. Malaysia and the Philippines in 1978 reached the 1969 levels of the Republic of Korea and Taiwan. As there have been considerable rises in the U.S. price of textile goods (about 50%) over the past ten years, a comparison in terms only of current prices is naturally misleading. However, real-term comparison may only shift the comparable past period by a few years backward.

It is estimated that the Republic of Korea registered a rise in textile exports of 3.4 times from 1973 to 1978; Taiwan, 2.2 times; Thailand, 3.4 times; Malaysia, 6.0 times; and the Philippines, 5.7 times. The rise for just the three years from 1975 to 1978 was 3.5 times for Malaysia, 3.7 times for the Philippines, and 4.8 times for Indonesia, indicating that the pace for those three years was particularly fast. Surprisingly enough, in the case of Indonesia, textile exports in 1979 were 5.6 times as high as the previous year, and it is to be noted that its textile exports rapidly rose to the levels registered by Malaysia and the Philippines in 1977. Indonesia, which hardly exported textiles in the 1960s, deserves special mention; in a short span of time it reached the level of Thailand in 1973 in terms of absolute dollar values. This rapid rise in exports was due in large measure to a significant devaluation of the rupiah (415 to 625 rupiah for US$1) in November 1978. Since Indonesia began at the near-zero level of exports, any export expansion would necessarily register a high percentage increase rate. The figures also do not reflect the quality of textile goods exported; Indonesian textiles are going to the Middle East in increasing quantities. However, the fact that Thailand, Malaysia, and the Philippines are "chasing" the NICs cannot be passed over. It must be taken into account that at a time when the NICs are facing rising wage costs due to inflation, the LDCs, taking advantage of relative low wages, have developed their

Table 9.   Values of Textile Exports from ASEAN and Asian NICs, 1968–79.

Unit: million US dollars

SITC	Thailand (65 + 841) A	Malaysia (65 + 841) A	Malaysia (65 + 841) B*	Malaysia (65) B*	Philippines (65 + 841) B	Philippines (65)	Indonesia (65 + 841) B	Singapore (65 + 841) A	Korea (65 + 841) A	Taiwan (65 + 841) A 1968, 69:A 1970~:B	Taiwan (65) B
1968	8.9	9.2	—	—		4.1		66.7	173.4	179.4	
1969	10.8	11.0	18.2	8.7		4.6		84.6	226.4	262.6	197.3
1970	9.6	16.2	21.2	9.1		5.4		84.7	298.3	410.2	236.8
1971	22.0	15.8	25.7	12.5	11.5	6.9		116.5	441.1	621.8	345.8
1972	46.6	26.6	41.9	20.7	35.5			165.6	616.2	833.7	559.2
1973	122.3	44.4	60.4	29.8	43.8			273.0	1,178.9	1,267.7	627.9
1974	140.1	61.6	79.7	40.2	55.6		4.4	264.9	1,439.3	1,522.1	648.9
1975	134.6	76.1	94.9	39.8	109.2		7.5	247.3	1,781.0	1,538.4	977.2
1976	239.1	108.7	141.3	63.9	147.6		7.9	361.2	2,800.0	2,298.0	921.7
1977	264.3	123.5	150.6	69.0				402.6	3,105.5	2,244.0	
1978	410.4	(265.0)**			203.6		21.0	563.7	4,056.8		1,163.2
1979							117.9	733.1	4,119.5B		1,564.0

Notes: * West Malaysia.
    ** Estimated by multiplying $ 121.6 million (SITC 65) in 1978 with the ratio (2.18) of 150.6/69.0 in 1977 in the B series.

Sources: A: UN, Yearbook of International Trade Statistics.
        B: Based on the Institute of Developing Economies information.
           Malaysia — Annual Statistics of External Trade.
           Indonesia — Indonesian Central Bureau of Statistics' materials.
           Korea 1979 — The Bank of Korea, Economic Statistics Yearbook. According to this, the 1978 figure is US$ 3,625.1
             million, which is lower than the A figure.
           Taiwan — based on original data from Taiwan.

textile industries to the point where they are attempting to outpace the NICs, at least in the speed of their growth. In this context, there is evidence of some boomerang effect from LDCs to NICs.

Taking advantage of this opportunity, let us quote some of the indices on the horizontal division of labor by industry computed by Toshio Watanabe (3). What is referred to here as the horizontal division of labor index is the same as the intra-industry trade index of Grubel and Lloyd. The horizontal division of labor index is computed in an equation as:

$$\frac{1}{n} \sum_{i=1}^{n} \frac{(\text{export} + \text{import}) - (|\text{export} - \text{import}|)}{\text{export} + \text{import}} \times 100.$$

The value of this index for all manufacturing in the Asian NICs increased from 8.9 in 1965 to 16.4 in 1970 and 27.4 in 1978. The index for textile goods was high but on the downturn (34.1 → 31.6 → 25.8). Horizontalization is indubitably in progress in the electrical machinery (3.8 → 20.4 → 22.4), transport machinery (0.5 → 6.8 → 10.6), precision machinery (2.5 → 3.3 → 16.5), and primary steel products (0 → 7.3 → 13.0) industries.

For the ASEAN nations, the index rose from 3.9 to 5.9 and 35.2 in all manufacturing for those years. With the advent of the 1970s the horizontalization became particularly conspicuous. In the textile and leather industries, the index rose from 4.8 to 19.0 to 30.7. It might be said, in general, that there had been a trend toward vertical specialization before 1970, but that the ASEAN nations entered a new phase in the beginning of the 1970s.

However, the evolution of horizontalization suggests that the division of labor can occur even in one and the same line of industries, resulting in a deepened mutual interdependence. Certainly this tendency is observed among the Asian NICs. Insofar as the ASEAN nations minus Singapore are concerned, however, it is regrettably true that their interdependence with Japan is not well developed. There definitely remain signs of one-way dependence. Japan's share in the ASEAN nations' exports (or imports) is extremely high (23–26% for the ASEAN members as a whole), as indicated in Table 10. However, the ASEAN nations' share in Japan's trade stands at 9–12%. The share of each member nation is even lower, 1–2%.

The percentage of trade among the ASEAN nations is also small; their trade with non-ASEAN nations is overwhelmingly dominant. As indicated in Table 11, trade dependence rates within the ASEAN area are already low, and should not drop much further, but there are some

Table 10. Characteristics of Japan-ASEAN Trade

(1978)

	Japan's share in ASEAN's total exports	Japan's share in ASEAN's total imports	ASEAN's share in Japan's total imports	ASEAN's share in Japan's total exports
Singapore	9.7	19.1	2.4	1.1
Philippines	23.5	26.8	1.6	1.3
Thailand	19.8	30.8	1.7	1.1
Malaysia	21.7	23.1	1.2	2.4
Indonesia	39.2	30.1	2.1	6.6
ASEAN	22.8	26.0	9.0	12.5

Source: Nihon-keizai Chosa-kyogikai, *ASEAN and Japan* (in Japanese), March 1980, p. 182.

Table 11. Intra- and Outside ASEAN Trade Ratios

		Intra-ASEAN trade	Outside ASEAN trade
Singapore	1960	46.5%	53.5%
	1970	26.9	73.1
	1978	17.1	82.9
Philippines	1960	3.1	96.9
	1970	3.2	96.8
	1978	5.2	94.7
Thailand	1960	20.6	79.4
	1970	7.3	92.7
	1978	9.1	90.9
Malaysia	1960	27.4	72.6
	1970	20.9	79.1
	1978	13.4	86.6
Indonesia	1960	22.4	77.6
	1970	16.8	83.2
	1978	11.6	88.4

Source: Nihon Keizai Chosa Kyogikai, *ASEAN and Japan* (in Japanese), March 1980, p. 348.

member nations whose rate has dropped in the past 18 years. The latest survey conducted by the Institute of Developing Economies (in Tokyo) suggests, however, that when the rate of trade dependence within the ASEAN region is computed only for manufactured products, it rose from 18.6% in 1970 to 22.8% in 1975 (4). Therefore, if there is progress in industrialization within the ASEAN region, the rate of intra-regional trade dependence may rise in the future. However, the higher rate of trade dependence for manufactured products still prevails because of the existence of a vertical division of labor. If industrialization hastens the development of a horizontal division of labor, one-way dependence will decline in favor of mutual dependence.

Future Prospects

To sum up, it is evident that rapid structural changes have emerged in the Asia-Pacific region's trade and industry that make it possible to call the area a growth region in the world. What kinds of predictions can be made about the future picture for the Asia-Pacific region on the basis of these facts?

(1) First, we can see the beginnings of the evolution of a horizontal division of labor, essentially of an intra-manufacturing type. This type is in remarkable contrast to the vertical division of labor which was predominant between agricultural and industrial countries in the prewar years, and it suggests a collapse of the established pattern of the LDCs, which is characterized by long-run stagnancy at an extremely low level, and an epoch-making change from the division of labor based on monoculture to a new type of intra-manufacturing division of labor. It is only natural, however, that the vertical division of labor still remains to an appreciable degree.

(2) A protracted downgrade of the so-called Kondratieff long cycle began at the time of the first oil crisis, so it would be a mistake to predict that favorable structural changes will occur at the same pace as in the past. However, the latest trend, in which the LDCs in the Asia-Pacific region have taken on the character of quasi-NICs, is clearly not temporary. The global economy may remain in stagnation, to be sure, but the author assumes that steady structural changes will continue in the next 20 years, with quasi-NICs tending to develop into full NICs.

(3) The development of a horizontal division of labor will not be the only change in the trade and industrial structure of the Asia-Pacific region. Now that energy consumption is limited and there is apprehension about the supply of energy, economic aid and overseas investment will increase, with emphasis on "comprehensive economic security" as a matter of course. With priority given in Japan to economic cooperation with Indonesia, China, Mexico, and Australia, it may become Japan's task to strengthen the energy and resource security of the Asia-Pacific region. This suggests that in addition to industrial adjustments associated with dynamic shifts in comparative advantages, industries in the region will also be affected by efforts to strengthen the security of energy and resources. Presumably, future changes will be significantly influenced by these two major factors.

(4) If it is assumed here that LDCs in the Asia-Pacific region are capable of joining in the ranks of NICs, in another 20 years LDCs and LLDCs may remain only in Africa and South Asia. If that is the case, the Asia-Pacific region will be transformed into a middle-class area in a global context. Economic cooperation is motivated both by the humanistic ideal of meeting "basic human needs" and by the rationales of "international industrial adjustment" and "international security." Economic cooperation based on humanitarian ideals may be needed only in specific parts of the world by the end of this century.

(5) Amidst these signs of change, the industrial structures of the United States and Australia are such that the strength of industry may be downgraded. This topic does not fall into the area of this study, and the author wishes neither to put forward his thoughts nor to draw conclusions about it. Changes in the roles of the two nations are an important issue that has yet to be discussed elsewhere. It will probably turn out that the changes are tied in with those concerning the trade and industrial structures of the Western Pacific nations.

(6) The roles played by the Soviet Union and China in the Pacific also will have a significant impact on the future of the Asia-Pacific region. The speed at which modernization progresses in China will be of particular significance.

It would be interesting to come up with a number of alternate scenarios for the future of the Asia-Pacific region with variations in a number of factors like the speed of China's modernization. The author believes it is high time such scenarios are drawn up, but again this does not fall under the aegis of this paper.

References

1. Shinohara, Miyohei. *Sangyo Kozoron* [Industrial Structure]. Tokyo: Chikuma Shobo, 1976, pp. 293–294.
2. Balassa, Bela: "Trade Liberalization and 'Revealed' Comparative Advantage," *The Manchester School of Economic and Social Studies*, Vol. 33, 1965; Grubel, Herbert G., and Lloyd, P. L.: *Intra-Industry Trade: The Theory and Measurement of International Trade in Differentiated Products*, London: Macmillan, 1975.
3. Kojima, M., Kasai, N., Watanabe, T., and Tanaka, T. *Japan and Asian NICs* (in Japanese). Tokyo: Sangyo Keizai Kenkyu Kyokai, 1980, p. 96.
4. Taniguchi, Koji (ed.). *ASEAN's Industrial Development and Intra-Regional Economic Cooperation* (in Japanese). Tokyo: Institute of Developing Economies, August 1980, p. 52.

7

A RENEGADE VIEW OF TRADE FRICTIONS

A U.S.-Japan Agreement on the Auto Issue

On May 1, 1981, the Ministry of International Trade and Industry came out with official measures concerning the export of automobiles to the United States. The measures, encompassing a limited span of three years till March 1984, are so formulated that (1) the quota for the first year is set at 1,680,000 passenger cars; (2) the quota for the second year is equivalent to the total computed by adding the first year's quota of 1,680,000 passenger cars to the figure which is obtained by multiplying the volume of market expansion by 16.5%; and (3) a study will be instituted on the question of whether a quantitative restraint is to be exercised, while keeping watch on changes in passenger car exports to the United States and taking account of trends in the American passenger car market.

To these measures, the general reaction in the auto industry and the press is that politics has pulled the rug out from under something which theoretically ought to have been economic in nature. Some people go so far as to fear lest the measures have repercussions in Europe and other regions, eventually leading to a collapse of the world free trade system.

I have no intention whatever of refuting the pertinence of such popular conceptions and coming out here with a counterargument. The argument which takes political pressure into account is persuasive in its own way Insofar as military security is concerned, Japan has remained a "free rider," so much so that there is no gainsaying that Japan is politically vulnerable when it is called on to meet security costs halfway. In this sense, it seems reasonable to regard the conclusion of the latest series of auto talks between Japan and the United States as a "political upshot." However, when it is concluded that something essentially economic, in a theoretical sense, has been completely dis-

This chapter was originally published in Japanese as "Boeki masatsu ron," in *Nissan Information*, July 1981.

regarded, I do have something to set forth, while admitting that I merely represent the opinion of the minority.

Free Trade Arguments as Popularly Understood

American industry, which once dominated the world as the ensign of free trade, exercised pressure on Japan in a series of talks on textiles, steel, and automobiles, and has economically weakened in the 1970s. It is a historical fact that American industry has increasingly tightened its protectionist posture in an attempt to make up for its economic enervation.

I will attempt here first of all to reappraise whether the so-called free trade which has been adopted by a nation such as the United Kingdom or the United States is really identical with free trade of the kind that has been idealized in the milieu of economics.

David Ricardo was the first economist to propound the theoretical framework for an international division of labor with free trade (the theory of comparative cost). In a nutshell, his is quite a terse proposition, which boils down to an argument that the relations between nations A and B will be more lucrative after the opening of trade than before its opening. The reason is that the opening of trade between the nations will enable them to purchase less costly goods from each other, thereby improving the real income of the two peoples. In the real-world application of this theory, however, a number of premises have escaped attention time and again.

(1) One is that the trade payments and receipts of both nations ought to be kept in balance. In fact, however, the United Kingdom and the United States, which were described as the forerunners of free trade in the prewar years, continued enjoying enormously favorable current balances of payments over a long span of years.

(2) An industry selected as the mainstay export industry of one country (e.g. auto manufacture) may be in a more advantageous growth position than an export industry in another country (e.g. agriculture), just when the comparative demand growth rate (income elasticity) and the comparative technical progress for the automobile industry are higher than those for agriculture. Such a dynamic factor was completely detached from the premises behind the theory of division of labor, which assumes away not only any dynamic intertemporal shift in comparative advantage for the industries but also the selective growth capability of the industries concerned. In this context, the textbook free-trade argument was very often static in nature.

One might go so far as to argue that both nations started from a hypothetical situation where the growth rate was zero and merely evaluated the effects after the opening of trade. The historical fact is, however, that those countries which had chosen as a mainstay export industry a line of business for which the comparative demand growth rate and the comparative technological progress were high rose to positions of world economic major power and relegated their colonies to the position of producers of primary products, for which the comparative demand growth rate and the comparative technological progress were slow. Thus disparities between North and South, such as we are witnessing today, are an inevitable consequence.

(3) The United Kingdom held sway over the world economy for a long period of time, and later the United States overtook the U.K. in steering the global economy. Today, Japan, taking advantage of the setback of some industries in the United States, is in pursuit of the United States, while the newly industrializing countries (NICs), leaping at the enervation of some industries in Japan, are on the track of Japan.

In a world where there are frequent share fluctuations and takeovers between nations, there are liable to be floods of exports of specific, important lines of merchandise. In the theoretical formulation of a static theory of free trade, however, the flavor added by such factors as this dynamism has been excluded from the analysis from the beginning. Nevertheless, there are signs that protectionism has been criticized only on the basis of this static framework.

(4) Given these factors, it might be pointed out that the relative rises and falls of certain countries have unmistakably occurred in the midst of the historical evolution of a free world economy. Under the provisions of GATT, however, a nation is authorized to impose emergency import restrictions, albeit for limited periods, if floods of exports have taken place.

Does this safeguard, as it is called, serve to shorten the life of protectionism? Not necessarily. The proponents of so-called free trade consider it basically feasible to conduct an industrial adjustment in a smooth manner as long as exceptional and transitory safeguards are authorized, and they base their argument on the point that free trade should be made the keynote in a medium- and long-range perspective.

However, the economic rise of one nation is usually tied closely to the economic downfall of another. The awareness of a probable downfall spurs a nation to go in for protectionsim. Consequently it follows that the textbook argument for free trade must be described as having been founded on the optimistic premise that an industrial adjustment may essentially be completed over a short span of time without a significant hitch in the national economy.

It has been argued time and again that floods of exports are an out-come of free trade. In no argument for free trade in the past, however, has there been any admission that the floods of exports constitute part of free trade. Some people lament that exercising control over these exports flooding local markets constitutes an admission of the necessity of administered trade.

In no way, however, is it tied in with an unconditional acceptance of administered trade to decelerate the excessive speed at which certain lines of merchandise are exported. Rather, this is no more than an at-tempt to ease the precipitous concentration, over a certain period of time, of the damage which is inflicted on a certain country by a flood of exports. Moreover, it must be admitted that such remedies are of effect in holding back a global proliferation of protectionism.

(5) Should the words "free trade" serve as a reminder of the prewar type of trade, then it should also be remembered that prewar "free trade" did not necessarily imply "free competition" in some sectors of merchandise. For example, the fact that the world's major oil dealers were able to beat down the prices of oil available from oil-producing nations and peg them at low levels for such a long time has nothing whatsoever to do with free competition but, rather, shows that the oil market had the characteristics of a buyer's monopoly (monopsony), operating in favor of buyers.

In reaction, the oil-producing countries have recently united to form a seller's monopoly. In modern economics, incidentally, it is called "bilateral monopoly" or "collective bargaining" when both buyer and seller become monopolists. The monopolistic strength of the oil-pro-ducing nations is so enormous at present that "oil-push" inflation has now permeated every nook and corner of the world. However, it is a gross mistake to contend that the world oil market in the prewar years was under a system of free trade.

Some economists who uphold the principles of free trade mock UNCTAD's NIEO (new international economic order) as a "new in-ternational economic disorder," but they fail to note that the buyer's monopoly had been a major characteristic of the world market in the colonial age.

(6) Should the actual process of free trade happen to be the process of a dynamic chase which has been described, each country should naturally give the nod to measures to promote, over a limited span of time, a promising industry which remains at a relatively low level at present but is likely to rise to the position of an export industry in the future. In fact, the developing countries must be described as having a right to do so.

In this sense, Japan is an example of the successful upbringing of "infant industries" on a braod scale, and it might be said that many NICs, following the example of Japan, are carrying out measures to boost their infant industries. When an attempt is made to nourish infant industries over a span of 5–10 years, and this attempt encompasses a large number of industries, a degree of protectionism may be justified, insofar as the industries are promising and the protection is of a time limit nature. Should the government and industry play into each other's hands and protectionism turn into something perpetual, however, it is only natural that the damage thus incurred should be colossal in dimension.

Arguments for Floods of Exports

The foregoing are my own views on the significant disparities that exist between the realities of free trade and its static ideal as envisioned in textbooks. As a matter of course, I hope that these views contain some suggestions applicable to the existing frictions over trade. When it is argued that control over exports runs counter to the principles of free trade, it should be noted that the proponents of this sort of argument are unaware of the fact that the theoretically built image of free trade is confounded by its existing dynamic image. If we could assume that free trade, as it is portrayed in a static perspective, leads to a perfect equilibrium, and that things do evolve in a smooth manner, then export control would be an evil, to be sure. But free trade of the kind which is expounded by proponents is not so static and perfect in nature; in many instances, it results in floods of exports. At no time have I discovered any economic theory in which this point is candidly admitted.

Schumpeter once eulogized, in an analysis of domestic economic development, the process of competition between businesses as "creative destruction." In the same vein, the dynamic interaction among nations, including floods of exports, might be glorified as the core of the actual process of world capitalism in the true sense.

Nevertheless, it is of importance to ascertain that free trade, as it occurs in the real world, has nothing whatsoever to do with free trade as a static ideal; it is dramatically dynamic, and takes on an entirely heterogeneous character depending on the vicissitudes of a given nation. If that premise is accepted, it must be looked upon as instinctual for a declining nation to stick to protectionism to a certain extent. "Freedom" and "protection" are two aspects which may alternately come to the fore, depending on the phase of world economic development.

Therefore, even if it is feasible to denounce as counter to free trade the protectionism which is generated almost as a matter of course, it must be taken into account that those who do so are confusing the dynamic and realistic process of free trade (which includes floods of exports) with the static image of free trade on which they are basing their argument.

In plain language, they recognize no other authority than the theory of free trade in a static pattern when they cry out for export control. In doing so, however, they are unconsciously approving and eulogizing floods of exports which have never been taken into account within the framework of that theory of free trade. This is a clear theoretical confusion, but they fail to note the difference between the two kinds of tree trade; they have fallen prey to the magic of the words "free trade," which are the same for both concepts but very different in substance.

When I take a look at the realities as they exist today, I am inclined to feel it an absolute imperative to prevent any extension of rigidity in the world economy resulting from widespread control over global trade. I also believe it necessary to smooth out floods of exports from "catching-up" countries, to moderate the counterpart nation's industrial adjustment, and to deter any rise of protectionsim.

For these purposes, safeguards or export controls for particular industries are inevitable and, in fact, necessary in a dynamic world, to some degree. Before we get down to the task of presenting realistic measures in an appropriate manner, it is necessary, more than anything else, to take a look at the individual issues that have arisen in the case of the inroads of Japanese passenger cars in world markets.

Frictions over Auto Trade

Logic apart, let us briefly look at the actual state of trade friction over the export of Japanese passenger cars to the United States and Europe.

Table 1 indicates how sharply the output of passenger cars and their imports fluctuated in the United States and the United Kingdom between 1965 and 1980. In the United States, output was down 32% over the 15 years, while imports soared 5.8 times. Above all, the imports of Japanese cars registered a stunning rise of 109 times in this period. The share of Japanese cars in all imports (c/b) leapt from 4% to 74.1%, and the share of Japanese cars in "output plus imports" (which is expressed by c/(a + b)) consequently reached 25% in 1980.

In the United Kingdom, output in the same period marked a significant drop of 46%, whereas imports soared an astonishing 15.5 times. Imports of Japanese cars rose 564 times. The share of Japanese cars in

Table 1. Output and Import of Passenger Cars in the U.S. and the U.K.

			U.S.				
	Output a	All imports b	Imports from Japan c	$\dfrac{b}{a}$	$\dfrac{b}{a+b}$	$\dfrac{c}{b}$	$\dfrac{c}{a+b}$
1965	9,335,227	559,430	22,127	6.0%	5.7%	4.0%	0.2%
1970	6,550,128	2,013,420	323,671	30.7	23.5	16.1	3.8
1975	6,716,951	2,572,557	711,902	38.3	27.7	27.7	7.7
1980	6,375,516	3,248,266	2,407,645	50.9	33.8	74.1	25.0
			U.K.				
1965	1,722,045	55,558	288	3.2	3.1	0.5	0.0
1970	1,640,966	157,956	5,017	9.6	8.8	3.2	0.3
1975	1,267,695	448,749	115,077	35.4	26.1	25.6	6.7
1980	923,744	863,080	162,535	93.4	48.3	18.8	9.1

Source: Computed on the basis of Nissan Motors' *Auto Industry Handbook* and Toyota Motors' *The Japanese Auto Industry*.

all imports jumped from 0.5% to 18.8%. In contrast to the case of the United States, however, the import share of Japanese cars in "output plus imports" remained at 9.1%. The share of Japanese cars (c/b) in the United Kingdom's total car imports rose to 25.6% in 1975 but dropped to 18.8% in 1980.

Table 2 indicates the shares of American and imported cars in the sales of passenger cars and also the changes in the share of large and medium cars, on the one hand, and small cars, on the other. Over the short span of two years from 1978 to 1980, sales of small cars were up 17.1%, whereas those of large and medium cars marked a sharp drop amidst skyrocketing oil prices. Against this background, the sales of Japanese cars, which featured compactness, lower fuel cost, and fewer breakdowns, marked an astonishing rise of 40.6%, while the sales of

Table 2. Passenger Cars Sold in the U.S.

Unit: thousand cars

	Cars sold	1978	1980	Change in 1978–80
American	Large, medium	5,684 (50.3)	3,190 (35.6)	−43.9%
	Small	3,624 (32.1)	3,388 (37.7)	−6.5
	Subtotal	9,308 (83.4)	6,578 (73.4)	−29.3
Imported	Japanese	1,357 (12.0)	1,908 (21.3)	+40.6
	European	636 (5.6)	482 (5.4)	−24.2
	Subtotal	1,993 (17.6)	2,390 (26.6)	+19.9
Total of cars sold in the U.S.		11,301 (100.0)	8,968 (100.0)	−20.6
Subtotal of small cars sold in the U.S.		5,617 (49.7)	6,578 (64.4)	+17.1

Source: Same as for Table 1.

large and medium cars of American make marked an alarming drop of 43.9%. The share of large and medium cars in total sales declined from 50.3% to 35.6% in two years, whereas the share of Japanese cars climbed from 12.0% to 21.3%. In the meantime, huge drops were registered by American automakers in their total car sales: down 23.6% for GM, down 42.9% for Ford, and down 42.4% for Chrysler.

Table 3 presents similar statistical data for the United Kingdom, West Germany, France, and Italy. In the case of the United Kingdom, sales of cars of British make in 1978–80 were down 18.8% and imports rose 9.3%, with Japanese cars showing a rise of 3.3%. Italy marked exceptionally big fluctuations, up 37.5% for Italian cars and up 54.4% for imported cars in the two years, but the import of Japanese cars remained up 9.7%. However, the situation was different for West Germany and France. Total sales of cars in both countries were on the downturn, whereas those of Japanese cars were up 158% in West Germany and up 55% in France.

Table 3. Passenger Car Sales in Major European Nations

		1978	1980	Change in 1978–80
U.K.	Domestic	806,872 (50.7)	655,442 (43.3)	−18.8%
	Imported	785,069 (49.3)	858,251 (56.7)	+9.3
	Japanese	174,494 (11.0)	180,190 (11.9)	+3.3
	Total sales	1,591,941 (100.0)	1,513,693 (100.0)	−4.9
W. Germany	Domestic	2,030,652 (76.2)	1,745,875 (72.0)	−14.0
	Imported	633,102 (23.8)	680,312 (28.0)	+7.5
	Japanese	97,419 (3.7)	251,990 (10.4)	+158.7
	Total sales	2,663,754 (100.0)	2,426,187 (100.0)	−8.9
France	Domestic	1,539,054 (79.1)	1,444,686 (77.1)	−6.1
	Imported	405,932 (20.9)	428,516 (22.9)	+5.6
	Japanese	35,355 (1.8)	54,897 (2.9)	+55.3
	Total sales	1,944,986 (100.0)	1,873,202 (100.0)	−4.7
Italy	Domestic	751,585 (62.9)	1,033,472 (60.2)	+37.5
	Imported	442,839 (37.1)	633,960 (39.8)	+54.4
	Japanese	1,366 (0.1)	1,498 (0.1)	+9.7
	Total sales	1,194,424 (100.0)	1,717,432 (100.0)	+43.8

Source: Same as for Table 1.

In the United States, the share of sales of Japanese cars leapt from 12% in 1978 to 21.3% in 1980, whereas the sales share rose only from 3.7% (1978) to 10.4% (1980) in West Germany and from 1.8% to 2.9% in France. It should be noted that the share of Japanese cars stands at 11.9% in the United Kingdom and 10.4% in West Germany, which represents half of the Japanese share in the United States. Herein lies the reason why there should be no need for Japan to make as big a compromise in talks with European nations, for the time being, as it has in talks with the United States (a self-imposed limit of a rise of 10–11% over the preceding year).

Newspaper accounts provide an unnecessarily exaggerated version of the issue of trade with Europe. European nations might also be described as excessively nervous about the inflow of Japanese cars.

Nevertheless, the marked fluctuations in the share of car sales by nation and by size, over a short span of time, are conspicuous sharp structural changes of the kind which cannot be dealt with by the static theory of free trade or the theory of an international division of labor. Japan must strive to minimize whatever disturbance it has created, now that it has produced in the United States and Europe the kind of impact which can hardly be adapted or adjusted to in the short run. There is no doubt that the world economy will maintain its strength if such endeavors make it possible to deter a rise in protectionism as a whole and to generally maintain free and dynamic trade, even though there may sometimes be localized restrictions on free trade.

International Behavioristic Principles

General Motors' global car strategy is so designed that a colossal amount of $80,000 million will reportedly be laid out in the 1980s to start the manufacture of "J-cars" (1,800 cc) in May 1981 and ultra-compact "S-cars" (1,000–1,300 cc) in the autumn of 1983.

Given this picture, Japan plans to exercise self-restraint on exports for two years and study, in the third year, the advisability of a quota system on the basis of the two years' achievement. What is desirable is for the American automakers to revitalize themselves in the meanwhile. If Japan's two-years' self-restraint only results in raising the prices of Japanese autos or those of American autos, thereby serving only to improve the business picture of American auto enterprises, the whole effort will end up merely giving rise to the appearance of the worst possible outcome of export control or of monopolies to restrict supply and initiate price rises.

Far from revitalizing American industry, this will create momentum to stiffen and degenerate it. If so, it might be beneficial to the United States for Japan to make a rearrangement so as to begin working for a steady increase in exports in the third year and giving an impetus to the U.S. auto industry, instead of merely coming out with measures to fix an export quota.

However, if it turns out that the American auto industry begins to show signs of self-revitalization, there will be a need to work for early abolition of the existing export controls. As things now stand, the probability is high that the outcome will be somewhere in between these two extremes. It is also possible that the American industry will show no convincing progress in the third year but that things will improve in, say, the fifth year.

In such cases, even if Japan is compelled to continue suppressing floods of exports by itself, in the hope of fulfilling its international obligations as a new major economic power and working for stable growth of the world economy and for the elimination of any excessive disturbances, it is absolutely necessary for Japan to see to it that there will be no wider rigidity due to the loss of a stimulus to world industry.

It will be an important task for Japan to work for an opportune harmonization of self-restraint (through export quotas) and the offer of an impetus (through quota relaxation) when engaged in negotiations. Self-restraint will be disadvantageous to Japan in the short run, whereas the offer of an impetus will be advantageous. In the same vein, self-restraint will benefit the industry on the other side of the negotiating table for some time, whereas the offer of an impetus will not. I must emphasize, however, that for the ultimate benefit of all the nations involved, it is necessary to work for harmonization of both elements.

It is only natural that a conclusion cannot be drawn in a clear-cut form. The major economic powers once held aloft a surrealistic and static concept of free trade, but in fact they colonized one country after another, under the ostensible pretext of free trade. In today's world no major power is able to take advantage of the concept of free trade for its own national interests.

Actually, free trade has been a concept that worked to the advantage of the strong. The weak found themselves in a relative disadvantageous position, with no alternative but to follow the principles of free trade as its logic dictated. What emerged was a one-sided economic domination by specific major powers. Such times are now buried in history. It is now the age of economic "multipolarization," in which NICs are running in hot pursuit of advanced nations and developing nations are catching up with the NICs. In this dynamic world, competition tends to become brutal, which stimulates a flood of exports. However, any effort to moderate this development would seem to be an attempt to bring the reality as close to the textbook ideal of free trade as possible.

It is high time for Japan, which has become a major economic power, to become aware of the merciless realities of the world economy and to formulate an "international behavioristic principle" under various dynamic conditions, instead of parroting the static, stereotyped textbook logic of free trade. Such international behavioristic principles are liable to be looked upon only as a concept from international politics, but they are the principles Japan has to look for in order to be able to grope in the midst of economic polarization for criteria on which to base dialogue with other countries of the world.

Gone is the time when a nation could adopt a haphazard way of doing things, disregarding acceptable, reasonable principles. Behavior in the international community has a variety of facets, including culture, society, politics, and economy. The lesson we have learned from the economic issue of trade frictions is the fact that perfunctory theories framed in a surrealistic and hypothetical world, in the years when Adam Smith and David Ricardo were predominant, are no longer workable. Recognition of this fact affords an unparalleled chance to ponder once again the way in which the principles of international behavior ought to be laid out in the economic sector.

Thus the settlement of the negotiations between Japan and the United States over the auto issue must not be construed as only a sign of the submission of economic principles to politics.

8

JAPANESE ECONOMIC GROWTH AND ITS IMPLICATIONS FOR AUSTRALIA

Japanese Economic Growth and Japan-Australia Trade

Over the period 1962–73, Australia's exports (X_A) increased fourfold, but at the same time Australia's exports to Japan (X_{AJ}) rose dramatically by some 800 %. In the years after the oil crisis (1973–77), however, the total value of Australian exports expanded by 43 %, and Australia's exports to Japan fell short of that by rising only 31 %. While Japan was experiencing high growth, Australian exports to Japan underwent a rapid increase, and the proportion of those exports within the total value of Australian exports (X_{AJ}/X_A) rose from 18.7 % in 1962 to 37.5 % in 1973. Following the oil crisis, this proportion fell to 34.0 % in 1976–77. In this way, it can be said that the effect of Japanese high economic growth on the share of Australian exports to Japan within total exports was considerable.

The changes in X_{AJ}/X_A can be seen in Table 1. During the period 1962–65, when investment in plant and equipment in Japan was temporarily stagnant, the ratio fell to 18–19 %, while between 1965 and 1970, when private investment rose quickly, X_{AJ}/X_A jumped from 18.7 % to 33.6 %. This reflects the medium-term cyclical increase in the ratio of private fixed investment to GNP from 15.3 to 20.7 %, and was obviously related to the time lag associated with long-term contracts. The X_{AJ}/X_A ratio went up to 35.5 % in 1971, fluctuated until 1975, and moved between 33 % and 37 % since then. On the other hand, private fixed investment as a percentage of GNP dropped from 20.7 % in 1970 to 15.8 % in 1975. Thus trends in the Japanese domestic investment environment were clearly reflected in the movement of X_{AJ}/X_A.

Oe well-knnown fact is that the share of Australian exports to Great

This is a translation of a paper which appeared originally in *Nichigo buretin*, No. 9, December 1978, entitled "Nihon keizai no choki keiro to nichigo keizai kankei." It was published in English in *Australia and Japan: Issues in the Economic Relationship*, edited by John Crawford and Saburo Okita, 1979.

Table 1. Two Indicators of Australia-Japan Trade

Year	X_{AJ}/X_A	X_{JA}/M_A
1962	18.7%	6.3%
63	18.5	6.5
64	19.1	8.0
65	18.6	9.3
66	22.0	9.3
67	24.0	10.4
68	27.8	10.8
69	31.6	11.9
70	33.6	13.4
71	35.5	15.5
72	36.0	16.0
73	37.5	17.5
74	37.4	18.0
75	35.7	17.7
75–76	32.9	19.5
76–77	34.0	20.7

Note: 1976–77 figures are for Australian fiscal years.
Source: 1962–75, *Commodity Trade Statistics*; 1976–77, Peter Drysdale and Kiyoshi Kojima, *Australia-Japan Economic Relations in the International Context: Recent Experience and the Prospects Ahead*, Canberra, Australia-Japan Economics Relations Research Project, 1978, Table 1.1.

Britain within total Australian exports showed a rapid decline in inverse proportion to the rise in the X_{AJ}/X_A ratio, which was of course brought about by Japan's high postwar growth. One other trend that can be discerned from Table 1 is the increase in the share of Japanese exports within total Australian imports (X_{JA}/M_A). While on the one hand X_{AJ}/X_A was exhibiting medium-run cyclical fluctuation, on the other hand X_{JA}/M_A was steadily increasing. This suggests that even during a slump in domestic investment Japanese exports continued to be in strong demand.

If the rise in these two ratios were clearly related to Japan's economic growth, estimating the effects of Japan's transition from 10 % growth to a stage of 4–5 % growth might not be too difficult. During the four-year period 1969–73, Australian exports to Japan rose 2.8 times, but in the four-year period 1973–77 they increased only 1.5 times. Naturally, this did not immediately affect Australia's domestic economic growth, and rather than directly reflecting the pace of the increase in Australia's total exports, it pointed to changes in the geographical pattern of trade. The consistent decline in the share of the United Kingdom and the continued rise in Japan's share is a trend that one cannot see changing rapidly in the years ahead, but the slower growth in exports to Japan after the oil crisis is certainly a real problem for Australia.

In these circumstances, it is worth considering the medium- to long-term outlook for Japanese economic growth, the potential for which is obviously relevant to the future of Australia-Japan trade.

The Background to Post-Oil Crisis Stagnation

Four or five years after the oil crisis the world economy at last returned to the level of activity immediately before the crisis, or in some cases slightly exceeded that peak In this the Japanese economy is no exception. The index of industrial output for September 1978, four years and nine months after the oil crisis, was 122.5 (1975 = 100), which was a mere 1.9 points above the November 1973 peak of 120.6. What brought about the recovery from slump and stagnation?

Increase in energy costs
According to the experience of a number of advanced countries after the oil crisis, energy costs rose by varying degrees from country to country. As can be seen from Table 2, in Japan, where oil dependence and dependence on its import are high, the rise in energy costs was the highest of the five countries at 4 2 times. Furthermore, it took longer than in other countries for the impact of this to be absorbed and for the price structure to adjust.

The effect of the oversupply of equipment and stocks
In the United States, where in recent years the growth rate has been not very different from Japan's, about 10 % of GNP has been channeled into private investment in plant and equipment. In Japan, however,

Table 2. Rise in Energy Costs (excluding primary electricity)

	Dependence on oil (1972, %)	Rise in costs 1975/1972
Japan	78.9	4.2
U.S.A.	47.5	2.8
U.K.	53.0	2.8
France	53.0	3.4
West Germany	71.8	2.9

Source: Japan Institute of Energy Economics, "Analysis of Energy Costs and the Ripple Effects of their Changes: A Study of the Effects on Major Industries and the Macro-economy," Report for the Economic Planning Agency Prices Bureau, March 1977, Tables 1–9, p. 17.

about 13 % was invested in this way in 1978, which suggests that Japan has that much more potential for increased capacity and strong pressures for an oversupply of plant. In the United States, the ratio of the value of stocks to sales in manufacturing industry was 1.62 in 1966, the peak year of the fixed investment cycle, and increased to 1.89 in 1970, the trough in the investment cycle. In 1976 the figure was 1.66; in 1977, 1.58; and by June 1978 it had fallen to 1.51, lower than the ratio in the investment boom of 1966. The index of stocks of finished products in mining and manufacturing industry in Japan was 127.9 in 1977 (1970 = 100) and 118.0 in September 1978. Even in the various recessions before the oil crisis the ratio had never reached 120, and so Japan shows a pattern contrasting with the under-stocking situation of the United States.

Thus, even though exports and public investment increased in any particular period, stocks of finished goods correspondingly fell without causing an inventory boom as in the past. It is certain that many industries are now adjusting their stocks, but overall this situation was one serious cause of the recession mentality prevalent after the oil crisis.

Increase in import dependence and the rapid fall in the size of the multiplier

In 1974, just after the rapid increase in the price of oil, the ratio of imports to GNP rose from the 10% of the past to a level of 15.2 %. This was the result of cost push, when viewed from the supply side, but from the demand side it can be seen as a fall in the size of the multiplier as the marginal propensity to import rose and the leakage ratio increased. After that, however, in 1975–76, the average propensity to import flattened out at 13.8 % and the marginal propensity to import probably fell somewhat. It must be realized as well that between mid-1977 and mid-1978, as the value of the yen continued to appreciate, the price index of imported goods dropped by some 20 %. At that time, the size of the multiplier was pushed upward by the sudden fall in the marginal propensity to import, and the recession was slowed to an extent by the higher value of the yen. Generally this point is not appreciated in public discussion.

Thus, just after the oil crisis, the drop in the size of the multiplier was a severe problem because of the relative price of imports, but today it seems that the drop in the marginal propensity to import through the higher value of the yen has increased the size of the multiplier.

Currency revaluation

Japan's exchange rate fluctuated around the 300 yen to the dollar mark from 1971 to 1976: 1971, US$1 = ¥314; 1972, ¥302; 1973, ¥280; 1974, ¥300; 1975, ¥305; 1976, ¥293. (In the same period, by contrast, the German mark gradually appreciated by 38 %, moving from US$1 = 3.27 M in 1971, to 2.36 in 1976.) The yen was then forced up rapidly from ¥293 in December 1976 to ¥240 in December 1977 and ¥180 in summer 1978. In other words, the appreciation of the yen was concentrated in the period 1977–78, allowing insufficient time for industry to adjust, and causing a strong polarization between industries like the automobile industry and those undergoing limited or structural recession. This is one reason why the recession mentality was not easily eradicated even in 1977–78.

The effects of lower growth

If the growth rate of a country were to be suddenly halved from 10 % to around 5 %, the shock would be concentrated most on the investment goods industry. However, in countries where growth was 4–5 % before the oil crisis, recession was not strongly felt even though their post-oil crisis growth rates were lower than that of Japan. In this way, the effect of the recession was sharper in Japan than in West Germany or the United Kingdom.

Constraints on Japan's Long-Term Path

There are several other factors which will act as a restraint in the longer term.

Energy restrictions

There are a number of countries where in the short term energy is becoming less of a problem, but if we think of the medium and long term, the oil-producing countries have reached the stage where they would prefer to control oil output at high prices rather than increase production of cheaper oil. To the extent that its effects on the average business can be measured, high growth will be possible in the immediate and short term, but 10 % growth appears impossible in the medium and long term. Furthermore, the likelihood of a suitable energy source alternative to oil in this century appears low.

Trends in the technological revolution

Around the time of World War II numerous new inventions appeared, including television, duralumin, synthetic rubber, radar, DDT, atomic power, jet engines, antibiotics, computers, and transistors. These formed the basis of the postwar technological revolution. American technology was spread throughout the world through the expansion of multinational enterprises and the export of technology, and helped push up world growth rates. Since the early 1970s, however, new inventions, new technologies, and new products have been remarkably few. Some commentators say that "the technological revolution has ended." This was realized before the oil crisis and is therefore particularly important.

The problem at present is that most modern industries of today have matured through progress in "hard" technology, as exemplified in the steel, automotive, and electronics industries, and are seemingly ill-prepared to develop "soft" technology. However, a "soft" technological revolution is not necessarily more difficult than one in "hard" technology. The proportion of machine tools with numerical controls has increased. Around 1970 almost no wristwatches were electronic, but electronic watches comprise more than 50 % of production today. This trend toward greater use of electronics in machinery may reflect the fact that new technological progress places more emphasis on systems technology. It is an example of the sophisticated interindustry exchange of technology developed in various industries. At the time the target industries of cars and computers moved ahead, growth was easy because goals were clear. We have now entered the age when the goal must be to strengthen soft, invisible technologies. Can Japan successfully cope with this difficult period? The more the problems are realized, the more we must move to a point where the tempo of technological revolution is assured.

Problems of the large national bond issue

As Japan's balance of payments surplus continues to reach ever higher levels, the need for positive fiscal policy is greater. The dilemma is one of rising budget expenditure, falling tax revenues and an increase in the amount of national bonds issued.

One drawback is that present deficit financing is not of a cyclical nature, and will not be removed if there is a return to full employment or full capacity utilization. Even if economic stimulus brought a return to full employment, "full employment deficit financing" would still remain, and might even increase.

Another complication is that, although the value of government bonds issued has been maintained at a level of about one-third of total General Account expenditure, it must be realized that it is now essential to begin to issue bonds in much larger quantities. Japan, in contrast to other advanced countries, has controlled interest rates and operated a "cheap money policy" which keeps rates below the market rates. This policy was not really a problem when the amount of bonds issued was relatively small, but as that value increases substantially, and the international market takes up these attractive securities, interest rates must in some way be liberalized.

In fact, bonds issued have after one year been bought by the Bank of Japan from city banks, although to prevent this practice from causing increased issuance of currency, one condition imposed was that industrial demand for equipment funds had to be at a low ebb. However, low economic activity cannot always be expected, and government bond issues will be a problem for some years to come.

In the event that the bonds are completely taken up by the market, it will be necessary for the terms under which bonds are issued to be liberalized, and for the types of bonds to be diversified and their international limitations to be lifted. At the same time it will be necessary for fiscal policy to follow the rules of the market mechanism. For that reason, if we are in too much of a hurry to overcome recession, we can reap the benefits of recovery in the short term, but will suffer a resurgence of inflation in the medium or long term. The decontrol of interest rates may, however, lead to serious conflicts among interest groups: financing institutions, share brokers, and postal savings depositors. Furthermore, since decontrol of interest rates is itself difficult, avoiding these will involve a new round of inflation in the medium term. Overcoming the dilemmas of the stagflation era is a real problem on its own.

For these reasons, the government will not find it easy to take a positive attitude to overcoming the recession. Adopting pure Keynesian policies will lead to some complications, and the difficulty of raising the speed of growth in the medium run is partly a result of this.

The "boomerang effect"

If the boomerang effect which we have described in earlier chapters leads to severe restraints on growth as a result of technology exports or the rapid overseas expansion of companies, it cannot be ignored. In the era of high growth, there were calls for substantial industrial reconversion, and even if the boomerang effect had appeared only temporarily, it would not have been very great. However, 4–5% growth is now the norm and industrial adjustment is by no means easy. While history has seen a distinct change from the century of Britain to the century of the United States, and while Japan to some extent had a boomerang effect on America, it is not always possible for the NICs today to replace Japan and other advanced nations in the short term, for reasons we have discussed.

In this way, then, we can distinguish several restraints on growth in the medium and long term. As a result, we cannot expect a return to 10% growth for Japanese industry in the future. If we think that 4–5 % is too low and prefer 6–7 %, this is only a difference of two percentage points, no more than the margin of error of the past. Those predicting growth of 8–10 %, however, are very few now.

Whatever the constraints are—energy shortages, the decline in technological development, the boomerang phenomenon, greater fiscal caution because of the dependence on government bonds—various pressures still operate, both from overseas for Japan to act as the engine of world growth and increase domestic demand so as to reduce balance of payments surpluses, and from within Japan to overcome the recession. In the medium term, maintaining a growth rate of 4–6% may be possible. While industry adjustment and the sophistication of the industrial structure need time to be carried through, at least Japan may be able to attain a medium-term growth rate somewhat higher than other advanced countries.

The Direction of Australia-Japan Trade

Predicting the future is difficult in the present uncertain age. Checking the weight of important commodities within the total value of Australia's exports to Japan, we find that 8 commodities made up 93.7 % in 1976–77 (iron ore 17.6 %, coal 26.4 %, bauxite 6.6 %, alumina 14.3 %, nickel ores and matte 9.3 %, wool 9.7 %, wheat 2.9 %, and sugar 6.9 %). Iron ore, coal, and alumina alone contributed 58.3 %. This commodity structure of exports to Japan changed dramatically in the 10 years from the late 1960s. In 1965–66, wool was the main component at 55.2 %, but dropped to 9.7 % by 1976–77. On the other hand, in 1965–66 iron ore accounted for only 0.6 % and coal 12.6 %, but by 1976–77 they accounted for 17.6 and 26.4 % respectively.

Australia's share of Japan's imports of main resource goods is set out in Figure 1. From it we can see that the share of iron ore from Australia went up dramatically, from 0.5 % in 1965 to 47 % in 1973, although it flattened out after that. Bauxite was 4 % in 1965, but 55 % in 1971, and stabilized thereafter. In that respect, Japan's dependence on Australia for iron ore will probably remain at about 45.9 % (the 1973–77 average), while dependence on Australia for bauxite will stay at approximately 56.8 % (the 1971–77 average). Nickel ores and matte started from zero in 1965 and had reached 34.9 % in 1977, but this is unlikely to remain stable. On the other hand, Japan's dependence on Australian imports of coal, wool, and wheat has fluctuated slightly, but there is no definite indication as to which way the trend is going. Recent three-year averages show coal at 34.9 %, wool at 85.3 %, and wheat at 17.9 %, and these could probably give some clue as to the future.

Table 3 presents data on the dependence of various Japanese indus-

Table 3. Dependence of Several Japanese Industries on Imports from Australia

	Australian exports of iron ore to Japan (a)	Australian exports of coal to Japan (b)	Value of output of Japanese steel industry (c)	$\frac{a}{c}$	$\frac{b}{c}$	Australian exports of wheat to Japan (a)	Output of Japanese flour industry (b)	$\frac{a}{b}$	Australian exports of sugar to Japan (a)	Output of Japanese sugar industry (b)	$\frac{a}{b}$
	\$ million	\$ million	\$ million	%	%	\$ million	\$ million	%	\$ million	\$ million	%
1962	1.2	40.9	2,010.4	0.06	2.03	29.0	322.7	8.98	17.9	502.0	3.56
63	1.3	40.7	2,244.6	0.06	1.81	24.7	362.6	6.80	49.4	572.6	8.63
64	0.9	58.4	2,779.6	0.03	2.10	33.7	376.5	8.96	51.3	560.3	9.16
65	3.0	89.1	3,046.4	0.10	2.93	29.3	398.2	6.85	25.1	506.0	4.96
66	24.7	106.4	3,957.5	0.62	2.69	25.3	428.7	5.90	30.2	494.6	6.11
67	97.7	116.6	4,488.5	0.62	2.60	34.9	441.5	7.91	29.9	580.1	5.16
68	163.9	154.8	5,313.1	3.08	2.91	50.5	449.0	11.24	27.3	832.6	3.28
69	273.5	208.8	6,662.9	4.10	3.13	83.2	461.2	18.04	41.3	702.2	5.88
70	421.6	246.4	7,933.2	5.31	3.11	57.5	464.7	12.36	51.6	856.3	6.03
71	514.9	264.0	7,557.5	6.81	3.49	29.7	508.1	5.84	54.1	944.5	5.72
72	526.4	354.1	9,335.9	5.75	3.79	52.5	632.0	8.31	97.1	1,111.9	8.73
73	777.6	504.4	14,407.6	5.40	3.50	14.5	879.0	1.65	111.4	1,151.2	9.68
74	972.1	711.9	15,796.9	6.15	4.51	122.9	901.8	13.63	127.4	1,726.9	7.37
75	1,001.9	911.8	11,493.9	8.72	7.93	139.5	1,037.5	13.45	131.6	2,189.0	6.01

(continued on next page)

Table 3 (continued)

	Australian exports of wool to Japan	Output of Japan's textile industry	$\frac{a}{b}$	Output of Japanese woolen yarn	$\frac{a}{c}$	Australian exports of alumina to Japan	Output of Japanese aluminum refining industry	$\frac{a}{b}$
	(a)	(b)	%	(c)	%	(a)	(b)	%
	$ million					$ thousand		
1962	254.6	4,761.2	5.35	483.2	52.7	—	34,398	—
63	297.6	5,393.7	5.52	515.0	57.8	—	40,593	—
64	314.0	5,768.8	5.44	551.1	57.0	3,095	36,022	8.59
65	284.8	5,958.3	4.78	562.9	50.6	3,663	41,168	8.90
66	321.2	6,546.8	4.91	630.1	51.0	6,257	43,005	14.55
67	297.6	7,298.1	4.08	617.8	48.2	7,072	49,952	14.16
68	299.4	7,973.4	3.75	598.9	50.0	10,451	51,905	20.13
69	315.1	8,652.2	3.64	662.1	47.6	12,909	57,672	22.38
70	276.2	9,763.8	2.83	681.7	40.5	21,419	76,803	27.89
71	234.7	10,558.3	2.22	657.9	35.7	31,865	93,372	34.13
72	376.8	13,145.5	2.87	908.9	41.5	35,233	99,192	35.52
73	815.7	19,122.2	4.27	1,502.9	54.3	28,707	135,114	21.25
74	423.5	17,634.6	2.40	1,179.4	35.9	51,078	174,331	29.30
75	409.6	16,821.3	2.44	958.4	42.7	52,227	200,390	26.06

Source: Output figures from Japanese Census of Manufactures (Commodities).
Note: Export and output figures are converted to US dollars using IMF conversion factors.

tries on imports from Australia—iron and steel, flour milling, sugar refining, textiles, and alumina. In the iron and steel industry, the 1970s show a much greater dependence on Australia than do output figures for the 1960s. If we examine the value of Australia's exports of wheat to Japan and Japanese domestic flour production, we can see changes, but there is an upward trend and a noticeable shift from other countries. In sugar, however, there is no trend in Australia's exports of sugar to Japan as a percentage of Japan's sugar refining industry output, only a slight cyclical movement.

If we compare Australia's exports of wool to Japan with the output of Japan's textile industry, dependence on Australia has naturally fallen with increasing use of synthetics. However, when we compare it to the output of Japanese woolen yarn, the dependence ratio has been fairly stable at between 40 and 50 %. In alumina, quite marked fluctuations are noticeable, although the 1970–75 average is 29.0 %.

It is probably fair to say that the effects of the severe shocks following the oil crisis have worn off. It is also no exaggeration to say that the increase in Japanese dependence on Australia that continued over the period 1960–70 has also stopped, except for a few commodities. There will probably be no recurrence of the investment boom to rapidly expand Japanese imports of iron ore, and there are fewer problems likely to cause rapid changes in the structure of Australian exports to Japan.

In that case, Australia's exports to Japan would seem to depend largely on the tempo of Japanese economic growth rather than on changes in the reliance on Australian imports. If we can rely on Japanese growth of 4–5% in the future, Australia-Japan trade in the near future will move in a pattern similar to that of the last few years (1975–78). This conclusion is not based on any particular calculations, but is a qualitative judgment derived from appropriate indices.

Figure 2 plots the proportion of imports from Japan within total Australian imports, by commodity. From 1965–66 to 1976–77, this increased rapidly from 9.1 % to 46.5 % in transport equipment, from 3.5 % to 13.6 % for machinery, and from 10.3 % to 45.4 % for electrical equipment. Steel rose somewhat from 41.2 to 65.3 %, but textiles, which peaked in 1973–74 at 32.4 %, fell to 23.1 % for 1976–77.

Australia's dependence on imports from Japan for important industrial products reflected the move to heavy industry in Japan's export structure, especially the relative increase in exports of machinery. Furthermore, even though various changes have occurred over the last few years, Japan's heavy industrialization has gone about as far as it can, so this percentage should not alter greatly in the near future. For this reason, we can say that the importance of Australia in Japanese

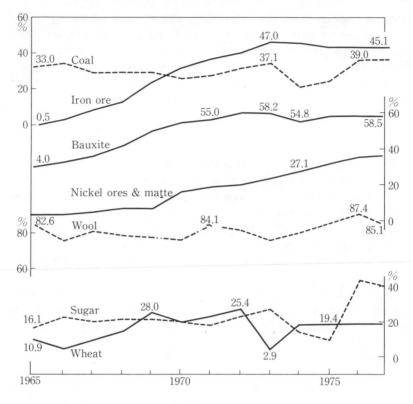

Figure 1. Imports from Australia as a percentage of Japan's major resource goods.

imports and the importance of Japan in Australian imports are now such that they have absorbed the secondary effects of the period of high growth of the past. However, while these figures reveal changes in the period of accelerating growth, we cannot expect similar fluctuations now that growth has slowed.

Instead, what will strongly influence the trade between the two countries in the future will generally be the growth rate of each country. If Japan's growth rises for the time being, Australia's exports to Japan will probably increase, while if Australia's growth path turns upward, Japan's exports to Australia will no doubt benefit. However, the various indicators do not reveal any consistent change in the short term. There are several points that should be kept in mind.

First, neither country should adopt excessively inflationary or deflationary policies but should seek a stable growth pattern. In Japan even before the oil crisis, for example, inflation was too high and the sudden reaction in controlling it involved some disagreeable policies for

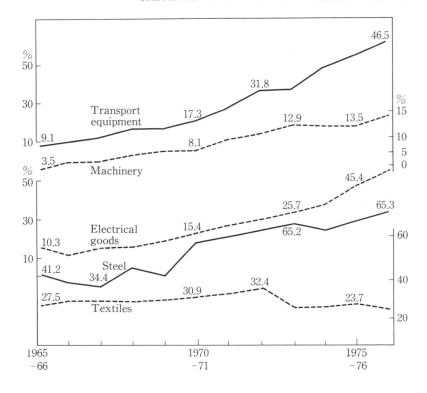

Figure 2. Imports from Japan as a percentage of Australian imports of major industrial manufactures.

a time. However, this does not occur without some ill effect on trading partners.

Second, one matter of concern in trade with Australia is that problems tend to arise occasionally in long-term contracts for primary goods. It is reasonable, of course, to wish to isolate the price of primary commodities from short-term fluctuations, but preventing losses from "cyclical price flexibility" may lead to the removal of what A.H. Hansen calls "structural price flexibility," which disrupts the world optimum resource allocation. In addition, an excessively high, long-term contract price aggravates worldwide stagflation. Furthermore, if the price of the primary commodity is very much higher than the unit cost derived from productivity and factor prices, or if it is set significantly lower, it is obvious that there is no structural price flexibility. If both these persist, structural price flexibility cannot be maintained and the development of smooth trade between the two countries will be obstructed.

Third, Japan should gradually relax controls on the import of primary commodities, while Australia should gradually reduce protection of its industries. Bilateral trade would naturally be stimulated by removal of these major obstacles.

Quantitative projections will show that the extent of change in the various indicators of each country's trade structure has been far less in recent years than in the past. Using the growth rates of each country as a basis, trends in bilateral trade and movement in the structure of trade will be much easier to predict in the future than they have been in the past.

III

DYNAMIC PATTERNS IN GROWTH AND CYCLES

9

POSTWAR ECONOMIC GROWTH: OVERVIEW OF THE 1970s AND THE COMING TWO DECADES

Postwar Industrial Growth in Two Leading Industries

The Japanese economy rapidly recovered from the extremely low trough and confusion that marked the years immediately following World War II. Today, after a lapse of one-third of a century, the Japanese economy has not only surged ahead of the level of other advanced nations' economies but has come so far as actually to threaten various industries of the Western nations.

As things now stand, there seems to be hardly any need to analyze in deta 1 how Japan's real GNP, industrial output, and exports have continued to rise at a fast pace as against those of other nations. Between 1965 and 1973 before the oil crisis, the average growth rate stood at 10.6 % in terms of real GNP and 12.5 % in mining and industrial production. It is quite evident that this was extremely high growth compared with that of other countries.

In this paper, an attempt will be made to examine how the output of two important and "symbolic" items in manufacturing industry, crude steel and passenger cars, have evolved in the United States and Japan over the last thirty years. As is discernible from Table 1, in the 1950s the Japanese steel and automobile industries were hovering at unquestionably lower levels than those of the United States. In 1955, Japan's crude steel output did not even reach 10 % of that of the United States. The output of passenger cars in Japan was so low as to be negligible. By 1980, however, the output of steel and passenger cars had soared to levels practically equal to those of the United States.

Why is it that these two items are "symbolic" as typical commodities of Japanese manufacturing industry?

First, in the 1950s both items were barely competitive in world markets, and their export prices were comparatively high. However, they now dominate world markets. In retrospect, this development is something even the Ministry of International Trade and Industry was

137

Table 1. United States vs. Japan in the Production of Two Major Commodities

	Crude steel production (million M.T.)			Passenger car production (thous. units)		
	USA (a)	Japan (b)	$\left[\dfrac{b}{a}\right]$	USA (a)	Japan (b)	$\left[\dfrac{b}{a}\right]$
1950	87.8	4.8	5.5%	6,666	1.6	0.0%
55	106.2	9.4	8.9	7,920	20	0.3
60	90.1	22.1	24.5	6,703	165	2.5
65	119.3	41.2	34.5	9,335	696	7.5
70	119.3	93.3	78.2	6,550	3,179	48.5
75	105.8	102.3	96.7	6,717	4,568	68.0
79	123.3	111.7	90.6	8,434	6,176	73.2
80	100.8	111.4	110.5	6,376	7,038	110.4

Sources: 1) Crude steel: Tekko Tokei Iinkai (Committee of Iron and Steel Statistics, *Tekko Tokei Yoran* (Handbook of Iron and Steel Statistics).
2) Passenger cars: Toyota, *The Japanese Automobile Industry* (in Japanese), 1973 and 1981.

unable to predict. Accordingly, these items symbolize the postwar development of Japanese industry.

Second, although it has been pointed out that by 1980 Japan came to rank with the United States in the output of steel and cars, it must of course be taken into account that the U.S. has a population twice as big as that of Japan. It follows therefore that Japan has come to a point where it may be able to produce roughly twice as much per capita as the U.S. in both commodities. To absorb the production, not only domestic but also external demand for these items must have been expanded to a significantly great extent. Already in 1980, the ratio of Japan's reliance on exports reached 31.3 % for rolled ordinary steel and 56.1 % for passenger cars. In fact, it is the rapid rise in the exports of both items that has enabled Japan to achieve an output per capita twice as great as that of the United States.

Third, of all manufacturing industries, steel is the most basic and highly capital-intensive. In contrast, the production of autos calls for sophisticated processing and assembly work. It could be described as highly technology-intensive, but in fact it is also labor-intensive. Moreover, the automotive industry involves a large number of affiliated subcontractors as an ancillary industry. Therefore, the fact that both the steel and auto industries have developed so rapidly in the postwar Japanese economy is indicative of the parallel development of both a capital-intensive industry and a labor-intensive industry. Furthermore, when the growth of auto subcontractors is taken into account it might be argued that both small and medium-sized businesses must have developed along with big businesses during the course of the general postwar expansion. This development also exemplifies the pattern of industrial development during the period. In the auto industry sub-contracted components and parts account for more than 60% of total cost. Therefore, to enable the automotive industry to equip itself to compete in world markets, both parent production complexes and sub-contracted smaller component and part manufacturers must improve their quality and cut costs through constant technical innovation.

Fourth, although it is a fact that the two industries are highly reliant on exports, they would have been unable to achieve the spectacular growth shown in Table 1 without a rapid expansion of the domestic market. The logic of this is that an expansion of the domestic market will facilitate sustained high growth of exports in the medium- and long-term perspectives by making it possible to reduce unit costs with the introduction of mass production. Certainly an expansion of domestic demand for steel may result in reducing the immediate supply for exports, and a reduction of the domestic demand may result in bringing about increased pressure on supply for exports, so much so that there are ways in which the domestic and external demands function in contradiction with each other in the short-term sequence of events. Nevertheless, it is a feature common to the steel and auto industries that an expansion of the domestic market has not conflicted with that of the export market in the medium and long term. The extent of diffusion obtained by dividing the number of passenger cars owned by the total population stood at 6.7% in 1969 but increased sharply to 20.4 % in 1980. This is unquestionably a clear indication of the rapid pace at which passenger cars have been diffused in Japan. It is hardly necessary to point out that the increased domestic demand for steel and its massive output have been sustained by the rapid rate at which the government's public works projects have been expanded year by year and by increased private fixed investment in various industries. In this context the parallel development of both domestic and export markets might perhaps be described as the two wheels of a cart which carries a continuous and cumulative expansion of two industries.

Industrial development in the postwar years has been characterized by the development of the capital-intensive steel and petrochemical industries as well as the labor-intensive automobile, electronic, apparel, and other industries. These basic industries, and the processing industries, have developed into what they are today after gradually moving towards internationalization by way of the following process: an expansion of domestic demand, followed by an expansion of exports, leading to inroads into foreign countries by overseas investment. Insofar as their development in the past goes, it is not the case that priority has been given to the labor-intensive industries alone or that increased favorable treatment has been afforded only to the capital-intensive industries. Rather, it might be argued that rapid development of industry as a whole has occurred while striving for a balance in the relationship between the two industries. Naturally, there must often have been unequal development of the two industries during the short-run business cycle or the medium-term cycle of fixed investment, but, in the long-term perspective, it is significant that the industries have developed concurrently and that, during the course of their parallel development, there has never been any tendency for either sector to restrict the other.

Another point that deserves attention is that the role played in the postwar development of Japanese industry by "borrowed technology" from the advanced nations was greatest in the earliest years, gradually decreasing over time. Every industry has progressively shifted to the promotion of its own technical innovations despite starting out with the introduction of foreign technology.

This certainly holds true in the case of the electronics industry, which has developed rapidly with the successive introduction of transistors, ICs, LSIs, and ultra-LSIs. Another example is the steel industry, which has been leading the world since 1970 or so; continuous casting technology was introduced on a large scale in the 1970s. Table 2 (A) shows the indices for per-unit consumption of oil fuels (including LPG and LNG), the yield ratio of steel products (final output of steel ÷ required quantity of steel products ingots), and the continuous casting ratio. Incidentally, the continuous casting method has been highly instrumental in saving energy and raising the yield ratio to a level much higher than that attained with the blooming method. Table 2 (B) suggests that Japan was ahead of all other nations in continuous casting ratio in the 1970s and also the most efficient nation in terms of the index for the unit energy consumption and in coke requirement per ton of pig iron production.

These factors are only an example of the technical progress that has been made by the Japanese steel industry. It has often been pointed out that the industry has taken advantage of the location of steelworks in littoral areas (thus reducing sea transport costs). However, the industry has not only taken advantage of foreign technology and the location of littoral steelworks but also moved ahead of the world in technical innovations, such as the installation of huge blast furnaces of the most efficient type with an intra-furnace capacity of more than 3,000 m³, the

Table 2. Indices of Technological Progress in Steel Industry

A. Time Series

	Oil consumption per unit of crude steel production (1973 = 100)	Final steel products relative to steel ingot production	Continuous casting ratio in crude steel production
1973	100.0	84.3%	21.5%
1974	97.8	85.8	26.7
1975	87.7	85.3	32.2
1976	87.3	86.2	36.3
1977	77.1	87.0	41.9
1978	71.2	87.9	47.9
1979	61.6	89.3	54.0
1980	43.1	89.5	58.7

B. Intercountry Comparison

	Energy consumption per unit of crude steel production (Japan = 100) —1978—	Coke (kg) per unit of pig iron production (ton) —1979—	Continuous casting ratio —1979—
Japan	100	423 kg	53.0%
USA	143	575	16.7
W. Germany	113	497	39.0
UK	147	578	16.8
France	116	514	29.5
Italy	110	480	46.4

Source: Nippon Steel Corporation, *Iron and Energy* (in Japanese), 1981.

rapid switch from open-hearth furnaces to revolving furnaces, the introduction of strip mills, and the raising of the continuous casting ratio. In this context, there has to be something which cannot be explained away as only the advantages of a latecomer using borrowed technology.

In the case of the automotive industry, it would be difficult in the limited space of this paper to describe all the various technological innovations that have been made. But it is not just because of their fuel efficiency that there has been such a tremendous rise in the global demand for small Japanese passenger cars. As has already been demonstrated by surveys in the Western nations, the frequency of malfunctions for Japanese passenger cars is significantly small. It is a fact that new ideas, know-how, and technical improvements have followed one upon another in each phase of the production process, and most Japanese automobile manufacturers have tried to pay attractive remunerations as incentives for creative suggestions. Nevertheless, it might be said that at the root of such creativity lies the typical Japanese worker's sense of solidarity, which enables engineers and skilled workers in each section to work together for upgrading productivity. This has been quite instrumental in improving individual techniques systematically. Automobile plants in the Western nations are decidedly influenced by the principles of individualism. Because of this tendency, ingenious contrivances are not cooperatively developed by workers. Efforts are confined to a mere integration of individual lines of work, with the consequence that malfunctions tend to take place at an early stage. This defect is noteworthy. It might be contended that at the heart of this matter lie differences in culture as well as differences in the systems of management and work. It should also be taken into account that, in recent years, an increasingly large number of electronic devices have been added to automobiles, and industrial robots have also stepped into the limelight. This development also marks the evolution of a new technology which Japan is bringing out ahead of all other nations in the world.

Table 3 indicates how Japanese automobile manufacturers have gone ahead internationally in the last 10 years as a result of their elaborate technical improvements. The ups and downs of the world auto industry are evident from this table, which shows how Japanese automobile manufacturers have progressed by leaps and bounds.

Factors Underlying High Economic Growth in the Postwar Years

In order to analyze the high economic growth in the postwar years, there is a need to take account not only of causative factors during the postwar period but also of the long-term factors which may have been in existence since before the war. In view of the limited space available here, however, an attempt will be made to enumerate some of the various factors in the postwar years which have contributed to the high economic growth rate.

(1) From the standpoint of international comparison, the ratio of defense expenditure to GNP is extremely low (0.79 % in 1970 and 0.90 % in 1980).

(2) Also from the standpoint of international comparison, the ratios of investment and savings are high. The personal savings ratio has been characterized by a long-run upward trend. The loans energetically advanced by city banks are instrumental in sustaining the rapid pace of private business investment. In the long run, the so-called overloans, which depend basically on loans from the Bank of Japan, have made it possible to make available greater amounts of capital expenditure for

Table 3. The Top 15 Producers of Passenger Cars in 1970 and 1980

Unit: 100 cars

		1970				1980	
		Volume of production				Volume of production	
Rank	Producer	Total	Passenger cars	Rank	Producer	Total	Passenger cars
1	GM	3,594	2,979	1	GM	4,753	4,065
2	Ford	2,658	2,017	2	Toyota	3,293	2,303
3	VW	1,621	1,518	3	Nissan	2,644	1,941
4	Toyota	1,609	1,068	4	Ford	1,888	1,307
5	Fiat	1,523	1,419	5	Renault	1,713	1,492
6	Chrysler	1,452	1,273	6	Peugeot-Citroën	1,647	1,446
7	Nissan	1,374	899	7	VW	1,632	1,517
8	Renault	1,160	1,055	8	Fiat	1,350	1,185
9	BLMC	962	789	9	Toyo-kogyo	1,121	737
10	Opel	821	812	10	Mitsubishi	1,105	660
11	Br. Ford	589	448	11	Honda	957	846
12	Peugeot	577	525	12	Opel	793	787
13	Can. Ford	566	410	13	Can. Ford	764	512
14	Citroën	540	471	14	Chrysler	758	639
15	Mitsubishi	457	246	15	Bentz	627	439

1980/1970 production ratio

GM	1.32	Chrysler	0.52
Ford	0.71	Nissan	1.92
VW	1.01	Renault	1.48
Toyota	2.05	Opel	0.97
Fiat	0.89	Mitsubishi	2.42

Source: Toyota, *The Japanese Automobile Industry* (in Japanese), 1973 and 1981.

plant and equipment beyond the limit of business internal accumulation.

(3) For the sustenance of high economic growth, there is a need for basic resources and energy as well as for capital goods to be imported rapidly. In order to attain this level of imports, it is also an important precondition to boost exports at a rapid pace. In a country like Japan where the endowment of resources and energy is limited, it is absolutely essential that exports be stepped up to achieve fast growth.

(4) As for the question of what kinds of export industries should be promoted, it was recognized (1) that income elasticity should be relatively high by international standards (or that the comparative growth rate of demand for the industry has to be high) and (2) that the comparative growth rate of technology must be high. Quite simply, autos, electronics, other machinery, and steel products may satisfy the two criteria. As a result, the share of machinery and equipment in total exports soared from 13.7 % in 1955 to 62.8 % in 1980, the first time the share of machinery in total exports has ever exceeded 60 % in any country.

(5) In the first half of 1981, the exchange rate was in the range of ¥210 to ¥220 to US$1. Until the "Nixon shock" in 1971, however, the exchange rate had remained pegged at ¥360 to $1 for many years. Considering the purchasing parity or relative price movement between the U.S. and Japan, this suggests that the yen at ¥360 to $1 was considerably undervalued and seemed to be highly stimulative for exports.

(6) Thus export-led growth may have given rise to a marked tendency to boost exports. But at the same time, domestic investment was also conspicuously stimulated by such a tendency. An investment boom will eventually entail improvements in quality and reductions in cost, thereby strengthening the ability to compete in export markets. With this in mind, it might be argued that there has evolved a "virtuous circle"-type feedback between exports and domestic investment, making it possible to also achieve a high domestic economic growth rate.

(7) The Japanese economy embraces a domestic market which caters to a population of over 100 million. In the case of a mass production industry, such as the automotive industry, the existence of an expansible domestic market is extremely advantageous. In this situation, unit costs may be reduced by increased domestic demand and mass production before the export-production ratio in growing industries begins to be boosted. In some important industries, as a matter of fact, domestic demand has been raised prior to, or at the same time as, a boost in exports. It is noteworthy that the process of shifting from a boost in

domestic demand to an increase in exports has actually occurred in the mass production industries.

(8) In the steel, petrochemical, automobile, and other industries, technology was first introduced from foreign countries, and what could be described as "borrowed technology" constituted the mainstream at one time. However, the importance of new technical innovations and know-how gradually increased. As a result, systems technology, the coalescing of techniques of a variety of production lines or industries, was widely adopted. For example, "mechatronix," a combination of mechanics and electronics, has evolved at a rapid pace. Now most machines are equipped with electronic parts, e.g. timepieces, machine tools, automobiles, organs, etc.

(9) The rapid growth of the Japanese economy in the postwar years has served to create an intensively competitive environment, and the industrial and export structures have therefore undergone varied and remarkable transformations. Kindleberger has emphasized that a high "capacity to transform" is one factor favoring rapid economic growth. In Japan, the share of textile products in total exports, for example, dropped from 37.3 % in 1955 to 4.9 % in 1980, while that of machinery and equipment rose sharply from 13.7 % to 62.7 %. This phenomenon is a fine example of a structural transformation.

(10) Nevertheless, it is well known that the government, through consensus with the business community, strongly supported the automobile, machinery, and other promising industries in their infancies. However, the protection of "infant industries" was eventually discontinued due to a liberalization of trade and capital and a lowering of customs duties (admitting that the adoption of these measures was stimulated by external pressures which came, for instance, in the form of the Kennedy Round). Furthermore, the conglutination between the government and the business community has not endured. It is important to point out, therefore, that apparently contradictory elements—a kind of government intervention in the form of support for "infant industries" and a sense of competition in the nation which stimulated growth—have coexisted behind the high economic growth of the postwar years.

As a matter of fact, pairs of contradictory elements have evolved: domestic investment vs. exports, big businesses (capital-intensive) vs. small businesses (labor-intensive). Restrictions on external competition and encouragement of internal competition look contradictory at first sight, but the development of the Japanese economy in the postwar years is evidence that the coexistence of such seemingly contradictory elements may have been important in the sustenance of industrial growth.

The 1970s—Before and After the Oil Crisis

In the period 1965-70, the Japanese economy found itself in a medium-term investment boom. This is shown in the ratio of private business fixed investment to GNP, which stood at 15.8 % in 1965 but rose to 21.1 % in 1970. At that time, I was of the view that the disproportionate growth of private fixed investment against GNP would be forced to undergo a downward adjustment within several years after 1971.

However, the money supply (M_2) continued to grow at high rates, 24.3 % in 1971, 24.7 % in 1972, and 23-25 % by around September 1973, when the announcement of oil price increases threw all economic indicators out of balance. It had been affected by the government's tenacity in holding to a fixed exchange rate and the adoption of "adjustment inflation" on the occasion of the international monetary adjustment in 1971, and by the Tanaka Cabinet's aggressive fiscal measures and plans for remodeling the Japanese archipelago. As a result, fixed investment in the private sector more or less revived, and it looked as though the tendency for a downward adjustment after 1971 was to fall away. This is shown by the rise of the fixed investment ratio to 18.5 %, albeit temporarily, in 1973. However, this ratio remained at 18.5 % in 1973 and never went beyond the 21.1 % mark set in 1970. Though slightly more than 18 % was chalked up in 1973-74, the rate continued to float downward, dropping to 14.0 % in 1978.

Two international economic events were of great significance to the 1970s. One was the "Nixon shock" of August 1971, and the other was the oil crisis towards the end of 1973. The "Nixon shock" signified an end to the fixed exchange rate system (¥360 to US$1) which had been in force for many years. It made inevitable revaluation of the yen to avoid increasing foreign currency reserves and the risk of "adjustment inflation" arising out of adherence to the ¥360 exchange rate. In actuality, the revaluation of the yen was realized by switching to an administered floating system. Resistance to this shift, and an orientation to adjustment inflation using aggressive fiscal measures for restructuring the Japanese archipelago, can be said to have persisted until 1973.

Nevertheless, the outbreak of the first oil crisis towards the end of 1973 was another important event. It exemplified an end to the high growth of the postwar world economy. Japan's real GNP growth dropped from 10 % on average before the oil crisis to almost 5 % after it, and this trend persisted for more than five years. In no way, therefore, can it be described as a short-term phenomenon.

Up to now, it has been possible to get over a balance of payments hurdle in a short span of time. It has also been possible to support the full employment ceiling with boosts in productivity. Nevertheless, the problems of resources and energy could not be easily cleared away. President Jimmy Carter once said that Japan, West Germany, and the United States should collaborate with one another and serve as a "locomotive" for the world in tiding over the global recession that followed the first oil crisis. Japan and West Germany did not follow the same line of thinking, but it stimulated inflationary expectations in America. And when people become deeply apprehensive about inflation, they begin behaving speculatively; the efficiency of the market mechanism is weakened and the effectiveness of aggregate demand administration is lost. The current realities of the American economy, which is plagued by high interest rates, have arisen from the fact that American inflationary psychology became all the more intense due to the Carter administration's policies.

From a historical perspective, there have been cases in which an aggressive policy stimulated inflationary speculation when the world economy came close to the threshold of the limit of resources and energy. President Carter's miscalculation lay in his advocacy of the "locomotive" theory, in utter disregard of the fact that the world economy had come very close to that limit.

Insofar as Japan was concerned, its growth rate was halved. By 1976, the United States's mining and manufacturing production index had returned to the previous peak of 1973, whereas it was as late as 1977 that the Japanese index went beyond the previous peak. Japan might perhaps be described as having stayed under the water line for four years.

As a result, the inventory-production ratio of finished commodities in mining and manufacturing industries in 1975 exceeded the 1970 level by 40%, and this excess persisted for five subsequent years. Therefore, while exports in 1976 were up 20% from the previous year (on a yen basis), inventory investment did not immediately recover due to the pressure of an excessive stockpile. Government investment also registered a rise of 19.6 % in 1977, but the pattern that was prevalent in the years of high growth, in which government investment stimulated inventory investment by the private sector and produced a subsequent boom in fixed investment, did not recur. In 1978, however, for the first time the growth rate of private business fixed investment exceeded 10 % because of replacement demand for machinery and equipment.

However, after the oil crisis consumption and housing construction in general grew at a slow pace. In 1974–78, real consumer expenditure and real housing construction by the private sector rose by 3.4 % and 1.2 % a year, respectively. But why is it that the rises of real GNP and mining and manufacturing production remained still higher than those of other advanced nations? One reason is ascribable to the fact that private fixed investment demand remained steady in the latter years of the 1970s. Another factor could be the increased exports from important industries. But one tendency which deserves special attention is that the exchange rate in 1975–78 became increasingly favorable to the yen (which increased in value from ¥305 to ¥195) whereas it had remained somewhat unfavorable (¥280 to ¥305) in the period 1973–75.

As a result, imported raw materials and energy became less expensive in 1975–78. In terms of supply-side observation, businesses enterprises seem to have profited by a lowering of unit costs. On the other hand, drops in the prices of imported raw materials in a situation where the exchange rate is in favor of the yen serve to reduce the propensity to import, which has an important impact on the value of the multiplier. When the marginal propensity to import goes down, the multiplier will go up. Therefore, the repercussions of rises in exports and fiscal outlays may have been reinforced in terms of effective demand analysis. Presumably, such a reason lay behind the fact that the exchange rate in favor of the yen had unexpectedly had no noticeable deflationary effects even on the export industries.

In order to avoid apprehension about inflation in an economic environment where resource and energy limits are foreseen, there is a need to keep the pressure of excess effective demand at a low level. In a low-pressure economy, not only will speculative moves towards inflation be restrained, thus sustaining the effectiveness of the market mechanism and of fiscal and monetary measures, but also the sustenance of low pressure will make it possible to retain the fundamentals of the economy in a favorable condition and to offset the balance of payments deficits which may arise in nations other than the oil-producing countries, by inducing the oil money from outside. Thus, the Japanese economy has been able to maintain its balance of payments in a healthy condition, since Japanese industry has been highly competitive in world markets and the pressure of effective demand has stayed low.

Issues for the 1980s

The Japanese economy has grown to the point where it is now described as "Asia's new giant." Moreover, with the advent of the 1980s, the international aspects of the Japanese economy have become of utmost importance. Let us analyze this problem in terms of Japan's economic relations with the Third World and the advanced nations.

In its relations with the Third World, Japan inevitably finds it necessary to give thought to the methodological theory and rationale of economic cooperation. In broad terms, the flow of funds for use in economic cooperation may be classified into three categories:

(1) Economic aid to satisfy basic human needs, in keeping with "humanitarian" thinking or justified by the need to preserve "international social security."

(2) Economic cooperation which may entail "international industrial adjustment." Overseas investment by the private sector will give rise to an industrial adjustment in both the giving and receiving nations. With the inroads of businesses and the export of technology, it may be expected that the export share of aid-receiving countries in world exports will increase in general.

(3) Economic cooperation for food, resource, energy, and (not for Japan, but for some nations) military security.

If by definition economic aid of the basic humanitarian type may be extended only to the poorest nations, then agricultural and food development, the development of small businesses, manpower formation, and investment in the infrastructure must all be taken into serious account even for Third-World nations which have developed to any noticeable degree. It might be useful to interpret humanitarian aid in a broader sense, to cover agricultural development and infrastructure investment for the less developed countries where conditions are relatively better than those in the LLDCs on the threshold of starvation.

Be that as it may, in the Asia-Pacific region, the Republic of Korea, Taiwan, Hong Kong, and Singapore have developed as newly industrializing countries (NICs). On the other hand, among the ASEAN member nations, the share of manufactures in total exports in 1979 exceeded 30 % for Thailand and reached 20–25 % for Malaysia and the Philippines, and the effects of industrialization were reflected in the structure of exports. In 1976–78 exports of textile goods rose by 72 % for Thailand, by 2.4 times for Malaysia, and by 1.9 times for the Philippines. In 1978–79, Indonesia registered a sharp rise of 5.6 times. Such developments might be taken as signs that these nations are advancing already from the status of LDCs to that of semi-NICs.

If so, there may be a sharp drop in the humanitarian economic aid required in the Asia-Pacific region by the end of this century. In this situation, the economic aid that Japan should offer as an economic superpower may be localized in Africa as far south as the Sahara Desert and in South Asia. In the Asia-Pacific region, an international division of labor will take place even within manufacturing industries; there will be signs of a shift from a "vertical" division of labor between agriculture and industry to a "horizontal" division of labor within industry itself. As a result, a heterogeneous pattern relative to the prewar international division of labor may make its appearance. The important role to be played by Japan in the Asia-Pacific region will be to develop this region into a group of the world's "middle-class" nations and work out a "horizontal" division of labor.

The third category of economic cooperation is tied in with international resource and energy security. It will be a vitally important task for the entire Asia-Pacific region to look for energy sources other than oil and become less reliant on the Middle East as well as to look for cooperation with Australia, Indonesia, Mexico, and other nations which possess energy resources. Economic collaboration of the kind which is designed to work for an inter-regional balance and development of energy is needed. So far, the energy problem has been mostly thought of as one facing the entire world and, at the same time, each nation, but it has to be approached also as a problem of regional security for the Asia-Pacific region. As a matter of course, Japan will have to play the role of a coordinator in this new approach.

It is perhaps inevitable for cultural frictions to make their appearance in the process of economic cooperation with the Third World. In the interest of minimizing such friction, it is necessary that economic cooperation be offered in a mutual spirit of understanding of heterogeneous cultures and values.

In its relations with the advanced nations, what problems will Japan encounter in the 1980s and 1990s? First of all, in promoting international collaboration for adjustment of total demand, as elucidated earlier, the mistakes involved in the "locomotive" theory of President Carter should never be repeated, especially when it is taken into account that we are on the threshold of the limit of resources. The advanced nations which find themselves in a maelstrom of inflation should collaborate with one another in an attempt to extricate themselves from it. If this task can be managed, crazy fluctuations between the exchange rates of the advanced nations may be avoided to some extent.

Having gone through a period of rapid economic growth, the NICs find themselves in a stalemate position at present. The cumulative deficits of the non-oil-producing developing nations are on the rise, making their financing increasingly risky. Thus it inevitably has become more difficult to work for a smooth recycling of oil money than it was after the first oil crisis. The task is to encourage the recycling of oil money through the channels of the World Bank, International Monetary Fund, Asian Development Bank, and other official international monetary agencies. To encourage this flow, what role should Japan play? Unless the attempt at recycling turns out to be a success, the maldistribution of oil money might propel the poorest nations to zero or negative growth and also intensify global inflation.

Another important problem with which Japan is directly confronted is "trade frictions" which arise in its economic relations with other advanced nations. Historically, world trade was once dominated by the United Kingdom and the United States. Therefore, the world economy might be portrayed in terms of the ups and downs of the major economic powers. However, the situation today is different from that which prevailed in the years of Pax Britannica and Pax Americana. The world economy has now fragmented. The United States has been closely pursued by Japan, with the NICs in hot pursuit. In turn, the LDCs are now on the track of the NICs. These developments might warrant the observation that we are now living in the era of the "great scramble."

Here Japan, sticking to a textbook approach, could censure the Western nations who abandon free trade and go in for protectionism. However, free trade theory of the kind which can be deduced from a textbook is worked out without giving any consideration to a situation where the sales of automobiles and television sets to specific nations could double in a matter of one year—a situation akin to a trade downpour. In such a situation, the importing nations could not adjust their industries quickly enough. Here lies the reason why GATT has worked out safeguards. But it is no glorification of totally administered trade to use export regulations as a kind of cushion. After all, they are only the other side of the coin of import controls. This means that there is a need to stick to the principles of free trade as a whole while adopting measures to even out exports of what could be described as the "torrential rain" type.

The important thing is that any attempt to boost exports at an excessively rapid pace gives rise to a clamor for protectionism which is not compatible with free trade. It might be argued, therefore, that Japan is now placed in a position to accomplish the difficult task of exporting in an orderly manner now that the world economy has entered a new phase.

Third, Japan must continue collaborating with other advanced nations in dealing with the question of energy. The output of oil by the OPEC nations, which stood at 30,759 thousand barrels a day in 1979, dropped by 22% to 24,122 thousand barrels a day on average in the period of January 1981 to June 1981. (This average fell to 20,678 thousand barrels a day in August 1981 as a result of a 33 % reduction.) The war between Iran and Iraq might be responsible in one way or another for the drop, but the principal reason is the efforts that had been made to cut down on oil consumption in conjunction with sharp rises in the global prices of oil. Partly because of this phenomenon, however, there are signs that oil prices may top out in spite of the long-term global oil strategy which is being enforced by the OPEC nations. These developments evidently demonstrate that international collaboration in the saving of oil is the most effective means to check the world inflation fanned by the oil crises. In Japan, there have been obvious efforts to escape from the excessive consumption of oil. In the Southeast Asian nations, conservation efforts are also being steadily made as well as attempts to replace oil with synthetic fuels. It is necessary that Japan continue its collaboration in these endeavors.

10

JAPAN'S HIGH SAVINGS RATIO: ITS DETERMINANTS AND BEHAVIOR PATTERNS
With Some Comparisons with Asian NICs

In the consumption function controversy, which mainly developed in the United States, it has been generally thought that the savings ratio tends to have a comparatively stable value in the long run, although for a comparatively short period of time only it can fluctuate subject to changes in current income as compared with previous peak income, in transitory income proportion, in growth rate, in the difference between expected and actual incomes, etc. Naturally, separate analyses have to be prepared regarding long-term change in the savings ratio and its inter-country differences. There are hypotheses which stress the importance of the percentage of aged population (life cycle hypothesis), the liquid assets-income ratio, interest rates, income distribution, etc. But most studies seem generally to have made an analysis on the assumption of long-term stability of the savings ratio.

When in 1958 I wrote a book in Japanese, *Consumption Function* (1), in which I made fairly detailed studies on the consumption-saving function in Japan, I had (in retrospect) been misled by this American belief in the long-term stability of the savings ratio. Having watched the savings ratio of workers rise from 2.0 % in 1951 to 9.2 % in 1955, and then to 12.6 % in 1958, I believed that the ratio would stabilize, sooner or later, at around 15 %. I criticized the projection of further increases in the savings ratio in Japan's economic plan at that time, based on the American experience and the consumption function theory. Ironically enough, however, the savings ratio of workers continued to rise, eventually reaching 24.0 % in 1974. To be quite honest, the fact that the savings ratio moved upward for such a long period of time betrayed our expectations.

This paper was submitted to the Conference on The Determinants of National Saving and Wealth, University of Bergamo, Bergamo, Italy, June 9–14, 1980, and is scheduled to be included in the forthcoming proceedings volume. It was published as Occasional Paper A–4 by the Asian Club, Tokyo, January 1981.

Since a secular increase in the investment-GNP ratio is observed in the recent Asian NICs (such as Korea, Taiwan, Singapore, etc.), it can be assumed that the savings ratio has also been moving upward for a long period of time. The experiences of Japan and other Asian industrializing nations thus have followed a considerably different pattern from that of the advanced nations.

Secular Upward Drift of Savings Ratios

Table 1 and Figure 1 show the long-term trend of savings ratios as compared to disposable incomes based on national income data, the Annual

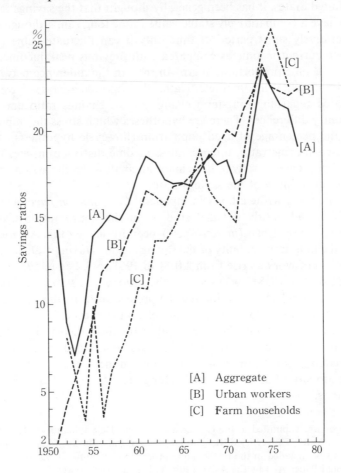

Figure 1. Personal savings ratios (aggregate, workers', and farm households').

Table 1. Savings Ratios in Macro and Micro Data

Fiscal year	Total gross savings / GNP		Personal savings / Personal disposable income		Workers' savings ratio** (cities with pop. of more than 50,000)		Farm household savings ratio (all Japan)
1951	30.4%		14.2%		2.0%		−%
1952	25.6		9.0		4.4		8.1
1953	25.4		7.0		5.8		6.0
1954	22.0		9.4		7.4		3.4
1955	26.2		13.9		9.2		10.1
1956	29.0		14.4		11.8		3.6
1957	31.1		15.1		12.5		6.2
1958	28.7		14.8		12.6		7.3
1959	32.1		15.7		13.9		8.6
1960	35.2		17.4		14.5		10.8
1961	38.6		18.5		16.5		10.8
1962	34.9		18.1		16.2	All Japan	13.6
1963	35.1		17.2		15.7	16.2	13.6
1964	35.1	New SNA	16.8	New SNA	16.8	17.1	14.4
1965	33.9	33.0	16.8	17.0	16.8	17.2	15.6
1966	35.6	34.7	17.1	16.7	17.4	17.6	17.1
1967	37.4	36.3	18.7	17.7	17.9	18.4	18.9
1968	38.9	38.1	19.2	18.6	18.4	18.6	16.6
1969	39.5	39.1	19.1	18.0	19.1	19.2	15.8
1970	40.3	39.7	20.8	18.2	20.0	20.3	15.4
1971	39.1	38.0	19.8	16.8	19.6	20.1	14.7
1972	39.2	37.8	21.0	17.2	21.3	21.6	18.8
1973	39.5	37.9	24.2	20.1	22.2	22.5	22.0
1974	35.6	35.1	25.5	23.6	23.8	24.2	24.6
1975	32.0	32.5	24.8	22.5	22.6	23.0	25.8
1976	32.2	32.1	23.8	21.5	22.2	22.6	24.1
1977		32.4		21.2	22.0	22.8	22.5
1978		32.4		19.1	22.4	23.0	22.6

Sources: National income data: Economic Planning Agency, *Annual Report on National Income Statistics*, and *Annual Report on National Accounts*, for new SNA data; workers' family budget data: Statistics Bureau of the Prime Minister's Office, *Annual Report on Family Income and Expenditure Survey;* farm household data: Ministry of Agriculture and Forestry, *Farm Household Economy Survey.*

  * Savings ratios in these surveys are computed with disposable income as the denominator.

 ** The years in this table are in terms of fiscal year (April–March), except workers' savings ratio which is in terms of calendar year.

Report on Family Income and Expenditure, and the Farm Household Economic Survey. The following points may be observed:

(1) The savings ratios in the national income data show that, except for 1951 when the Korean War broke out, the personal savings ratio showed a rising trend. Since cyclical fluctuations in corporate savings and government savings are greater, and the relative proportions of these are larger in the early stages, the long-term upward trend of the total gross savings ratio is not so conspicuous. However, it is quite clear that even these total gross savings ratios were 28.6 %, 36.5%, and 38.4 % for the periods 1951–60, 1961–70, and 1970–73, respectively.

(2) The workers' savings ratio showed a more drastic upward trend, posting a huge increase from 2.0 % in 1951 to 23.8 % in 1974.

(3) The savings ratio of farm households did not show an upward trend before 1961: its fluctuation corresponded to the fluctuation of the annual real income growth rate of farm households. However, the savings ratio began to show a sharp increase from 10.8 % in 1961 to 25.8 % in 1975, which almost corresponds to that of the urban workers' savings ratio.

(4) These uptrends became stalemated after the oil crisis. However, it is amazing to note that the savings ratio still maintained a high plateau of more than 20 % while the GNP growth rate slowed down by half, from 10 % to 5 %.

(5) During the 10-year period from 1952 to 1961, the average personal savings ratio in national income data was 13.4 % while the savings ratios in worker and farm households' family budget surveys showed 10.9 % and 7.5 %, respectively. Thus the personal savings ratios on a macro basis are distinctly higher than those in the micro survey data. The comparatively higher savings ratios of nonfarm individual proprietors and nonprofit organizations may account for this gap, simply because in the personal sector not only workers and farmers but also nonfarm individual proprietors and nonprofit organizations are included. In the past, Kawaguchi and I tried to calculate the higher savings ratios of individual proprietors and nonprofit organizations based on the gap between the macro and micro data (1, 2). However, according to the Family Savings Survey conducted by the Statistics Bureau of the Prime Minister's Office, the savings ratio (against pre-tax income) in 1963 was 14.4 % for workers' households against 21.6 %, 49.0%, and 28.2 % for merchants and craftsmen, unincorporated businesses, and executives of corporate enterprises, respectively. During the 10-year period from 1952 to 1961, there was such a gap between the macro and micro data, but this was reduced considerably in the latter

half of the 1960s and 1970s as the savings ratio increased in general.

The average personal savings ratio during the 10-year period from 1968 to 1977 was 19.8 % in the national income data (new SNA), while the Workers' Household Survey (cities with more than 50,000 populations) and the Farm Household Survey reported 21.1 % and 20.0 %, respectively, with the difference being reducible to a margin of error.

(6) Another interesting point worthy of note is that even at a time when Japan had almost finished catching up with the level of advanced nations, its savings ratio remained extremely high. The personal savings ratio during the 10-year period from 1968 to 1977 stood at approximately 20 % on average, which is quite high by international standards. During the same period, the average personal savings ratio was 6.9 % in the U.S.A., 7.9 % in the U.K., 14.9 % in West Germany, and 14.0 % in France.

Therefore, there are two questions which need to be asked. One is why the savings ratio remained unusually high even after Japan had caught up with the advanced nations. The other is why this continual up-trend in the savings ratio was maintained throughout the whole postwar period.

Factors Behind the High Personal Savings Ratio

Authors writing in Japanese who have tried to explore the reasons for Japan's higher savings ratio include the present author (3), Hisao Kanamori (4), and Ryutaro Komiya (5), while works by Komiya (6), Saburo Okita (7), Tuvia Blumenthal (8), Toshiyuki Mizoguchi (9), and the present author (10) are all available in English. One of the common features in these analyses is that none of them attempts to explain the high savings ratio on the basis of any single hypothesis. On the other hand, no econometric attempts seem to have been made so far to find the secrets behind Japan's high savings ratio by employing an international cross-section analysis. I do not intend to tackle this difficult task, but would rather like to review some major factors here.

I should like to avoid repeating the detailed discussion of various factors which I have undertaken elsewhere. I will, however, briefly list some of the factors which have been reviewed in the past.

(1) *The high savings ratio of individual proprietors.* If the personal savings ratio as defined by national income data is to be discussed, the personal savings ratio of Japan may be higher than those of the advanced nations, as there are proportionately more individual proprietors in Japan. Thus, if a comparison is made between two countries

with the same growth rate, the personal savings ratio would be higher in the country where the relative proportion of individual proprietors (with their higher savings ratio) is high.

(2) *Insufficiency of social security benefits.* For example, social security benefits as a ratio of national income in 1960 were 19.5 % in Germany, 18.1 % in France, 13.5 % in Sweden, and 12.9 % in the U.K., while they were only 5.1 % in Japan. The extent of family security, so to speak, is greater than social security in Japan, and this makes it necessary to have more savings for one's twilight years.

(3) *Bonus effect.* The percentage of non-regular income (e.g. bonus payments) in the total amount of income in Japan is comparatively high. According to a study by Ryohei Magota (11), temporary income including bonuses during the period 1955–57 accounted for 16.4 % of income in Japan compared with 8.3 % in Italy, 1.4 % in the U.S.A., and 0.8 % in the U.K. Although bonuses are not necessarily windfalls, and many people expect them as part of their regular income, it is easily possible to compute a statistically higher savings ratio from bonus income than that from other regular income.

(4) *Assets effect.* The postwar hyper-inflation tremendously reduced the real value of liquid asset holdings. If we use total cash and deposits outstanding as a proxy for liquid assets and divide this by national income, converting it as relative to 1935, then we find that this index was reduced to 46.5 % in 1952. It was not restored to the 1935 level until 1965 (10). Therefore, during this long period, there seems to have remained a positive gap between the desired and actual levels for liquid assets, and this may be one of the secrets of the high savings ratio. Even after the liquid asset·national income ratio surpassed its prewar level, the desired level with respect to these assets as "stock" may well have continued to surpass the actual level, due to the aspiration of people for a higher standard of living which was accelerated during the period of high-pitched economic growth.

This does not apply to liquid assets alone. The Japanese people after the war had inadequate housing facilities, and there was always a tendency to move to costlier houses. Those who lived in apartments were trying to move to their own homes, and those who lived in their own houses sought more spacious and better homes. This may have contributed to the high savings ratio.

(5) *Age composition.* Colin Clark once mentioned that, in the life cycle process, one saves while young so that one can live on those savings when one gets older. Under this assumption, a country with a higher composition of younger people would have higher savings ratio, while a country with more aged people would have smaller savings ratio.

Kanamori raised questions about this hypothesis (4). Based on family income and expenditure data (1959) for Japan, he measured savings on a vertical axis and disposable income on a horizontal axis. Then he discovered that the curve derived from the data classified by age of household head showed a steeper slope than the curve obtained from the data merely classified by income class, and that, at the 30-year age point, the former cut through the line of the latter from below. This led to an observation that once a household head reaches 30 years of age, the household's savings ratios exceed those of the uniform average income bracket, and thus Kanamori insisted that in postwar Japan the savings ratio becomes rather higher as the age of household head increases.

Criticizing this view, Mizoguchi maintained that older Japanese household heads often tend to have a young couple living with them, and that the fact that they receive lump-sum retirement payments would also contribute to the high savings ratio (9).

Making an international comparison, Komiya pointed out that when a wage curve is drawn as a function of the years of service in each country, the slope of the curve for Japan is much steeper than that for other countries, and he maintained that this is an important background of the higher savings ratio of families with older household heads.

Regarding these points, I would like to point out that wage statistics classified by age show a tendency toward a higher bonus ratio against regularly paid wages as the worker's age increases. The ratio of the bonuses and other special allowances paid during 1976 as against the monthly regular wages in June 1977 for male workers in manufacturing was as follows: 1.28 for 17 years of age and under, 2.87 for 20–24 years of age, 3.41 for 30–34 years of age, 3.60 for 40–44 years of age, and 3.75 for 50–54 years of age, with a slight decline after the retirement age. It seems that the bonus hypothesis can also be applied to this aspect.

The international cross-section model based on Modigliani's life cycle hypothesis (12) seems to have succeeded in detecting the effect by which a decrease in the ratio of population aged 65 and over would cause an increase in the savings ratio. This may occur in the cross-section analysis. However, the ratio of population aged 65 years and over in Japan, as a time series, increased as follows: 4.9 % in 1950, 5.3 % in 1955, 5.7 % in 1960, 6.3 % in 1965, 7.1 % in 1970, and 7.9 % in 1975; at the same time sharp increases in the savings ratio continued to occur. This does suggest that as far as the time series are concerned, some other factors may have been more important than the life cycle factor.

Another point which bothers me in the traditional life cycle model is the assumption that savings accumulated in youth are to be spent after retirement and no bequest is left. However, in a strongly community-oriented society like Japan, this community consciousness exists not only among members of a society at a given point in time but also between generations. In other words, because of this stronger community orientation, it appears to me that the propensity to bequeath is greater than in other countries.

Incidentally, in international comparisons, a fairly close association is found between the ratio of population aged 65 and over and the already mentioned social security benefit·GDP ratio, and therefore the social security factor and the age composition factor may constitute two sides of the same coin (13).

(6) *Lack of consumer credit.* Although the use of installment credit for purchases of durable consumer goods such as automobiles has recently become more popular, this system has not been in general use for a long time in Japan. Therefore, compared with America and European nations where installment buying is more common, saving for major purchases is part of the higher savings ratio in Japan.

(7) *Growth rate.* This factor generally appears in combination with the bonus effect mentioned above. It is sometimes assumed that "relative income"—actual income as compared with a "standard" income—is a determinant of the size of the savings ratio. If previous peak income is used as the standard income, this assumption becomes the well-known relative income hypothesis advocated by Modigliani (14) and Duesenberry (15). In this hypothesis, when each year's income is compared with the previous year's, the difference (i.e., the growth rate) is considered as determining the savings ratio.

However, when a kind of permanent income is used as standard income, no matter whether it is presented in a Milton Friedman-style formula (16) or in a Modigliani-Brumberg-style life cycle hypothesis (17), the ratio of transitory income to actual income should play an important role in determining the savings ratio. In an economy experiencing high growth, the ratio of transitory income naturally becomes larger, increasing the savings ratio in turn. In postwar Japan, the growth rate was high; therefore, the savings ratio was also high.

(8) *National character and demonstration effect.* Buddhism and Confucianism are the two traditional philosophies which built up the values of the Japanese people. In Confucianism, labor and thriftiness were considered virtues, and this way of thinking may well be stronger in rural areas, depending upon the extent of urbanization and industrialization. I once made a graph plotting workers' savings ratios and disposable incomes in 46 prefectures, as based on the National Survey

of Family Income and Expenditure conducted in 1959 (10). (This is a special comprehensive survey covering 31,000 households.) I discovered that for the industrialized prefecture group and the less industrialized prefecture group, parallel curves sloping downward to the right could be drawn, which indicate that for both groups, the higher the income, the lower the savings ratios. As this cross-section relationship was obtained from a survey conducted during the period September-November, it does not include any bonus effect. However, since this result is exactly opposite to the Keynes Law that the higher the income, the higher is the savings ratio, I have called my empirical relationship the "Contra-Keynes Law."

The slope of these curves shows that as urbanization proceeds and income rises, the propensity to consume will become higher, aided by the demonstration effect, thus making the savings ratio lower. Therefore, when in future urbanization is further developed in local areas, the savings ratio may well become lower as a long-term trend.

In order to make my analysis simpler, I broke the 46-prefecture survey data down into the following nine regions. Hokkaido in the north, Tohoku, Kanto (including Tokyo, Yokohama), Hokuriku (facing the Japan Sea), Tokai (including Nagoya), Kinki (including Osaka, Kobe, Kyoto), Chugoku (including Hiroshima, Yamaguchi), Shikoku, and Kyushu (including Fukuoka and Nagasaki). I repeated the analysis, using the same survey data, for 1974; the 1974 survey covered 46,000 households. For 1974 the addition of Okinawa brought my number of regions to 10. The regional-data curves for 1959 and 1974 are shown in Figure 2.

The 1959 chart in Figure 2 shows the same downward-sloping curves I had obtained from the 46 prefectures in the same year. However, the 1974 chart is completely different from that of 1959. The first point to be noted is a considerable tendency toward income level equalization among regions during this 15-year period. As the 1974 chart shows, the average disposable (monthly) incomes of workers in the industrialized Kanto, Kinki, Chugoku, Tokai, and Hokuriku regions were all within the range of ¥163,000 to ¥168,000. If Kanto-area income represents 100 on a scale, income in the Hokuriku area was 85 in 1959; in 1974, Hokuriku income rose to 99 on the scale. In regions such as Tohoku, Hokkaido, Kyushu, Shikoku, and Okinawa, where industrialization was delayed, we can still see an inter-regional relationship in which the lower the income level, the higher the savings ratio. However, in the five industrialized regions it is worth noting that, even after almost similar income levels had been achieved, there still remains a large gap in the savings ratios, ranging from 14.0 % (Hokuriku) to 8.9 % (Kinki), even

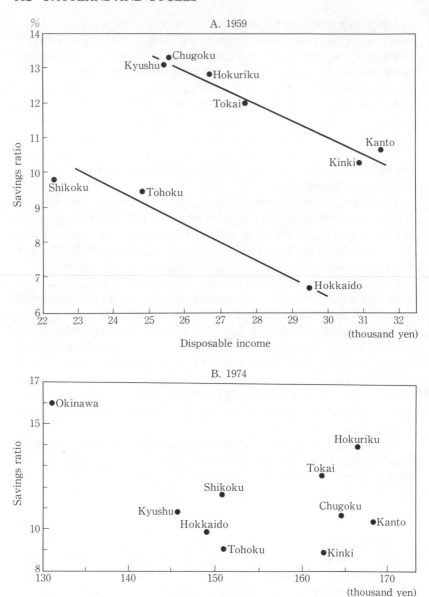

Figure 2. Inter-regional differences in savings ratios associated with per-household income in workers' households.

Source: Statistics Bureau of the Prime Minister's Office, *National Survey of Family Income and Expenditure*, 1959 and 1974. This survey is comprehensive and covers the September-November period, so the savings ratios reported are independent of the bonus effect.

ignoring the bonus effect. The fact that there still remains a difference in the savings ratio in the Hokuriku and Tokai regions, even after some degree of equalization of income levels with those of the Kanto and Kinki regions, may indicate that traditional values are still dominant in these relatively backward areas.

Naturally, as it can be speculated that the income growth rates of the Tokai, Hokuriku, and Chugoku regions must have been higher than those of the Kanto and Kinki regions during the period of income equalization, it may be hypothesized that as a result comparatively high rates of savings had emerged in Tokai, Hokuriku, and Chugoku in 1974. If this is the case, it may be assumed that once income levels are equalized among regions and income growth rates are also equalized, the regional differences in savings ratios should decrease in size sooner or later.

One problem remaining is whether or not the ratio of population aged 65 and over has anything to do with these savings ratio differences. As against the savings ratio by region shown in Table 2 displayed according to size, however, the ratio of population aged 65 and over does not show any significant negative association.

Table 2. Regional Differences in Workers' Savings Ratios and the Ratios of Population Aged 65 and Over, 1974

Region	Savings ratio, 1974 (A)	Ratio of population aged 65 and over, 1975 (B)
Okinawa	16.0%	7.0%
Hokuriku	14.0	9.5
Tokai	12.0	8.0
Shikoku	11.7	10.8
Kyushu	10.8	9.7
Chugoku	10.7	10.1
Kanto	10.4	6.3
Hokkaido	9.8	6.9
Tohoku	9.1	8.6
Kinki	8.9	7.5

Sources: (A) Statistics Bureau of the Prime Minister's Office, *National Survey of Family Income and Expenditure*, 1974.
(B) Ibid., *Japan Statistical Yearbook*, 1978.

Reasons for the Rise in the Savings Ratio

We learned from Table 1 that the savings ratio was not only high but also showed a sharp upward trend. Why did this tremendous increase continue? The following reasons can be mentioned.

(1) At least during the postwar rehabilitation period when the real

per capita income was smaller than its prewar or wartime peak level Y/Y_0, the ratio of postwar current real income (Y) to peak real income (Y_0), was smaller than 1. Up to the point when Y/Y_0 becomes equivalent to 1, Y and Y/Y_0 will increase almost proportionately. According to the relative income hypothesis as based on the habit-persistance theory, the savings ratio is considered to depend upon Y/Y_0. In other words, as long as Y/Y_0 continues to increase, the savings ratio is also expected to increase. However Y/Y_0 is supposed to halt its upward movement as soon as Y reaches the peak income. Therefore, although a separate explanation may be needed concerning the long-continued upward movement of the savings ratio even after $Y = Y_0$ has been achieved, this may be at least one of the explanations for the increases in the savings ratio.

(2) Second, as long as the desired level of liquid and physical assets is higher than their actual level, additions to these assets will continue. The postwar liquid assets ratio, obtained by dividing cash · deposits outstanding by national income, was lower than the prewar level until 1965, as already mentioned, when it finally reached the 1935 level. Per-capita real income level had reached the prewar peak level around 1955. Therefore, even after the prewar peak in the flow of real income had been attained, unsatisfied desire in stock terms still continued, and this desire for liquid assets could be construed as one of the reasons for an increase in the savings ratio. In addition, unfulfilled desire in terms of physical assets not only was created by destruction caused by the war, but also became greater because of the fundamental change in the quality of life which was brought about by the postwar consumption revolution centering on durable goods.

(3) The third point to be noted is that the sharp increase in the savings ratio of workers' households shows a close association with the phenomenal increase in the proportion of temporary income (such as bonuses) in the worker's total before-tax income. If the temporary income which mainly consists of bonuses is completely considered a windfall, there is a validity in the application of the so-called permanent income hypothesis, associating increases in transitory income with increases in the savings ratio. In other words, the long-term increase in the temporary income ratio may be considered one of the important factors behind the long-term increase in the savings ratio. However, as mentioned already, many workers seem to have come to expect to receive at least similar amounts as bonuses in June and December every year. Certainly the bonus ratio is subject to business fluctuations. An increase in the bonus ratio when business is booming is naturally high, while under

sluggish business conditions bonuses will be stagnant. However, no bonus has ever been drastically reduced in the past. Therefore, we would like to attach more importance to people's custom of applying a higher rate of savings to bonuses, treating a bonus as expected "extra" income rather than a windfall. Those who receive a lump sum retirement payment will show a higher propensity to save, despite the fact that the amount and the time of its payment are anticipated. The same thing can be said of bonuses. However, there is no denying that some portion of bonuses will have certain windfall characteristics.

The five-year average savings ratio of workers (in cities with populations exceeding 50,000) for 1956–60 was 13.1 %. An observation of the five years for 1966–70 reveals that this figure increased to 18.6 %. However, the growth rate of real disposable income per household changed from 6.2 % in 1956–60 to 6.0 % in 1966–70. In other words, although the savings ratio increased by 5.5 points just when there was almost no change in workers' real income growth rate, an interesting point is that as a matter of fact an almost identical increase of 5.4 points (from 14.0 % to 19.4 %) in the temporary income ratio was observed during this period. In this case, the growth rate and the temporary income ratio actually showed different movement patterns!

(4) The next point is that not only did the savings ratio of workers' households show a long-term upward trend; the savings ratio of farm households also showed a parallel increase in the 1960s. Growth of the real income of farm households did not manifest any acceleration, particularly during this period. The average annual growth rates of farm households' real incomes were 8.2 % for 1961–65, 7.6 % for 1966–70, and 7.3 % for 1971–75, respectively. Nevertheless, the savings ratio for farm households jumped from 10.8 % in 1961 to 25.8 % in 1975. What are the reasons behind this?

Figure 3 shows the temporary income ratio (temporary incomes and bonuses of a household head ÷ before-tax income) for workers, together with the non-agricultural income ratio (non-agricultural income ÷ total farm income) for farm households. On the one hand, the temporary income ratio of workers' households, which was 8.4 % in 1951, sharply increased to 23.0 % in 1974 before it settled down to 19.0 % in 1978 after the oil crisis. On the other hand, the non-agricultural income ratio of farm households, which was 30.7 % in 1951, continued to increase, reaching 70.6 % in 1977. This is due to the fact that the number of households which were engaged in farming as a major occupation (full-time) in the total number of farm households dropped sharply from 50.0 % to 12.9 % in the 1950–78 period, while

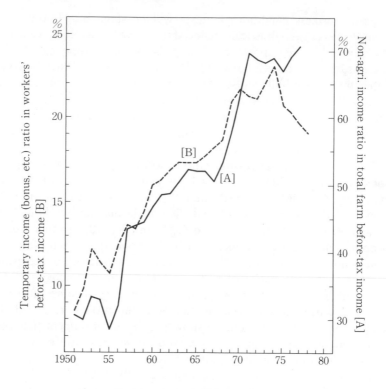

Figure 3. Temporary income of workers' households and non-agricultural income of farm households.

the ratio of side-work (or part-time) farming households continued to increase from 50.0 % in 1950 to 65.7 % in 1960, 84.4 % in 1970, and 87.1 % in 1978.

Therefore, the proportion of farm household members working in nearby factories or similar businesses increased tremendously. Since an increasingly larger portion of the wages they received took the form of bonuses, it is quite evident that the influence of bonuses on the savings ratio is seen not only in workers' households but also in farm households. Therefore the increase in the savings ratio of farm households is attributable to two factors. One is the increase in the non-agricultural income ratio, and the other is the increase of the bonus ratio in workers' income. Thus, the increase in the non-agricultural income ratio played an important role in transmitting the long-term increase in the savings ratio of workers' households to farm household's saving and consumption patterns.

Savings Ratios by Income Class Associated with Absolute and Relative Incomes*

Next, I would like to utilize the statistics on "monthly income and expenditure on an annual average basis per worker's household classified by annual income class" from the Annual Report on Family Income and Expenditure. Then I would like to compute savings ratios for each annual income class in order to compare them with the average disposable income by income classes in Figure 4. In order to facilitate comparison of disposable incomes over time for 1963, 1965, 1975, 1976, and 1978, average disposable income by annual income class in each year is divided by the consumer price index so that all the figures can be converted into real terms of 1970 prices.

A graph similar to Figure 4 appears in one of my books (19); it confirms that, at least for the three years 1954, 1958, and 1959, the savings ratio curves were almost overlapping one another. If such is the case, as far as these three years are concerned, the savings ratio was a function of real disposable income even when classified on an income class basis. In other words, to the real income will correspond an identical savings ratio, and if real income continues to increase year by year, the savings ratio will be obliged to increase as an aggregate as well.

A similar result is observed in Figure 4 here as far as the two years of 1963 and 1965 are concerned. However, the real disposable incomes which I employed for the 1961 book were in terms of 1951 prices, while those shown in Figure 4 are in terms of 1970 prices. But when the savings ratio curve is redrawn on a common real income basis, taking into account the increase in consumer prices for 1951-70, I found that the curves for each year (1954, 1959, 1965, etc.) were almost overlapping. Consequently, the behavior of the workers' savings ratio supports the absolute income hypothesis over this long period.

However, after the oil crisis, the savings ratio curve, which had so far always shown an upward slope to the right, reversed to a downward slope to the right. The curve for 1975 was characterized by an increase in the savings ratio for the lower income class and a decrease in that for the highest income class. As shown in Figure 4, this reverse trend eased in 1976 and 1978, and the curve began to be normalized. How can this reversed phenomenon be explained? In the oil crisis period, when abnormal price rises resulted from people's reluctance to sell and aggressive buying, the lower income classes might, because of anxiety over coming inflation and resultant concern over their real in-

*The analysis developed in this section was first presented in (18).

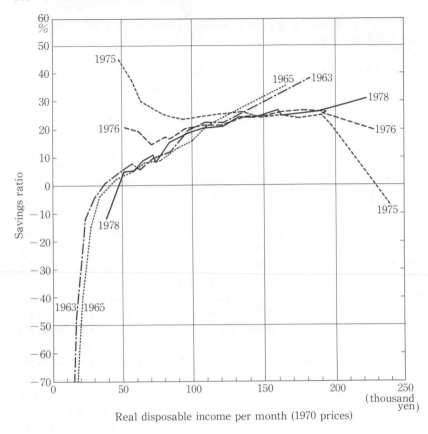

Figure 4. Savings ratios by income class for workers' households.

come, have tried to reduce their consumption; this, in turn, would have brought about an increase in their savings ratios. In appearance, inflation seems to drive consumers away from saving because of the losses in the real value of their deposits outstanding. However, as the lower income classes generally have fewer liquid assets, this will result in more serious anxieties about the future which, in turn, might have worked to reduce consumption due to the lowering of "expected real incomes."

On the other hand, as higher income classes have more liquid assets, they are not motivated to increase their savings ratio in circumstances where they are afraid of future inflation. Speculative expenditure for commodities whose prices are expected to rise sharply may in fact be accelerated, if only temporarily. What is more, if their confidence in ever-rising bonuses as an important base of the savings ratio is shaken, decreases in the savings ratio of the higher income classes seem inevitable.

The above analysis of savings ratio by income class is based on absolute real disposable income. However, it is necessary to review the "relative income hypothesis" in which relative income, as compared with the average income in the society as a whole, is considered a determinant of the savings ratio. According to this hypothesis, in a country such as the United States where the savings ratio has shown a long-term stability, a household which is close to the average income level of the society may still maintain a constant savings ratio even if its absolute real income increases year after year. This hypothesis also assumes that in a higher income class a higher savings ratio will prevail than in a medium income class, while in a lower income class the savings ratio will be lower. In short, according to this reasoning, the savings ratio is determined as a function not of the absolute income, but of the household's relative position on the social income scale.

The Report on Family Income and Expenditure of Japan presents statistics in which the surveyed households are divided into five groups by relative income level from the lower to the higher income classes, and the income, expenditure, and savings in these "five percentile income classes" are indicated. Therefore, data can be derived on the movement of the savings ratio of each income class divided into quintiles.

If the savings ratio curves in Figure 5 were to overlap, this type of relative income hypothesis would be proved in Japan. However, as the savings ratios curve for the four years 1963, 1965, 1970, and 1973 continued to show an uninterrupted upward shift, the relative income hypothesis does not fit for this period of time. As far as the period prior to the oil crisis is concerned, Figure 4, which measures real disposable income by the horizontal axis, seems more appropriate as it shows the savings ratio curves overlapping one another.

However, as is also seen in Figure 4, the two years 1974 and 1975 in Figure 5 also show a remarkable rise in the savings ratio of lower income classes and a sharp decrease in the savings ratio of the highest income class. In 1976 and 1978 a normalization of the slope is observed, but this is attributable to the fact that some abnormal moves are hidden, since the samples included at both ends of the upper and lower income classes are greater in Figure 5 than in Figure 4.

In any case, I would like to add that the relative income hypothesis tested above is in substantive content not a case of habit persistence but rather of socio-psychological factors at work, i.e., the so-called demonstration effect.

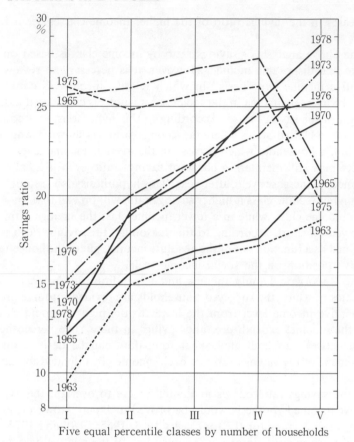

Figure 5. Savings ratios by five equal percentile classes for workers' households.

The above analysis probes the savings behavior of workers only in the micro data classified by income class. How would it look if an attempt were made to observe the savings or savings ratio on a time series basis alone?

Deflating the data for workers' households by the consumer price index (1975 = 100) and denoting real disposable income by Y_{dr} and real savings by S_r, we get the following result for 1963–78:

$$S = -20936.8 + 0.3251\ Y_{dr} \qquad\qquad \bar{R}^2 = 0.9876$$
$$ (1670.7) \quad\ (0.0094) \qquad\qquad\ \ \text{D.W.} = 1.3399$$

$$S_r/Y_{dr} = 7.49 + 0.0000719\ Y_{dr} \qquad\qquad \bar{R}^2 = 0.9575$$
$$\phantom{S_r/Y_{dr} = } (0.69)\ \ (0.0000039) \qquad\qquad\quad \text{D.W.} = 1.8766.$$

When the income class data are aggregated in a time series, the influence of the oil crisis is actually not so evident except in 1974. The savings ratio in 1974 was 24.3%, only a little higher than the theoretical value of 22.6% obtained by the second formula above, even in that post-oil-crisis year. Thus, even on a macro basis, the absolute income hypothesis appears to be applicable, simply because, as Figure 4 shows, the savings ratio curves were basically almost overlapping each year of the absolute real disposable income.

However, the validity of this seemingly old-fashioned absolute income hypothesis may be only superficial. A deeper study reveals that behind it lies a long-term rise in the bonus ratio. Furthermore, behind the long-term rise in the bonus ratio there may lie the persistence of a high postwar growth rate and an increase in the domestic investment ratio.

In terms of habit persistence the relative income hypothesis does not seem to fit either. Comparing the 1967-69 and 1972-73 periods, the annual growth rates of workers' real income per household were about 6.0% in both periods, while the former period showed a savings ratio of 18.7% and the latter period a higher savings ratio of 22.8%. The annual growth rate for the five-year period 1969-73, prior to the oil crisis, was 6.0% on the average; this growth rate was reduced to 1.0% during 1974-78, after the crisis. Nevertheless, the average savings ratios during these two periods were 20.7% and 23.1% respectively. Thus the savings ratio, despite a slowdown in the growth rate, did not manifest any corresponding major decline, proving once again that a simple growth rate hypothesis is not applicable here either.

Total Saving and Its Composition

So far, we have mainly analyzed personal savings as based on micro family income and expenditure survey data. However, in addition to personal savings, corporate and government savings also contribute to total domestic savings. It is necessary to study how the compostion of savings as a whole has moved based on national income statistics.

In terms of the net savings composition, which does not include fixed capital consumption allowances, the personal sector, as shown in Table 3, had a share of approximately 50% throughout the 1950s and 1960s. In the meantime, the relative composition of corporate savings was more than 20% during the 1956-60 and 1966-70 periods, which included big investment booms; during the 1951-55 and 1961-65 periods, which included the medium-term investment stagnation of the Juglar cycle in private fixed investment, the relative composition dropped to ap-

Table 3. Composition of Domestic Savings

A. Net Savings Composition

Fiscal year	Percentages		
	Personal savings	Corporate savings	Government savings
1951–55	46.2	16.9	36.9
1956–60	50.3	20.5	29.2
1961–65	50.7	17.5	31.8
1966–70	49.8	23.1	27.1
New SNA			
1970	45.5	28.2	26.3
1971	49.4	22.1	28.5
1972	49.6	22.1	28.3
1973	55.9	12.0	32.1
1974	82.5	−12.2	29.7
1975	90.7	− 2.9	12.2
1976	91.2	−3.5	12.3
1977	88.5	− 0.9	12.4
1978	79.8	3.4	16.8

B. Gross Savings Composition*

Fiscal year	Percentages		
	Personal savings	Corporate savings	Government savings
1951–55	44.3	27.0	28.7
1956–60	44.1	33.0	22.9
1961–65	41.3	35.1	23.6
1966–70	41.3	38.0	20.7
New SNA			
1970	38.2	43.3	18.5
1971	40.0	41.1	18.9
1972	40.4	40.7	18.9
1973	44.9	33.5	21.6
1974	60.9	19.8	19.3
1975	66.4	24.9	8.7
1976	66.6	24.8	8.6
1977	65.6	25.7	8.7
1978	60.6	28.1	11.3

Sources: Economic Planning Agency, *Annual Report on National Income Statistics* and *Annual Report on National Accounts* for new SNA data.
* For old data, accidental damage to fixed capital is allotted to corporate, personal, and government sectors in the same proportion as those of depreciation charges.

proximately 17%. At the same time, the share of government savings increased to 36.9% and 31.8%, respectively, during these two medium-term stagnant periods, and declined in the 1956-60 and 1966-70 periods when the investment booms took place.

The point to be particularly noted is that the share of the personal sector sharply increased, to 86.5%, for the 1974-78 post-oil-crisis period, while the corporate sector share dropped drastically, to minus 3.2%. As it entered the phase of large-scale issue of government bonds, the surplus in the government current accounts dropped to an average of 16.6% relative to total net savings.

I once made an estimate, based on national income statistics and the money flow table, that during the 12-year period from 1956 to 1967, 67% of personal net savings was transferred as financial surplus to other sectors, particularly to the corporate sector (10). In Japan, the indirect channeling of personal sector surplus to various enterprises through loans from monetary institutions has been much more prevalent than direct financing through the capital market. During the high-growth period, enterprises made investments in plant and equipment which accounted for two to three times their gross internal accumulation, including depreciation allowances. And most of the financial resources for these investments came indirectly from the personal sector. Compared with European and American enterprises, which have high internal financing ratios, Japanese enterprises depend to a greater extent upon external funds. (The ratio of corporate net savings to total domestic net savings during the period 1966-70 was 38.1% in the U.S., while it stood at 23.1% in Japan.) In 1974 the stagnation of private investment began; at the same time, surplus funds in the personal sector began to be directed toward the government sector, which had entered an era of large-scale issue of government bonds, rather than to the corporate sector.

A slightly different picture can be derived from studying savings in terms of their gross composition, estimated by allocating fixed capital consumption allowances into three sectors. Needless to say, compared with the net composition, the shares of personal and government sectors declined to a certain extent, while the corporate sector gained in its share. According to this analysis, the relative composition of the corporate sector during the period 1970–73 before the oil crisis was 39.7% on average in gross terms, while during the 1974–78 period, after the oil crisis, the figure eased to 24.7%, as compared with minus 3.2% in net terms.

Having achieved 36.8% for 1966-70, 35.7% for 1971-75, and 31.0% for 1976-78, the share of the domestic gross investment in GNP of Japan has been extremely high by international standards, and it continued to be high even after the oil crisis. This ratio is almost equivalent to those which Asian NICs finally reached after their rapid expansion in the latter half of the 1970s. What is important is that a majority of Japan's high domestic investment was financed from domestic sources without dependence upon an inflow of foreign capital. Since the latter half of the 1960s, Japan has been a capital-exporting country, and, as shown in Table 4, during the period 1976-78 an amount equal to approximately 4% of domestic gross investment was lent overseas.

Table 4. Domestic and Foreign Investment

(million yen)

Fiscal year averages	Domestic gross investment a	Surplus of the nation on foreign a/c b	Net lending to the rest of the world c	$\dfrac{b}{a}$	$\dfrac{c}{a}$
1951–55	1,811.3	24.4	39.8	1.3%	2.2%
1955–60	3,978.8	11.1	−10.3	0.3	−0.2
1961–65	9,222.5	−52.7	−73.9	−5.7	−8.0
New SNA
1966–70	21,764.0	613.4	471.5	2.8	2.2
1971–75	41,822.9	548.8	449.1	1.3	1.1
1976–78	59,146.8	2,568.9	2,435.6	4.3	4.1

Corporate savings are a reservation from corporate profits. Figure 6 compares the savings ratio from after-tax corporate disposable income with the annual real GNP growth rate. In the calculation of the corporate savings ratio, both the net ratio (A) which excludes capital consumption allowances and the gross ratios (B) including these allowances are shown in Figure 6.

Particularly during the period 1965-78, large differences are observed in figures, depending upon whether old or new SNA data are used, but there is no fundamental difference in the pattern of fluctuations. In any case, a broad trend can be derived from Figure 6: corporate savings change in close association with the annual fluctuations of GNP growth rate for the most part. The use of Modigliani's "cyclical income index," $Y - Y_0/Y$ (Y_0 is the highest peak real income in the past), instead of the growth rate, $Y - Y_{-1}/Y_{-1}$, might have been more appropriate (14), but about the same result is expected as there has been no negative growth of real GNP in Japan except in 1974, the year of the oil crisis.

Brief Comparisons with Asian NICs

Is a similar upward trend in the personal savings ratio observed in Asian NICs? Table 5, first of all, confirms that the total domestic investment

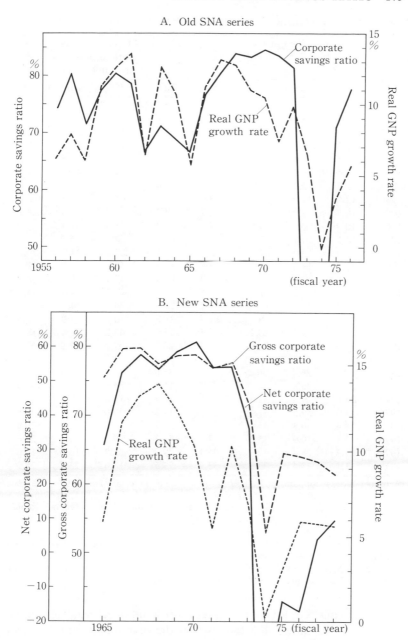

Figure 6. Corporate savings ratio and real GNP growth rate.
Sources: Economic Planning Agency, *Annual Report on National Income Statistics* (A); *Annual Report on National Accounts* (B).

Table 5. Investment, Exports, and Deficits in Foreign Accounts in Ratio Terms

	Domestic gross investment/GNP			Exports/GNP		Deficit in foreign a/c as a ratio of domestic gross investment**		
	Korea	Taiwan	S'pore*	Korea	Taiwan	Korea	Taiwan	S'pore
1951	%	14.5%	%	%	10.2 %	%	31.2%	%
1952		15.4			8.1		40.0	
1953	16.0	14.1		2.1	8.7	40.3	36.9	
1954	11.7	16.1		1.0	6.5	46.2	52.2	
1955	11.8	13.4		1.6	8.3	58.7	32.5	
1956	9.4	16.2		1.4	9.1	114.6	42.8	
1957	15.3	15.9		1.5	9.6	63.7	33.2	
1958	12.9	17.8		2.0	11.7	61.8	44.2	
1959	10.7	19.0		2.7	12.5	63.3	45.8	
1960	10.9	20.3	9.5	3.3	11.3	78.4	37.3	
1961	13.1	20.0	12.8	5.3	12.9	64.9	35.7	
1962	13.0	19.0	14.3	5.2	13.1	83.5	34.7	70.7***
1963	18.5	17.8	16.0	4.8	17.8	58.1	4.0	87.7
1964	14.6	19.4	20.0	6.0	18.9	47.9	−1.2	58.8
1965	15.1	23.2	21.1	8.5	18.6	42.2	15.4	54.9
1966	21.7	22.6	19.7	10.3	20.8	39.0	4.6	37.6
1967	22.1	24.7	19.7	11.4	21.8	40.1	8.9	38.0
1968	26.8	25.3	23.1	13.1	23.9	43.2	12.4	18.3
1969	28.8	24.6	26.4	13.1	26.3	37.9	3.5	31.2
1970	26.9	25.7	32.5	14.2	29.7	34.8	0.9	50.2
1971	22.7	26.4	36.2	15.7	35.0	42.8	−9.3	53.7
1972	21.7	25.8	37.4	20.2	41.8	24.8	−24.4	38.9
1973	25.6	29.3	34.3	30.1	46.8	14.8	−18.1	20.9
1974	31.0	39.5	37.4	28.2	43.7	40.0	19.9	46.6
1975	29.4	30.8	35.1	28.1	39.5	35.5	12.7	26.6
1976	25.5	30.9	35.3	32.8	47.8	9.5	−6.3	29.6
1977	27.3	28.4	32.9	35.1	49.7	2.2	−16.4	19.6
1978	31.1	28.4	33.3	33.7	53.5	18.6	−23.8	25.9

Sources: Korea, Singapore: IMF, *International Financial Statistics*; UN, *Yearbook of National Account Statistics*.
Taiwan: Directorate-General of Budget, *National Income of the Republic of China*, Dec, 1979.
*Ratios for GDP.
** Deficit in foreign a/c stands for the excess imports of goods and services plus net factor income paid to abroad.
*** Singapore figures for 1962–68 stand for the excess imports of goods and services, and do not include net factor income from abroad.

ratio as against GNP had a long-term up-trend in Korea, Taiwan, and Singapore and shows that the rises in the investment ratios are connected with the increase trend in the export-GNP ratios in Korea and Taiwan. In other words, a feedback relationship is observed between investment-led growth and export-led growth, which made possible an upward trend of a virtuous-circle type. Thus, in countries which are not endowed with basic resources the emergence of this kind of growth process seems unavoidable, if they really intend to pursue a high rate of growth.

Furthermore, Table 5 reveals that the continuance of the high growth process resulted in excess imports of goods and services plus net payment of factor incomes abroad for a considerable period of time. Comparing this amount with gross domestic investment, all three countries show quite high figures. Naturally, all deficits in foreign accounts will not be reflected in net borrowings from abroad, since a considerable portion of them are also embodied in payments to governments (e.g. military aid). However, unlike the case of Japan, it is worth noting that a sharp increase in domestic investment was related to the continuance of the foreign account deficit. Of these three countries, only Taiwan rapidly improved in its domestic investment dependence upon the foreign account deficit after it entered the 1960s.

Table 6 shows a shift in the savings composition of Korea and Taiwan in terms of net savings. In Taiwan, where price increases have been relatively moderate, the proportion of personal savings is relatively higher with only small fluctuations. Compared with the situation in Japan, the share of personal and government savings is equally high while that of corporate savings is relatively low.

As indicated in Table 7, the personal savings ratio in both Korea and Taiwan was below 10% up to 1962. However, was it merely coincidental that early in the 1960s in Taiwan, when the personal savings ratio exceeded 10%, the deficit in the foreign account relative to domestic investment (Table 5) became smaller at the same time? Compared with Taiwan, a lower personal savings ratio continued in Korea, reflecting the fact that the progress of inflation in Korea was very rapid.

Are the upward tendencies in the personal savings ratios in these two countries by any chance related to a rise in the aged population ratio, as predicted by the life cycle hypothesis? The ratio of population aged 65 and over in Taiwan (20), for example, was 2.5% in 1952, 3.0% in 1970, and 4.0% in 1978. While the total population registered an increase of 2.11 times during the period 1952-78, the population aged 65 and over marked a drastic increase of 3.36 times during the corresponding period. During this period, the savings ratio did increase, offsetting an expected decline in the savings ratio due to a rise in the aged population ratio. This is similar to the experience of Japan, and it shows that an observation based on time series data is considerably different from an analysis derived from an international cross-section.

During the same time period, an acceleration was observed in the real

Table 6. Net Savings Composition in Korea and Taiwan

	Percentages		
	Personal savings	Corporate savings	Government savings
Korea			
1953–55	84.6	2.7	12.7
1957–59*	44.8	11.7	43.5
1961–65	10.8	29.0	60.2
1966–70	12.1	16.3	53.6
1971–75	43.9	23.7	32.4
1976–78	48.9	18.3	32.8
Taiwan			
1951–55	26.8	23.8	49.4
1956–60	37.5	24.0	38.5
1961–65	61.1	22.2	16.2
1966–70	57.3	23.3	19.3
1971–75	56.7	16.3	27.0
1976–78	50.1	18.1	31.8

Sources: Korea: 1953–61: The Bank of Korea, *National Income in Korea*, 1978; 1962–78: Economic Planning Board, *Handbook of Korean Economy*, 1979.
Taiwan: Directorate-General of Budget, *National Income of the Republic of China,* Dec. 1979.
* In the case of Korea, the figures in 1956 and 1960 show extremely erratic changes, so in the computation of the average ratios the two years are omitted.

Table 7. Personal Savings Ratios in Korea and Taiwan

	Korea	Taiwan		Korea	Taiwan
1951	—%	5.5%	1965	0.2%	11.7%
1952	—	2.5	1966	5.0	15.2
1953	7.2	2.9	1967	1.7	15.2
1954	5.3	2.7	1968	3.8	13.0
1955	4.1	3.6	1969	9.1	11.1
1956	−2.4	3.9	1970	5.8	16.5
1957	5.5	4.1	1971	4.6	19.6
1958	4.3	5.5	1972	5.4	21.0
1959	2.0	4.6	1973	11.9	24.3
1960	−2.2	6.3	1974	9.1	20.1
1961	−0.2	7.6	1975	5.5	16.2
1962	−1.2	8.7	1976	9.3	18.5
1963	4.0	11.5	1977	12.6	20.8
1964	4.1	13.7	1978	15.0	21.3

Sources: Korea: 1951–60: The Bank of Korea, *National Income in Korea*, 1978; 1961–78: Econ. Plan. Board, *Handbook of Korean Economy*, 1979.
Taiwan: Directorate-General of Budget, *National Income of the Republic of China*, Dec. 1979.

GNP growth rate in the two countries (Table 8). Correspondingly, an upward tendency was also observed in the personal savings ratio. However, the personal savings ratio in Korea during the period 1961-70 did not show a parallel upward movement. In the case of Taiwan, while the growth rate marked a gain of only 2.1 points from 8.1% to 10.2% between 1954-60 and 1971-78, the personal savings ratio rose by as much as 16.2 points from 4.0% to 20.2%, and a far steeper increase in the personal savings ratio was realized even though the two indices were moving in the same direction. Thus, the case of Taiwan appears quite similar to that of Japan.

Table 8. GNP Growth Rate and Personal Savings Ratio in Korea and Taiwan.

	1954–60 annual average	1961–70 annual average	1971–78 annual average
Korea			
Real GNP growth rate	3.7%	8.4%	10.3%
Personal savings ratio	2.4%	2.8%	9.2%
Taiwan			
Real GNP growth rate	8.1%	9.7%	10.2%
Personal savings ratio	4.0%	12.4%	20.2%

Incidentally, according to the extensive household income and expenditure survey conducted in Taiwan in 1975 covering 3.01 million households, the total savings ratio was 14.7% of disposable income, which is not considerably different from the 16.2% (national account figures) shown in Table 7 (agricultural employers 62.7%, agricultural own-account workers 14.0%, non-agricultural employers 17.1%, non-agricultural own-account workers 14.1%, agricultural employees 9.3%, non-agricultural managers, administrators and professionals 21.6%, office staff, salesmen and service workers 15.1%, industrial workers 11.7%). The number of households is divided into ten equal sectors in order of size of distributed disposable income; the savings ratio by class, in order from lower to higher income classes, is as follows: I. 2.7%, II. 6.6%, III. 7.0%, IV. 8.3%, V. 8.8%, VI. 10.7%, VII. 12.6%, VIII. 14.3% IX. 16.6%, and X. 26.4%. The average of these ratios is 14.7%. In this regard, a similar relationship which is also seen in other countries is confirmed. In the 1978 survey (covering 3.37 million households) corresponding to that of 1975 described above, the savings ratio obtained from the total samples was 21.5%, almost identical with the 21.3% national account figure in Table 6 (21).

Secular rise in the savings ratio has thus existed also in the Asian NICs. If, however, the bonus system only exists in Japan, how are we to explain the secular tendency of rising savings ratios in these countries? One could introduce the Kaldorian macro income distribution theory to account for it, but a number of people dislike this theory.

However, it turns out that the bonus system has existed in Taiwan and Korea. In Korea, the government adopted it in 1974, and private corporations may have adopted it much earlier than that. Businessmen and economists told me that about 200–400% of monthly regular income has been paid as bonuses recently (14.2–33.3% as a ratio of annual total income) in Korea.

In Taiwan, a bonus survey has been conducted since the middle of 1972, and the bonus·total income ratio was 14.8%, 12.5%, 13.0%, 13.7%, 18.0%, 16.2%, and 14.8% for the years 1373 to 1979, according to Taiwan annual statistics on wages and employees (Executive Yuan, Republic of China).

Moreover, I was informed that the bonus system has so far existed also in Hong Kong, Singapore, Thailand, etc. If so, the parallel movement of the bonus ratio and the savings ratio which we found may not be a Japan-specific phenomenon. Therefore, there remains a strong case for exploring how the bonus ratio has changed in the East and Southeast Asian countries, as a background to the secular rise of the savings ratio.

References

1. Shinohara, Miyohei. *Shohi Kansu* [Consumption Function]. Tokyo: Keiso Shobo, 1958.
2. Kawaguchi, Hiroshi. *Chochiku no Kozo Bunseki* [Analysis of Savings Structures]. Tokyo: National Association of Local Banks, 1960.
3. Shinohara, Miyohei. "Why the Savings Ratio Is So High" (in Japanese). *Nihon Keizai Shimbun* [Japan Economic Journal], April 1961.
4. Kanamori, Hisao. "Why the Japanese Savings Ratio Is High" (in Japanese). *Keizai Geppo*, Economic Planning Agency of Japan, October 1961.
5. Komiya, Ryutaro. "The Supply of Personal Savings" (in Japanese). In *Sengo Nihon no Keizai Seicho* [Postwar Economic Growth in Japan], ed. by the author. Tokyo: Iwanami Shoten, 1963.
6. Komiya, Ryutaro. "The Supply of Personal Savings." In *Postwar Economic Growth in Japan*, ed. by the author. Berkeley: University of California Press, 1966. Translation of (5).
7. Okita, Saburo. "Savings and Economic Growth in Postwar Japan." *Asian Studies*, Vol. 6, No. 1, February 1964.
8. Blumenthal, Tuvia. *Saving in Postwar Japan*. Harvard East Asian Monograph, 1970.
9. Mizoguchi, Toshiyuki. *Personal Savings and Consumption in Postwar Japan*. Tokyo: Kinokuniya, 1970.

10. Shinohara, Miyohei. *Structural Changes in Japan's Economic Development*. Tokyo: Kinokuniya, 1970.
11. Magota, Ryohei. "International Comparison of Real Wages." In *Nihongata Chingin Kozo no Kenkyu* [Studies in the Japanese Pattern Wage Structure]. ed. M. Shinohara and N. Funabashi. Tokyo: Rodohogaku Kenkyusho, 1961.
12. Modigliani, Franco. "The Life Cycle Hypothesis of Saving and Intercountry Differences in Saving Ratio." In *Induction, Growth and Trade* (Essays in Honour of Sir Roy Harrod), ed. W. A. Eltis, M. F. Scott and J. N. Wolfe. Oxford: Oxford University Press, 1970.
13. Fukaya, Masahiro. "International Comparison of Public Sectors as a Life Security System" (in Japanese). In *Fukushi-zaigen to shite no Sozei to Shakai Hokenryo to no Sentaku* [Alternative between Tax and Social Insurance Premiums in Financing Welfare Expenditures]. Tokyo: Finance Institute, 1979.
14. Modigliani, Franco. "Fluctuations in the Saving/Income Ratio: A Problem in Economic Forecasting." *Studies in Income and Wealth*, Vol. II, 1948.
15. Duesenberry, James S. *Income, Saving and the Theory of Consumer Behavior*. Cambridge, Mass.: Harvard University Press, 1949.
16. Friedman, Milton W. *A Theory of the Consumption Function*. Princeton: Princeton University Press, 1957.
17. Modigliani, Franco, and Brumberg, "Utility Analysis and the Consumption Function: An Interpretation of Cross-section Data." In *Post-Keynesian Economics*, ed. K. Kurihara. New Brunswick, N. J.: Rutgers University Press, 1954.
18. Shinohara, Miyohei. "Saving-Consumption Behavior" (in Japanese). In *Gendai Keizaigaku Sainyumon* [Modern Economics Revisited] by the same author. Tokyo: Kunimoto Shobō, 1978.
19. Shinohara, Miyohei. *Seicho to Junkan* [Growth and Cycles in the Japanese Economy]. Tokyo: Sobun-sha, 1961, p. 209.
20. *Taiwan Statistical Data Book*. Council for Economic Planning and Development, Executive Yuan, Republic of China, 1979.
21. *Statistical Yearbook of the Republic of China*. Director General of Budget, Accounting and Statistics, Executive Yuan, Republic of China, 1977 and 1979.

11

POSTWAR CYCLES RE-EXAMINED: KONDRATIEFF, JUGLAR, AND KITCHIN CYCLES

The Limitations of Keynesian Economics

Half a century has already passed since the Great Depression of the 1930s, bringing us into the 1980s. The 1930s were characterized as a dismal ten years of deflationary stagnation. The decade following the oil crisis at the end of 1973, however, will be remembered as a period in which the world economy most decidedly suffered from stagflation (that is to say, inflationary stagnation).

Since the end of World War II, a great number of economists have been trained as Keynesians, or have switched to Keynesianism under the influence of the dominant economic thought of the period. Generally, they are apt to believe strongly in the possibility of aggregate demand management. Certainly full employment was achieved in the postwar period, and growth was accelerated. However, as Milton Friedman had predicted even prior to 1955, the postwar years were emancipated from the critical strains of a great depression but not from the peril of inflation. The fiscal and monetary authorities were not, as most Keynesians had anticipated, omnipotent. They tried to overcome recessions when they occurred, but were not always mindful of suppressing inflationary tendencies. Policy discussions conducted by Keynesian economists have also strongly reflected such a tendency.

Keynesianism was effective during times of depression; it had validity even when effective demand was expanding, as long as productive capacity was increasing as a result of fixed investment. The balance of payments ceiling was no more than a temporary barrier to growth. Even the full employment ceiling was no obstacle as long as technological progress continued. Supported by technical progress, productivity made great gains even in a very short period of time, and thus it was possible to increase the "full employment output" level year after year.

The ceiling on resources and energy, however, eventually began to be recognized as the most serious. Naturally, the technology for exploiting mineral and fuel resources has continued to improve, so this ceiling has not been immutable. In the past it has tended to rise with technological progress. Nevertheless, the secular growth rate of the world economy has thus far considerably outdistanced upward shifts in the limits of resources and energy.

Even before World War II such a tendency was clearly identifiable. Around the peaks of Kondratieff's long waves (the duration of which is about 40 to 50 years), the world economy always reached a basic resources barrier which drove prices upward in rapid leaps. After the war, however, world economic growth accelerated, a phenomenon to which the shift from the gold standard to a managed currency system seems to have greatly contributed. The major impact of the postwar emergence of a flood of new technologies and new commodities based on wartime discoveries and inventions should also be cited. The third of a century following World War II was a truly unprecedented age of phenomenal technological innovation. Advanced technology, particularly that of the United States, has been transferred to other countries at an unparalleled speed and scale via technology exports and the overseas activities of multinational corporations. As a result, world economic growth rapidly accelerated, and since it far surpassed progress in extending the limits of the world's resource supply, arrival at those limits was inevitable sooner or later.

We have several problems. First, Keynesian economists have believed that they should prescribe a therapy of "reflation" for depression and "disinflation" in inflationary situations. However, as J.M. Buchanan has suggested, Keynesianism has actually tended to lead to a political economy of inflation due to the political dynamics of democracy.

Second, once an economic policy is adopted which attempts to eliminate unemployment in the neighborhood of the resource and energy ceiling, the effectiveness of aggregate demand management must necessarily be impeded by the emergence of inflationary expectations and speculation. The vicious spiral of "inflationary expectations → high interest rates → tight money policy → stagnation" has thus characterized the early 1980s in the United States and Great Britain. The usual brand of Keynesianism is no longer applicable in these circumstances.

Third, Keynesian policies were indeed effective in achieving full employment and in accelerating growth. However, not only did they become ineffective in combating inflation; they have also been powerless to moderate the amplitude of business cycles. The so-called "political cycle" or "policy cycle" has preserved a relative regularity, partly due to the existence of "policy lag," in spite of strong government and central bank intervention.

Fourth, as the resource ceiling is approached, monetarism will revive.

Just as J.R. Hicks suggested in his famous paper, "Keynes and the Classics" (1937), monetary policy is much more effective than fiscal policy in combating inflation around full employment—or near the resource ceiling.

Fifth, Keynesian economics has a strong bias toward "short-run" cyclical analysis, mostly from the demand side. For the most part, it seems to be restricted to studies of the inventory cycle in particular. As a result, studies of the fixed investment (Juglar) cycle of 7 to 10 years, or of Kondratieff's long waves, have tended to be excluded from most Keynesian macroeconomics textbooks.

Kondratieff Long Waves

In searching for a framework within which to reconstruct the dramatic events of the half-century following the Great Depression, one is reminded of Joseph Schumpeter's old-fashioned procedure of simply combining a number of business cycles—the Kitchin, Juglar, and Kondratieff cycles. The simple Keynesian approach, without any consideration of the above cycle differences, cannot be effectively applied in an analysis of the dynamic processes at work in the world economy since the 1930s. Therefore, let us take up the three important cycles in turn, beginning with the 40- to 50-year Kondratieff cycle.

A brief sketch. There seem to be a number of reasons for analyzing the world economy in terms of the Kondratieff cycle. Since World War II a great number of countries have demonstrated rates of economic growth double or triple those experienced in the prewar period. (The United States and Australia are notable exceptions.) Now that these nations have encountered a ceiling on natural resources, however, they are shifting course toward a path of low and stable growth. One might view this phenomenon as a curtain-raiser for the globe's coming of age as "spaceship earth"—the first event of its kind since the beginning of capitalist development. However, it seems far more reasonable to understand it instead as a downswing of the Kondratieff long wave.

The reason for adopting the latter view is as follows: The currently perceived ceiling on resources would not have been reached without the achievement of long-term rapid growth following World War II. If the present situation is to be understood in the context of the dynamics of capitalism, we should not adopt an approach which treats the high rate of world economic development during the past 30 years in complete isolation from previous experience. The current situation is not our first encounter with such a resource ceiling. Even before the war, resource shortages were often experienced at the peaks of the

Kondratieff cycle. Buoyant increases in the prices of basic resources have always occurred at such times.

Kondratieff's original paper on the long wave was published in Russian in 1925, then translated into German in 1926. An abridged English translation became available in 1935. According to Kondratieff, three long waves could be identified from the late 18th century to World War I (Table 1). If the trough of the third long wave is assumed to be 1933, then the duration of the waves ranges from 60 years for the first wave to 37 for the third.

Table 1. Kondratieff's Long Waves

	Trough	Peak	Trough	Duration
First	1789	1814	1849	60 years
Second	1849	1873	1896	47 years
Third	1896	1920	(1933)	37 years

Kondratieff concluded that such a long-term cycle indeed exists, based on his observations of nine-year moving averages of time series of prices, wages, interest rates, coal and iron production volumes, etc. The cycle is more evident in the value series than in the time series based on volume. Later on, Kuznets identified a growth cycle of about twenty years from the volume series, and Arthur Lewis named it the "Kuznets cycle." However, the Kondratieff cycle is far longer.

Kondratieff pointed out four interrelated phenomena at work in this longest of cycles: (1) war and revolution, (2) technological innovation, (3) the volume of gold production, and (4) agriculture.

Those who stressed the first factor noted that the Napoleonic Wars (1792–1815) occurred at the peak of the first wave, the Franco-Russian War (1870–71) and the American Civil War (1861–65) took place at the peak of the second wave, and finally World War I came at the crest of the third wave. Before Kondratieff published his paper, the Dutch economist S. de Wolff had presented in 1923 an analysis based on the war hypothesis. In Japan, the economic impact of war was considered very important by economists like Kaname Akamatsu. Such economists emphasized the role of great wars and their mutual feedback relation with economic phenomena in bringing about the long wave.

Schumpeter emphasized the second factor, technological innovation, as the major one in the cycles. According to him, the first wave was generated by the British industrial revolution centering on the cotton spinning industry; the second was brought on by the rise of the iron, steel, and railroad transportation industries; and the third was a cycle initiated by the rise of such new industries as electrical equipment, chemicals, and automobiles.

The importance of the third of Kondratieff's factors, gold production, had already been pointed out by Gustav Cassel as early as 1918. However, it was Alvin H. Hansen who, in his book *Business Cycles and National Income* (1951), presented in a most clearcut and ingenious way the causational relationships among gold production, general productive activities, the price of gold, and the general price level.

The fourth factor is the role of agriculture. Since the price elasticies of supply and demand for primary products are generally low, the prices of such products rise sharply at the peak of a long wave. However, this is followed by equally drastic price declines, with higher rates of price increase and decrease for primary products as compared to changes in the general price level. This phenomenon in the downswing has a tendency to further accelerate the decline in the undeveloped nations' terms of trade relative to the developed nations. In this sense, primary industry on one hand becomes the limiting factor defining the "ceiling" for the rise of the long wave and hence for the long-term expansion of nonprimary industries; on the other hand, however, as a factor accelerating secular deflation, it plays a role in increasing the amplitude of the cycle. In the context of the present day, the term "primary products" should naturally include basic raw materials and energy resources.

Re-evaluation of the Kondratieff cycle in the contemporary context. The first difficulty in evaluating this cycle by extending it beyond World War I is the question of whether or not World War II constitutes another peak in the long wave. Although price controls and rationing were adopted during the war, prices were nevertheless relatively stable in such countries as the United States and Great Britain. Only after the war, in the defeated countries like Japan, did hyper-inflation occur due to drastic decreases in production. In terms of price indices, therefore, a peak in the long wave was not achieved.

Hence, in their book *The Kondratieff Wave* (1972), James B. Schulman and David Rosenau treat the World War II period as an exception. They identify instead the era of the Vietnam War as the long wave peak which follows that of World War I. Of course, this approach is likely to induce some debate.

Whatever one may conclude with regard to the periodization problem, the relevance of the four factors—war, technological innovation, gold production, and resource limitations—in the observation of the postwar long wave should be clarified at this point.

1. *War.* Certainly, the Vietnam War was "local" in the sense that it

was confined to a limited geographic region. But its economic impact must be viewed as worldwide since it in fact accelerated U.S. inflation, which led to increased gold outflows, which precipitated the "Nixon shock" and ultimately an excess liquidity inflation on a worldwide scale. There can be no doubt that, due to its repercussions in the world economy, the Vietnam War played a significant role in pushing the long wave up to the limits of resources availability.

2. *Technological innovation.* The post-World War II period has been characterized as an era of upsurge in technological and industrial innovation, in electronics, space, and marine industries, in extensive use of oil and nuclear energy, computerization, giant blast furnaces, the emergence of ethylene plants, etc. Moreover, technological innovation has been marked by the combined use of diverse techniques, or systems technology. The postwar international transfer of technology among advanced countries and between advanced and less developed countries through technology exports and the activities of multinational corporations was without historical precedent. Here is one major reason why growth rates have doubled or trebled after the war for almost every country in the world, with a few exceptions such as the United States.

3. *Gold production.* This hypothesis is naturally outdated due to the decline in the status of gold in the world. However, if the concept is expanded and generalized as a "money-supply" hypothesis, it takes on tremendous importance. In countries where inflation has intensified, we have always found that the inflation has been preceded by extremely rapid increases in the money supply. It will be imperative for anyone investigating the upswing of the postwar Kondratieff cycle to probe the international causational processes connected with money supply increases. The phenomenon may have something to do with the war factor, together with the international currency system.

4. *Resource limitations.* This is the most important factor at present. Even before World War II, resource scarcity produced sharp increases in the prices of primary products and basic resources. At present, however, the role of this factor has expanded to such an extent that it cannot even be compared to the prewar period. The point is that, in the Kondratieff long wave, secular expansion will proceed very dynamically through the combined impetus of technological innovation, war, and monetary expansion. Eventually, however, it will hit a resource ceiling. This is the essential characteristic of the long wave.

Peculiarities of the Kondratieff cycle. Very often analysts have stressed only one aspect of the long wave, ignoring others. For instance, the war factor only (Wolf) and technological innovation only

(Schumpeter) have sometimes been emphasized in a one-sided fashion. Such partial approaches are misleading.

The fact that the Kondratieff cycle is the longest one indicates that the factors operating in the cycle are historically not unitary but complex and manifold. Thus, we cannot ignore any of the three factors, war, technological innovation, and monetary expansion, which operate together as major mainsprings driving the cycle; nor can we afford to overlook the resource ceiling. These are the essential features of the Kondratieff cycle, and no one-sided theory which fails to take all of them into account will succeed in explaining the long-term dynamics of the capitalist process.

Consequently, our problem here is not to determine which of the factors we should select for exclusive analysis. Rather, some multidimensional and organic way of orienting the four factors vis-à-vis one another will be imperative in order to properly understand the contemporary state of the world economy.

In this sense, Schumpeter's methodology was unfortunately one-sided. His motivation for theorizing about the long wave solely in terms of technological innovation is understandable, for his theory of economic development was based on the role of entrepreneurs as the agents of innovation. However, to assume that it is possible to understand the long cycle in isolation from any and all wars is to engage in a very partial analysis.

The key characteristic of the long cycle in the contemporary era may be its international "synchronization," the fact that its peaks and troughs affect all countries at the same time. The significant fact about the Vietnam War thus is not simply that it occurred, but that a war which affected the entire world ended. In the same way, not just a few countries but the the great majority of the nations of the world ran into the resource ceiling almost simultaneously in the 1970s. In the short-term inventory cycle, peak and trough years vary from country to country. In the fixed investment, or Juglar, cycle, international synchronization occurs to a certain extent, but not always. However, in Kondratieff's long cycle, such synchronization will inevitably take place, for the fact that every country is bound to encounter the resource ceiling is uniquely characteristic of this cycle.

It is unfortunate from the standpoint of grasping the dynamics of capitalism that world economists have in recent decades been so inclined to devote attention to the Kuznets cycle, while almost completely forgetting the Kondratieff cycle. The approximately twenty-year Kuznets cycle was originally identified as the growth cycle, while the Kondratieff cycle is derived mainly by observing price index levels. Thus, it is possible for the Kondratieff cycle to be in a downswing when the Kuznets cycle is at a peak. International synchronization is not always an essential condition for the Kuznets cycle, but it is indispensable for the long Kondratieff cycle

The Kondratieff cycle can be formulated in the contemporary context as a kind of "limit cycle theory" (or "billiard table" theory). The dynamic upward pressure arising from the combination of technical innovation, war, and monetary expansion pushes the world economy to the limits of resource and energy supplies. In the prewar period, this phenomenon was followed by a secular deflation, but this has been transformed into a secular stagflation (simultaneous stagnation and inflation) due to the growth of Third World power, particularly that of the oil-producing countries.

By organizing the roles of technical innovation, wars, monetary expansion, and resource limitation in terms of a "limit cycle" theory, the long-term dynamics of capitalism can be understood in a more effective and integrated way. If a long wave is so understood, whether or not the cycles are regular is relatively unimportant because irregular influences may be introduced by the outbreak of wars. Therefore, whether the duration of the cycle is thirty or fifty years is of no consequence. More important is a grasp of the dynamic role played at the international level by each of these four factors in the long-term historical development of the Kondratieff cycle.

A comment on Rostow's analysis. In his two most recent books, *World Economy: History and Prospect* and *Getting There From Here* (both 1978), W.W. Rostow has presented an analysis of the peak and trough years of the long wave diametrically opposed to that outlined above. He does not appear to seriously depart from the traditional analyses of prewar peaks and troughs. However, Rostow's version of fluctuations in the fourth and fifth long waves completely differs from ours. In his analysis of the fourth long wave, he identifies 1933 as a trough in a cycle which peaked in 1951; then, according to him, the long wave went into a downswing, bottoming out in 1972, the next postwar trough. Moreover, he believes the 1970s and 1980s will be an upswing of the fifth long wave. This interpretation is entirely contrary to my own view that since the 1970s the Kondratieff cycle has been in a downswing.

This divergence of opinion arises from the fact that Rostow's analysis primarily depends upon relative price movements between primary products and manufactured goods (terms of trade) for the dating of peaks and troughs. According to Rostow, the terms of trade for primary products peaked in 1951 and continued to decline until 1972.

From the early 1970s, however, they began to rise, boosted by oil prices after the end of 1973. Since Rostow depends almost exclusively on the terms of trade, he mechanically assumes that the long wave will go into an upswing after 1972.

Rostow insists that in such a new phase, Keynesian policies based on demand-side analysis will not be valid, and that policies stressing the supply-side importance of new technology and increased investment are required. This is true enough, but at the same time it is also undeniable that since the 1970s technical progress has generally stagnated. Certainly, at present we appear to be in the gestation phase leading to the next period of flourishing technological innovation. Such a prosperous period, however, may be another one or two decades away.

Rostow interprets as a downswing of the Kondratieff cycle the postwar world economy's most prosperous period, 1951 to 1972, in which economic growth accelerated and flourished, and innumerable new technologies emerged as well. Such an unrealistic interpretation of the cycle suggests itself to him as a result of an analysis biased toward the mechanical observation of terms of trade movements, and ignoring other factors and the unique ways in which they combine with one another. Thus, we are obliged to reject the analysis that Rostow presents in these two new books.

Returning to our starting point, I would like to reconfirm the necessity of understanding the Kondratieff long cycle from a comprehensive perspective which deals simultaneously with all four of the key phenomena of technical progress, wars, monetary expansion, and resource limitations. A broad and integrated comprehension of this cycle can facilitate a realistic understanding of long-term capitalist development.

The Medium-Term Juglar Cycle

Private fixed investment and the Juglar cycle. Shorter than the Kuznets cycle, which lasts an average of 20 years, and longer than the inventory cycle of approximately 40 months, the Juglar cycle occupied the premier position in prewar business cycle analysis. After the war, however, the Juglar cycle was for some reason pushed aside in favor of the Kuznets and inventory cycles, and in many countries it was almost completely forgotten. Indeed, in the midst of accelerating growth, concern was on the whole focused on growth rather than cycles. Nevertheless, if, as we will see below, private fixed investment cycles clearly existed in the postwar period in both Japan and the United States, the persistent disregard of the Juglar cycle must necessarily be reevaluated.

Figure 1 charts fluctuations in the ratio of private fixed investment to GNP and the growth rate of gross fixed capital stock in postwar Japan. Ideally, one should make use of the new data revised in the summer of 1978 in accordance with the new System of National Accounts. These data, however, can only be obtained for the years from 1965 onward. Therefore, the movements shown in Figure 1 for the years 1946 to 1965 are based on the old time series and capital stock data. The ratio of private non-residential fixed investment to GNP repeats three almost ten-year cycles in the years 1946–55, 1955–65, and 1965–77. Changes in the growth rate of gross fixed capital stock also correspond to these movements. In this sense it is difficult to deny that in the postwar Japanese economy an unmistakable and well-contoured medium-term cycle occurred three times.

According to the new SNA data, however, this private fixed investment ratio fell further for two years after 1975, from 16.0 % in 1975 to 15. 0% in 1976 and 14.1 % in 1977. This may reflect the influence of the long cycle's downswing after the oil crisis, thus accelerating the decline in the private fixed investment ratio. It can be interpreted as having prolonged the downswing of the medium-term cycle. Nevertheless, from 1978 onward this ratio rises from 14.3 % to 15.3 % and then 15.7 %. Thus we see here the inflection point of the Juglar cycle.

When the private fixed investment ratio has been in the upswing phase of a cycle, the expansion in private fixed investment has been larger than that in GNP. That is, disproportionate growth in fixed investment has prevailed. However, when this ratio has been on the decline, reverse unbalanced growth in fixed investment, i.e., investment stagnation, has occurred. The fact that these two phenomena move in the same direction as, and parallel to, fluctuations in the fixed capital stock bears witness that the so-called capital stock adjustment takes about ten years.

Let I_t^e stand for the firm's net planned investment in plant and equipment, K_t for fixed capital stock at the beginning of the period, and K_t^e for planned fixed capital stock; we obtain the equation

$$I_t^e = K_t^e - K_t. \tag{1}$$

If Y_t^e is expected effective demand for the period, and C_{at} is the productive capacity corresponding to fixed capital stock at the beginning of the period, we have the following equations:

$$K_t^e = \alpha Y_t^e \tag{2}$$

$$K_t = \beta C_{at}. \tag{3}$$

Substituting equations (2) and (3) into equation (1), we obtain:

$$\frac{I_t^e}{Y_t^e} = (\alpha - \beta) + \beta \left(\frac{Y_t^e - C_{at}}{Y_t^e} \right). \tag{4}$$

From this equation it is possible to obtain cyclical changes in the planned fixed investment ratio I_t^e/Y_t^e corresponding to expansions and contractions in the gap between expected effective demand Y_t^e and production capacity C_{at}. Changes in $(Y_t^e - C_{at})/Y_t^e$ will arise from surpluses and shortages in the fixed capital stock. To the extent that they induce changes in I_t^e/Y_t^e, they give rise to the cyclical adjustment of fixed capital stock. In other words, this process of fixed capital stock adjustment may in fact be interpreted as manifesting itself in waves of about ten years' duration.

Issues connected with the Juglar cycle. Very sharply defined Juglar cycles for the United States can be seen in Figure 2. A medium-term cycle of nine to ten years from peak to peak and from trough to trough is clearly obtained.

The existence of the Juglar cycle, which Western economists had completely forgotten after the war, raises the following issues:

(1) From 1961 to 1966, long-term prosperity continued in the United States. Not once did the boom subside. As a result, some American economists began to speculate that the business cycle was obsolete. Prevailing opinion at the time pointed out that Keynesian fiscal-monetary policies during the period had been skillfully conducted, and policy devices such as "operation twist" and the interest equalization tax had been successfully introduced in rapid succession. It is important, however, to underscore the fact that this period happens to correspond to an upswing in the Juglar cycle. If Kennedy and Johnson had been in power in the downswing phase of the medium-term cycle which prevailed during the Nixon administration, their policy maneuvers probably would not have succeeded so well.

(2) A comparison of Figures 1 and 2 shows that the Juglar cycles in Japan and the United States are almost opposite in the occurrence of peaks and troughs—that is, we find a reversed cycle. For example, in 1961 the United States was at the trough in the Juglar cycle, but Japan was at the peak of the investment boom. This reverse calls to mind the reverse association which Brinley Thomas pointed out in construction and migration cycles between the United States and the United Kingdom, although of course the reason for the case of the Juglar cycle does not lie in migrations of people. It is not possible to delve further into this subject here; but the mere fact that these two Juglar cycles are almost reversed seems not to have even occurred to many people.

(3) For Japan, the amplitude between the peaks and the troughs for the fixed investment ratio is large at approximately five percentage

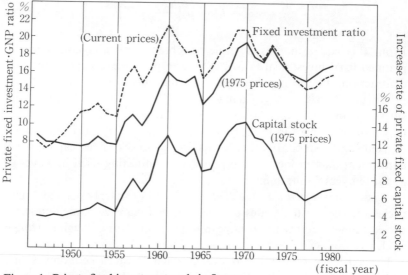

Figure 1. Private fixed investment cycle in Japan.
Source: Economic Planning Agency.

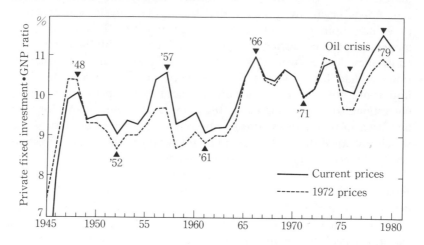

Figure 2. Private fixed investment cycle in the United States.
Source: Council of Economic Advisors, *Economic Report to the President*.

points. In the U.S. this value is a small 1.5 to 2 percentage points. In the U.K., it is difficult to even detect a medium-term cycle in this ratio. This suggests the possible hypothesis that the greater are the cyclical oscillations in this ratio, and the more active a role a nation's firms take in the dynamics of the investment process, the higher the trend growth rate will tend to be, beyond the Juglar cycle. At least, one cannot help but gain a strong impression to that effect from comparing these three countries.

Certainly, no major business downturn occurred in the postwar period before the oil crisis. This fact greatly curtailed interest in the medium-term cycles caused by the dynamics of fixed investment. In every nation in the postwar period entrepreneurs' desire for fixed investment increased, and at the same time, the uncertainties involved in investing were vastly reduced by the rapid growth. Nevertheless, it was a great mistake to have completely forgotten about the cyclical fluctuations in the investment ratio arising out of the dynamics of the investment process itself.

The Juglar fixed investment cycle has not only been recognized in Japan and the United States; it can also be statistically derived in the Asian NICs. In Figures 3 and 4, the Juglar cycles in Korea and Taiwan are derived from both national income statistics and trade statistics. The only difference in the statistics utilized here from the two countries is that in Taiwan the gross *private* fixed investment (excluding residential building) is used as a ratio to GNP, and in Korea gross *domestic* fixed investment is used.

In Korea, we see two peaks, exactly ten years apart, in fixed investment-GNP ratio, in 1969 and 1979. In terms of share of capital goods in total imports, an identical ten-year period occurs between peaks, this time in 1968 and 1978. Korea differs from Japan and the United States in that the fixed investment ratio did not undergo any major downward adjustment as a result of recession: we find only minor fluctuations in that ratio during 1970–76, and it can be assumed that the ratio remained almost constant during this period due to the rapid growth potential of the Korean economy. In terms of the share of capital goods imports, however, a distinct decline took place in 1969–74.

The latest Korean five-year economic and special development plan, for 1982–86, predicts a fixed capital formation ratio of 29.7 % (for 1981) to 31.7 % (1986) in 1980 prices; however, it seems more likely that the ratio will show a declining tendency after 1980, in view of the fact that the share of capital goods imports has already sharply decreased, from 33.9 % in 1979 to 23.0 % in 1980. The 30 % level for the capital formation ratio seems excessively optimistic.

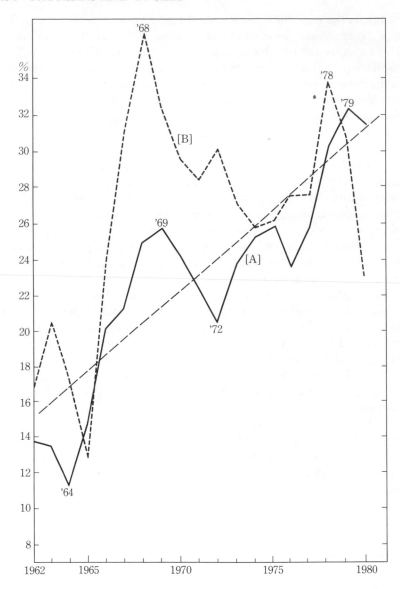

Figure 3. Fixed investment cycle in Korea.
Notes: [A] Gross domestic fixed investment-GNP ratio.
        [B]: Share of capital goods in total imports.
Source: Economic Planning Board, Korea, *Major Statistics of Korea's Economy*,
         1981.

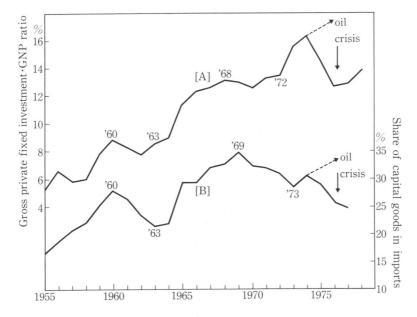

Figure 4. Fixed investment cycle in Taiwan.
Notes: [A]: Gross private fixed investment-GNP ratio.
       [B]: Share of capital goods in total imports.
Sources: [A]: Directorate-General of Budget, Accounting and Statistics, Executive
             Yuan, *National Income of the Republic of China*, 1919.
        [B]: Council for Economic Planning and Development, Executive Yuan,
             Taiwan Statistical Data Book, 1979.

In the case of Taiwan (Figure 4), we also see a Juglar cycle in the
fixed investment ratio and the capital goods import share. The fixed
investment ratio showed an eight-year cycle, with peaks in 1960 and
1968; the capital goods import share, a nine-year cycle. A major difference from the Korean case is that both the investment and trade ratios
collapsed downward in Taiwan from 1975 onwards, while in Korea the
fixed investment ratio continued to increase, probably because of the
introduction of oil money.

   Thus in the cases of these two Asian NICs, where dynamic growth
has continued, we find the occurrence of distinct Juglar cycles.

   Schumpeter once believed that the dynamism of capitalism could not
be analyzed without "cycles." According to him, growth was no more
than a reflection of cycles. His concept of "result trend" simply manifests it. In this sense, we must bear in mind that Japan, where the fixed
investment ratio fluctuated most dynamically in the medium term, had the
highest postwar growth rate. Disregarding this fact, many Keynesians

have nevertheless devoted their efforts to analyses of the growth process far removed from any discussion of cycles.

The Kitchin Cycle

Short-term cycles and inventory investment. The approximately 40-month cycle known as the inventory cycle is named for Joseph A. Kitchin. Schumpeter has pointed out, however, that in 1923, at about the same time that Kitchin was writing, William Leonard Crum, working from a study of the month-to-month discount rates on commercial bills in New York, also discovered a cycle having a mean value of 40 months and a standard deviation of 12.7 months.

According to the periodization of the National Bureau of Economic Research (NBER) in the United States, short-term cycles from 1854 to 1970 averaged 49 months in length. The average for the postwar period 1945–1970 was also 49 months. During the postwar years, however, the average *expansion* phase of this cycle was 39 months, and the average contraction period 10 months. For the entire 1854–1970 period, the average expansion lasted 31 months, and the average contraction lasted 18 months; thus the average expansion period has lengthened while the period of contraction has become shorter in the postwar period.

As can be seen from the Economic Planning Agency's business cycle reference dates shown in Table 2, six cycles in the postwar Japanese economy (excluding the first, which may contain some errors in dating) have an average expansion period of 34 months, contraction period of 13 months, and total duration of 47 months. If the two periods after the "Nixon shock" and the oil crisis are excluded, the average duration of Japan's contraction period becomes 11 months for the years

Table 2. Reference Dates for Business Cycle Fluctuations

	Trough		Peak		Trough		Duration (months)		
	Mo.	Yr.	Mo.	Yr.	Mo.	Yr.	Expansion	Contraction	Entire cycle
Cycle 1			6	1951	10	1951		4	
Cycle 2	10	1951	1	1954	11	1954	27	10	37
Cycle 3	11	1954	6	1957	6	1958	31	12	43
Cycle 4	6	1958	12	1961	10	1962	42	10	52
Cycle 5	10	1962	10	1964	10	1965	24	12	36
Cycle 6	10	1965	7	1970	12	1971	57	17	74
Cycle 7	12	1971	11	1973	3	1975	23	16	39

Source: Economic Planning Agency, *Japanese Economic Indicators,* Feb. 1977.

1951 to 1965, very similar to that of the United States. It was under the impact of these severe shocks from about 1970 onward that Japan's contraction period lengthened to 16 or 17 months.

The data in Table 2 also show that during the boom periods of 1956–57 and 1959–61, the expansion period of the short-term cycle lengthened from the 27 months that it had been prior to these booms, to 31 and then to 42 months. From 1962 to 1965, during a medium-term stagnation in fixed investment, it declined to 24 months. It abruptly lengthened to 57 months during the expansionary phase of the medium-term cycle, then shrank again to 23 months within the medium-term contractionary downswing.

Thus emerges the general principle that the expansionary phase of the short Kitchin cycle lengthens while the Juglar cycle is in an upswing, and contracts while it is on the downswing. Moreover, the periods of contraction were fairly stable at 10 to 12 months until the Nixon shock, but as a result of it and the oil crisis of 1973 it subsequently lengthened to 16 or 17 months.

This short Kitchin cycle is generally termed the "inventory cycle." It should be noted, however, that it may be viewed from two standpoints. One holds that it is a cyclical fluctuation which arises endogenously from inventory shortages and surpluses. The other contends that the upswing of the inventory cycle continues during an expansionary phase until instability is introduced by an encounter with the balance of payments ceiling or the full employment ceiling; thereafter, the economy enters a recessionary downswing as a result of policies aimed at decelerating the economy.

Issues connected with short-term cycles. As a matter of fact, many postwar recessions began with the introduction of policies of restraint implemented as the economy came up against the balance of payments ceiling on growth. Figure 3 shows that in Japan, even after the positive payments balance has begun to subside into a downswing, policies of restraint have still not been implemented. Rather, the growth cycles of money supply and mining and manufacturing output actually enter a recessionary downswing only after a considerable time lag.

The response lag of firms and consumers is thought to play a major role in short-term cycles. In addition, if one considers some time lag inevitable in the implementation of fiscal and monetary policies, the emergence of a regular policy-lag cycle in the implementation of policies may be unavoidable. Ever since Oscar Lange, the expression "political cycle" has been used. Much attention has in fact been devoted to the inevitability in the U.S. economy of an "election cycle," which accompanies the holding of presidential elections every four years,

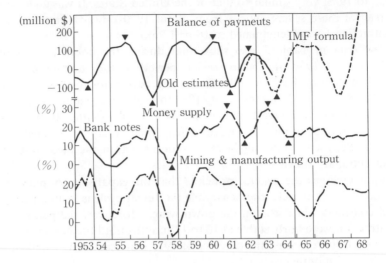

Figure 5. Balance of payments and the growth cycle of money supply
and industrial output. Balance of payments figures are four-
period moving averages.

Note: Money supply and mining and manfacturing output figures are
four-period moving averages of the rates of change vis-à-vis the
same period for the previous year. The shaded areas are recessionary periods according to the Economic Planning Agency's
"reference dates" for business cycles.

rather than a policy lag cycle. Stimulatory policies are adopted prior to
elections in order to win popularity, and then restrictive policies are
pursued in an effort to rectify the resulting situation *ex post facto.*

In any case, if one accepts the idea that a lag still exists in policy
implementation, it will at the very least be difficult to eliminate the
cycle which arises *because of* this policy lag. The Keynesian economists
succeeded in achieving full employment and accelerating growth, but
insofar as they failed to conquer inflation and bring cycles under control, this policy lag will require our attention.

Many Keynesians became convinced that it is to a certain extent possible to overcome cycles by means of aggregate demand management.
Yet Keynesian policies failed both to conquer inflation and to subdue
business cycles. Why? As Yukio Noguchi et al. show in *A Study of the
Public Decision Making Process in Budget Formation (Yosan hensei ni
okeru kokyoteki ishikettei katei no kenkyu)* (1977), it is almost entirely
possible to explain all the public sector variables, which tend to be treated

as exogenous variables in macroeconometric models, as endogenous variables instead by using lagged functions.

In other words, to the extent that Keynesianism is called upon in the mammoth Japanese ship of state finance, small turns at the ship's wheel are of no avail. The ship moves slowly, with a considerable lag. Herein lies the secret of how the "policy cycle" arises from the policy lag. Thus, even under Japan's government-sponsored modified capitalism, a comparatively regular short-term cycle remains. The cycle arising from this lag differs somewhat from the above-described cycle based on the dynamics of fixed investment in that it is passive. In order to circumnavigate the pitfalls of the Keynesian bent for disregarding cycles, this point must not be overlooked.

SUPPLEMENTARY CHAPTER

TECHNICAL PROGRESS AND PRODUCTION FUNCTION BY INDUSTRY

Theoretical Background—The Concept of Capital

In the measurement of technical progress, neoclassical economists have often adopted the so-called "residual method," in which technical progress is assumed to be a residual unexplained by variations in capital and labor inputs. In this case, they are obliged to regard technical progress as "disembodied," apart not only from labor but also from capital equipment. Therefore, the neo-classical concept of technical progress is mostly "disembodied" technical change, as far as its measurement is concerned. In the preparatory stage of this analysis, we tried to explore alternative methods to explain more concretely the actual development of technological progress by industry. Due to the usual insurmountable underlying data difficulties, we are obliged to ride this convenient neoclassical vehicle, which is in fashion and easy to utilize.

The concept of "total factor productivity" is not free from the limitations of the residual method, although sophistication can be introduced, as seen in a number of studies conducted by E. F. Denison and J. W. Kendrick incorporating the quality differences inherent in labor and capital equipment and other factors.

However, there is another fundamental issue, presented by Joan Robinson, which is less apparent at first sight in the concept and measurement of capital.

As is well known, one of the aims of determining the production function is to make clear the role of marginal productivity in income distribution by factor shares. However, the magnitude of capital stock itself, when introduced into the production function, is not independent of the level of the interest rate. If the value of capital is nothing but the

This is a summary of a long 1974 Japanese paper entitled "Measurement of Technical Progress by Industry" in *Keizai Bunseki* (Economic Analysis) No. 48, July 1974, published by Economic Planning Agency of Japan]. Kiyoshi Asakawa cooperated in the preparation of basic data and the procedure.

sum of future expected returns discounted to present values by the interest rate, the latter must be assumed beforehand in such derivation of capital stock valuation. Since the value of capital is not derivable without this assumption, any attempt to explain the interest rate itself via a production function in which the concept of capital is used as an explanatory variable may involve a serious dilemma or circular reasoning.

Joan Robinson's criticism, paraphrased above, seems irrefutable, and if she is right, the computation of the production function may be nonsense. However, as J. R. Hicks pointed out in Chapter 1 of his *Capital and Time* (1973), the concept of capital has two dimensions, "forward-looking" and "backward-looking" characteristics. The first views capital from the demand side, and can be derived by discounting the series of future expected returns. It determines the demand price of the capital stock. On the other hand, the concept of capital to be introduced in the production function should be derived from the supply-side concept of capital, and therefore be of a backward-looking nature. In the latter case, the value of capital stock may not be of a volatile character, fluctuating in accordance with future expectations and uncertainty.

As a matter of course, the value of capital at its supply price is not the usual quantum unit. Since various facilities and equipment of a heterogeneous nature are to be added up in the computation of total capital, they must be in value terms. However, even though the value of capital to be introduced in the production function must be of the backward-looking type, it would be inappropriate to use accounting values, in which the valuation differs according to differences in the date of purchase or acquisition of each piece of equipment. In other words, such book values are essentially "heterotemporal," probably useful in managerial decision-making, but in the analysis of the national economy or industries they should be converted to some common time frame. For the purpose of our present study, the preparation of a real-value capital stock series is needed, so a constant price series had to be compiled.

In order to derive such a series, the value of capital stock outstanding must first be decomposed into flows of fixed investment according to the year of acquisition, converted into constant prices with 1965 as the base, and then resummed. The capital stock series derived in this way has 1) the character of a backward-looking type or supply-price series, and also 2) real or constant price values. It has been used in the following production function analysis.

Basic Data

The basic data for 1960–71 come from the financial statements of major corporations, classified into twenty-one segments of manufacturing. The number of corporations totaled 154, and all of them are listed on the Tokyo Stock Exchange. The tangible fixed assets of each corporation are converted into 1965 prices and exclude "construction in process." Adjustment of capital stock data was made with respect to variations in the utilization rate of equipment. As a proxy, the real value of sales as a ratio to real fixed capital stock (after trend elimination) is adopted as the utilization rate. The variability of capital stock is not as large as its level, and, assuming that sales reflect fluctuations, the ratio of the two by industry was used as an index representing the degree of equipment utilization in each corporation after trend elimination.

The number of employees in each corporation was adjusted according to the monthly working hours statistics of the Ministry of Labour (the so-called *maikin tokei*). By so doing, labor series also are adjusted by their degree of utilization.

As the output of the production function, value added in constant prices (deflated by the wholesale price indexes of each industry) is utilized. Note that in the derivation of the equipment utilization rate, the real value of sales is used in order that the rate not be influenced by fluctuations in the value-added ratio.

Time-Series Production Function

Before going into the computation of the time-series production function, an overall sketch of the annual average growth rate of output (Y), capital stock (K), and labor (L) for 1960–70 by industry subsector may be useful. Table 1 indicates this; if the growth rate of, for instance, manufacturing as a whole for the total 154–company sample is examined, the virtually identical figures of 14.1% and 14.2% for the growth rate of Y and K contrast sharply with that of L at only 2.2%. This relation holds true for almost all sectors of manufacturing. At first glance, capital stock growth seems to have played the predominant role in output growth.

Coefficients of the production functions of the Cobb-Douglas type [$Y = AK^{\alpha}L^{\beta}$ and $Y/L = A(K/L)^{\alpha}$] were computed from the data, and are indicated in Tables 2 and 3 respectively. The latter function is a special case of the former, in which the sum of the two coefficients $\alpha + \beta$ is assumed as unity. In manufacturing as a whole $\alpha + \beta$ computed from the Cobb-Douglas function of the former type is 1.1989 and

Table 1. Annual Average Growth Rates of Output, Capital, and Labor (1960–71)

	Output (Y)	Capital (K)	Labor (L)
Flour milling	11.3	12.0	1.4
Edible oil	9.1	12.7	2.2
Cotton spinning	7.6	7.6	−1.0
Synthetic textiles	15.2	12.6	0.0
Paper and pulp	9.0	9.4	−0.9
Chemicals	14.2	14.5	−1.3
Drugs and medicines	17.9	15.8	5.5
Glass	14.9	13.2	3.0
Cement	8.8	10.7	−0.9
Petroleum refining	9.5	14.0	1.1
Blast furnace	12.7	15.2	2.0
Open and electric furnaces	10.6	17.0	2.6
Special steel	10.8	12.9	1.0
Non-ferrous metals	7.6	11.9	−5.6
Electric wire and cable	11.0	14.3	1.5
Machine tools	9.2	12.3	1.8
Bearings	14.8	15.4	0.7
Automobiles	22.8	24.3	10.0
Heavy electric equipment	15.3	11.8	4.5
Light electrical appliances	22.0	17.2	5.0
Optical instruments	23.3	21.1	7.1
Total	14.1	14.2	2.2

Notes: K and L are adjusted by the utilization rate of equipment and manhours, respectively.

Annual average growth rates are computed from mere comparison of 1960 and 1971 by compound interest calculation. "Blast furnace" and "open and electric furnaces" designate types in the iron and steel industry.

not extremely different from unity. However, the extent of variation from unity varies from industry to industry.

Moreover, in the linear homogeneous production function of Table 3, the total manufacturing coefficient α is 1.0152 and almost unity, although the range of α varies from 1.38576 in light electrical appliances to 0.76985 for open and electric furnaces. The almost parallel growth of Y and K in various sectors of manufacturing manifested in Table 1 is more clearly shown in the computed values of α. In the production function of Table 2 ($Y = AK^\alpha L^\beta$), among the six industries in which β, the coefficient of labor, is statistically significant, removal of those with negative β-values leave only a few labor-intensive industries: machine tools, bearings, and automobiles. This result may tentatively support the *a priori* choice of the formula $Y/L = A (K/L)^\alpha$.

R^2 is very close to unity in every industry. However, it is widely held that during the rapid economic expansion of the 1960s, rapid technolog-

Table 2. Time-Series Production Function ($Y = AK^\alpha L^\beta$)

	Constant term	α	t-ratio	β	t-ratio	R^2	Standard error	D. W. ratio
Flour milling	-1.04942	0.88148	(17.330)	0.32160	(1.192)	0.9805	0.02228	1.502
Edible oil	-0.54206	0.82528	(5.421)	0.28674	(0.300)	0.8293	0.07857	1.484
Cotton spinning	1.81730	1.03534	(9.987)	-0.49228	(-0.874)	0.9429	0.03016	0.993
Synthetic textiles	6.92081	1.28293	(24.495)	-1.83936	(-2.581)	0.9823	0.03117	1.494
Paper and pulp	-3.05655	1.02467	(13.299)	0.48395	(0.693)	0.9854	0.01726	1.376
Chemicals	-1.24693	0.99713	(12.205)	0.15913	(0.201)	0.9925	0.01867	1.111
Drugs and medicines	1.19977	1.34316	(24.938)	-0.64745	(-4.406)	0.9977	0.01218	1.500
Glass	-1.48623	1.09903	(7.611)	0.15295	(0.228)	0.9786	0.03504	0.854
Cement	0.21164	0.87523	(9.990)	-0.05682	(-0.091)	0.9520	0.03118	1.354
Petroleum refining	0.60269	0.87193	(10.004)	-0.13220	(-0.148)	0.9244	0.05131	1.820
Blast furnace	1.39101	0.88034	(25.370)	-0.21986	(-0.940)	0.9966	0.01160	2.101
Open and electric furnaces	-0.29363	0.77106	(4.545)	0.22100	(0.196)	0.9180	0.06273	2.046
Special steel	-1.12083	0.88607	(14.890)	0.28686	(0.618)	0.9816	0.02724	1.217
Non-ferrous metals	-0.29905	0.71224	(4.632)	0.30487	(0.978)	0.9273	0.02667	2.516
Electric wire and cable	2.89306	0.76912	(10.714)	-0.44580	(-0.982)	0.9744	0.02545	1.123
Machine tools	-7.52146	0.49257	(5.338)	2.30479	(4.306)	0.9702	0.02859	1.084
Bearings	-2.45607	1.00281	(46.816)	0.50449	(3.677)	0.9958	0.01599	1.148
Automobiles	-1.16891	0.67033	(7.708)	0.54866	(3.072)	0.9967	0.01780	1.289
Heavy electric equipment	-2.27134	1.21155	(15.747)	0.17160	(0.892)	0.9923	0.01969	0.933
Light electrical appliances	-1.70162	1.22297	(6.164)	0.12363	(0.205)	0.9922	0.02849	0.572
Optical instruments	1.35677	1.37949	(20.477)	-0.69549	(-3.558)	0.9956	0.02214	0.770
Total	-1.60815	0.97566	(24.270)	0.22325	(0.960)	0.9990	0.00666	1.862

Table 3. Time-Series Productivity Function,

$$\frac{Y}{L} = A\left(\frac{K}{L}\right)^{\alpha}$$

	Constant term	α	t-ratio	R^2	Standard error	D. W. ratio
Flour milling	−0.28819	0.90320	(20.887)	0.9574	0.02196	1.379
Edible oil	−0.16075	0.83614	(6.921)	0.8100	0.07461	1.493
Cotton spinning	−0.53420	1.08926	(15.551)	0.9563	0.02942	0.710
Synthetic textiles	−0.72708	1.29571	(21.258)	0.9762	0.03651	1.049
Paper and pulp	−0.60400	0.97839	(30.830)	0.9885	0.01677	1.237
Chemicals	−0.49275	0.98307	(44.083)	0.9944	0.01775	1.150
Drugs and medicines	−0.13628	1.19240	(35.561)	0.9914	0.01673	0.719
Glass	−0.48770	1.15990	(19.280)	0.9712	0.03364	0.917
Cement	−0.57473	0.89335	(17.489)	0.9652	0.02969	1.343
Petroleum refining	−0.45833	0.85989	(11.595)	0.9239	0.04893	1.787
Blast furnace	−0.36557	0.82990	(44.535)	0.9945	0.01260	1.934
Open and electric furnaces	−0.32636	0.76985	(9.813)	0.8965	0.05951	2.047
Special steel	−0.36289	0.90359	(22.663)	0.9790	0.02608	1.203
Non-ferrous metals	−0.21515	0.70665	(22.966)	0.9795	0.02531	2.528
Electric wire and cable	−0.08857	0.66632	(15.259)	0.9547	0.02784	1.326
Machine tools	−0.05303	0.78930	(9.504)	0.8904	0.04472	0.548
Bearings	−0.25107	1.01895	(31.373)	0.9889	0.02472	0.695
Automobiles	−0.18117	0.85904	(23.560)	0.9805	0.02133	0.675
Heavy electric equipment	−0.27710	1.38498	(20.337)	0.9740	0.02642	0.426
Light electrical appliances	−0.02782	1.38576	(28.325)	0.9865	0.02809	0.610
Optical instruments	0.05116	1.24217	(30.555)	0.9883	0.02670	0.676
Total	−0.42522	1.01521	(88.340)	0.9986	0.00667	1.600

ical progress was prevalent in every sector of manufacturing. Therefore, a further modification in the time-series production function lies in the introduction of a time trend factor. Actually,

$$Y = AK^{\alpha}L^{\beta}e^{\tau t} \tag{1}$$

$$Y/L = A(K/L)^{\alpha}e^{\tau t} \tag{2}$$

are computed, but in view of the computational result already described, description of the results of the latter may suffice. As Table 4 shows, in manufacturing as a whole, τ, the coefficient of t, is not statistically significant; moreover it becomes negative, a counter-sign to what is expected in this period of high technical advance.

Negative signs are observed in seven industries, contradictory to our expectation; in some of these industries, ten t-ratios indicate a statistical significance. Interestingly, there is a negative association between the signs of the coefficient τ and the changes of α when the time-trend is introduced in the productivity function as follows:

Table 4. Productivity Function with a Trend Factor

$$\frac{Y}{L} = A\left(\frac{K}{L}\right)^{\alpha} e^{rt}$$

	Constant term	α	t-ratio	β	t-ratio	R^2	Standard error	D. W. ratio
Flour milling	−0.16745	−0.63187	(1.605)	0.01160	(0.694)	0.9740	0.02255	1.354
Edible oil	−0.04307	0.42323	(0.756)	0.02186	(0.757)	0.8015	0.07626	1.565
Cotton spinning	−0.04655	−1.15200	(−0.887)	0.07883	(1.727)	0.9636	0.02688	1.027
Synthetic textiles	0.27292	−1.06786	(−1.166)	0.11855	(2.584)	0.9848	0.02916	1.644
Paper and pulp	−0.38984	0.63971	(2.258)	0.01506	(1.203)	0.9890	0.01641	1.894
Chemicals	−0.37845	0.72340	(1.769)	0.01731	(0.636)	0.9940	0.01830	1.011
Drugs and medicines	−0.14896	1.28625	(4.781)	−0.00395	(−0.352)	0.9905	0.01752	0.699
Glass	−0.31170	0.75507	(2.321)	0.01925	(1.265)	0.9728	0.03268	1.155
Cement	−1.16406	1.63559	(2.456)	−0.03619	(−1.118)	0.9660	0.02933	1.389
Petroleum refining	−0.40512	0.79959	(1.166)	0.00335	(0.089)	0.9155	0.05155	1.776
Blast furnace	−0.52056	1.13863	(6.849)	−0.01755	(−1.866)	0.9956	0.01128	1.239
Open and electric furnaces	−0.40697	0.99172	(2.406)	−0.01436	(−0.549)	0.8887	0.06170	1.857
Special steel	−0.44401	1.34251	(5.818)	−0.02430	(−1.925)	0.9835	0.02314	1.493
Non-ferrous metals	−0.25037	1.00987	(7.730)	−0.02126	(−2.366)	0.9860	0.02094	2.714
Electric wire and cable	−0.08439	0.63294	(2.635)	0.00181	(0.142)	0.9498	0.02932	1.373
Machine tools	−0.00854	1.47729	(7.037)	−0.03222	(−3.409)	0.9468	0.03114	0.803
Bearings	−0.25249	0.97917	(3.302)	0.00255	(0.135)	0.9877	0.02604	0.729
Automobiles	−0.10844	0.57794	(3.961)	0.01410	(1.975)	0.9849	0.01878	1.088
Heavy electric equipment	−0.26323	1.04317	(23.472)	0.01292	(8.959)	0.9971	0.00884	1.406
Light electrical appliances	−0.13313	0.80171	(7.873)	0.02881	(5.893)	0.9969	0.01343	1.106
Optical instruments	−0.03307	0.98247	(3.653)	0.01443	(0.977)	0.9883	0.02676	0.690
Total	−0.44794	1.08144	(7.764)	−0.00323	(−0.477)	0.9985	0.00695	1.464

	Value of τ	Changes in α
Cement	$- 0.03619$	$+ 0.74224$
Machine tools	$- 0.03222$	$+ 0.68799$
Special steel	$- 0.02430$	$+ 0.43892$
Non-ferrous metals	$- 0.02126$	$+ 0.30322$
Blast furnace	$- 0.01755$	$+ 0.30873$
Open and electric furnaces	$- 0.01436$	$+ 0.22187$
Light electrical appliances	$+ 0.02881$	$- 0.58405$
Cotton spinning	$+ 0.07883$	$- 2.24126$
Synthetic textiles	$+ 0.11855$	$- 2.36357$

In other words, the time trend seems redundant in this function, indicating that multi-collinearity exists between K and t. Thus, the introduction of t fails to make clear the part played by the technical progress in the 1960s.

It seems necessary, therefore, to return to the original simple productivity function, $Y/L = A(K/L)^\alpha$, where the parallel growth of Y and K seems to identify the "neutral technical progress" as defined by the late Roy Harrod. The so-called "Harrod-neutral" is defined as technical progress which maintains the relative income shares between capital and labor inter-temporally unchanged under the condition of constant capital-output ratio (K/Y). In this case, the constancy of capital-output ratio (K/Y) and yet the constant relative share of capitalist income $(r\ K/L$, where r denotes interest rate) stand for the unchanging rate of interest.

In the general production function $Y = f(K, L)$, if we further denote the efficiency of capital by $A(t)$, and the efficiency of labor by $B(t)$, then $Y = f(A(t)K, B(t)L)$. If $A(t) = B(t)$, then $Y = A(t)f(K, L)$ obtains. In this case, $A(t)$ will designate "Hicks-neutral" technical progress, which maintains unchanging relative income shares under constant capital intensity (K/L) between two different points in time. Under the required condition of constant relative shares of capital and labor $(rK/wL$, where w is the real wage rate), this means the constancy of relative factor prices w/r. By contrast, in "Harrod-neutral," technical progress $A(t) = 1$, and therefore $Y = f(K, B(t)L)$. In this case, technical progress emerges due to the "labor-augmenting" rise of $B(t)$, and will not influence the magnitude of capital-output ratio (K/Y). Hicks-neutral technical progress will maintain the constancy of K/L, whereas the Harrod-neutral type will maintain the constancy of K/Y.

According to the 1960s' manufacturing data for major Japanese business corporations, K and Y grew proportionally, and therefore

K/Y remained almost constant overall. From this fact, we are inclined, influenced by neoclassical textbook knowledge, to assume that technical progress of this period in manufacturing was "Harrod-neutral." However, this judgment may be superficial. Actually, in the 1960s, rapid qualitative changes occurred in the machinery and equipment newly installed in every segment of manufacturing. Therefore, technical progress in this period was not neutral in the sense of its separability from $f(K, L)$, K or L, but was "embodied" in the capital stock. If such technological innovation did not develop, then the rise in the capital-output ratio would have been inevitable for the achievement of mass production and economies of scale. Due to such "embodied" technical progress, the stability of the capital coefficient in manufacturing as a whole had been realized. Consequently, stability of the capital coefficient and "Harrod-neutral" technical progress should not be confused.

Insofar as it was made clear that the net contribution of technical progress could not be analyzed by the mere addition of $e^{\tau t}$, it should further be understood that the magnitude of α, the coefficient to capital in the time-series production function, was highly influenced by technical progress during this period.

Cross-Section Production Function

In view of the continuity over time of the data on Y, K, and L, the time-series production function may be superior to the cross-section function, which is fitted between industries or corporations. For instance, in comparing the food-processing and steel industries, some qualitative differences may still remain which cannot be explained by the variations of K and L. Nevertheless, a much greater influence may have been introduced due to the rapid technical progress on the computed value of α in the time-series production function than in the cross-section function. Therefore, it may be of some significance to compare the time-series function to the cross-section function—that is, to compare the differences in α, if any, for each function.

Tables 5 and 6 are the results of fitting the data among 21 industries. The coefficient of determination, R^2, is much higher in the case of $Y = AK^\alpha L^\beta$ than for $Y/L = A(K/L)^\alpha$. In the former, R^2 ranges from 0.9352 to 0.9631, and in the latter from 0.3945 to 0.6494. However, it must be recognized that α is quite similar in Tables 5 and 6 (e.g., 1960: 0.43249 vs. 0.44086; 1971: 0.28749 vs. 0.28997). Moreover, β, the coefficient of labor, is statistically significant in the cross-section function, whereas in the time-series function (see Table 2) it was rarely significant.

Another decisive difference from the time-series case is that the value

Table 5. Cross-Section Production Function
$$Y = AK^{\alpha}L^{\beta}$$

	Constant term	α	t-ratio	β	t-ratio	R^2	Standard error	D. W. ratio	$(\alpha + \beta)$
1960	0.40810	0.43249	(6.812)	0.44544	(6.068)	0.9631	0.08666	1.809	0.8779
1961	0.27760	0.35976	(5.187)	0.55804	(6.986)	0.9603	0.09108	1.725	0.9178
1962	0.28472	0.36268	(4.925)	0.55827	(6.679)	0.9549	0.09630	1.625	0.9210
1963	0.39578	0.39215	(5.612)	0.51131	(6.466)	0.9555	0.09273	2.103	0.9035
1964	0.33694	0.36409	(5.236)	0.55899	(7.162)	0.9555	0.09478	1.815	0.9231
1965	0.33094	0.40993	(5.631)	0.51113	(6.124)	0.9477	0.10447	1.693	0.9211
1966	0.33134	0.41230	(5.096)	0.51736	(6.795)	0.9542	0.09710	1.327	0.9297
1967	0.31547	0.35382	(5.199)	0.59629	(8.091)	0.9578	0.09523	1.376	0.9501
1968	0.42637	0.32663	(4.620)	0.61159	(8.100)	0.9538	0.09840	1.443	0.9382
1969	0.53650	0.31686	(4.125)	0.61197	(7.469)	0.9477	0.10493	1.675	0.9288
1970	0.63258	0.29304	(3.502)	0.62444	(6.923)	0.9352	0.11650	1.588	0.9175
1971	0.30668	0.28749	(3.800)	0.70213	(8.375)	0.9513	0.10808	1.542	0.9896

Table 6. Cross-Section Productivity Function,

$$\frac{Y}{L} = A\left(\frac{K}{L}\right)^{\alpha}$$

	Constant term log A	α	t-ratio	R^2	Standard error	D. W. ratio	A	$\Delta A/A$
1960	−0.13925	0.44086	(5.781)	0.6184	0.10420	1.865	0.7257	—
1961	−0.09402	0.36511	(4.924)	0.5376	0.09744	1.715	0.8053	10.97
1962	−0.07499	0.37204	(4.812)	0.5256	0.10136	1.584	0.8414	4.48
1963	−0.04712	0.40655	(5.339)	0.5790	0.10151	2.096	0.8972	6.63
1964	−0.01917	0.37852	(5.223)	0.5678	0.09951	1.768	0.9568	6.64
1965	−0.03267	0.42220	(5.604)	0.6032	0.10872	1.687	0.9275	△3.06
1966	0.00429	0.42716	(6.168)	0.6494	0.10046	1.496	1.0099	8.89
1967	0.07923	0.36871	(5.488)	0.5928	0.09586	1.528	1.2001	18.83
1968	0.13026	0.34728	(4.930)	0.5382	0.10045	1.610	1.3498	12.47
1969	0.19371	0.34022	(4.398)	0.4784	0.10804	1.923	1.5621	15.73
1970	0.23488	0.31815	(3.746)	0.3945	0.12057	1.835	1.7174	9.94
1971	0.25729	0.28997	(3.783)	0.4264	0.10532	1.562	1.8084	5.30

of α in cross-section ranges from 0.28 to 0.44; the average value is 0.359 in Table 5 and 0.373 in Table 6. This is considerably different from the near unity α in the time-series production function, indicating that the influence of technological progress upon the value of α is not as distinctly revealed in cross-section, where the possible inter-industry technological differentials may be absorbed within the inter-industry price dispersion to a considerable extent. However, in the time-series function, the impact of technological innovation upon the value of α seems to be remarkably high. If so, the values of α computed by the time-series or cross-section production function cannot be interchanged even when the functional form is identical. Any approach based upon the assumption that the character of α is the same whether it is derived from cross-section or time-series is therefore completely misleading.

Incidentally, in the computed results of $Y/L = A(K/L)^{\alpha}$ in Table 6, even if the variation of α is not large, the value of intercept A follows a rising trend; moreover, the annual movement of $\Delta A/A$ closely reflects the ups and downs of the business cycle.

By combining the cross-section productivity function in each year with the time-series productivity function F in Figure 1, we can see that, first, technical progress had brought about the upward drift of the cross-section productivity function for the 1960–71 period, and second, the rising shift of the cross-section function is now embodied in the rather higher value of α ($\doteqdot$ 1) than those derived from the cross-section functions each year.

It still remains to be discussed if the value of α in the cross-section

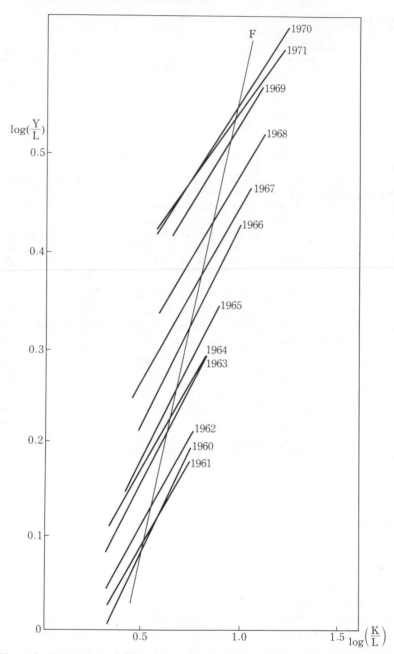

Figure 1. Intersection of the cross-section and time-series productivity functions.
Notes: *F* is the time-series productivity function of Table 3: $\log(Y/L) = -0.42522 + 1.01521 \log(K/L)$. Cross-section functions are based on Table 6.

production function is acceptable, but it should be pointed out that it is much less disturbed by technical progress than in the time-series function.

Furthermore, the constancy of the capital coefficient (K/Y) in manufacturing corporations seems once more due less to the fact that the increase in capital efficiency was not included in the fixed capital stock, and more to the proposition that "embodied" technical progress had suppressed any possible rise in the capital coefficient (which may nevertheless have occurred due to mass production and expansion of scale). Technical progress was unlikely to have been Harrod-neutral or merely labor-augmenting. The apparent stability of the capital-output ratio and the near-unity value of α in the time-series function should be understood in this light.

Integration of Time-Series and Cross-Section Functions

It may be of further interest to extend our analysis by introducing the two dummy variables "years" and "industries" in an integrated function in which both time-series and cross-section variables are pooled. Denote the dummy (0 or 1) for "years" as $Dy_1, Dy_2, \ldots, Dy_n$ (where $y_1, y_2 \ldots y_n$ stand for the n years), and for "industries" $D_{I_1}, D_{I_2}, \ldots, D_{I_m}$ (where $I_1, I_2 \ldots I_m$ stand for the m industries); then the following equations can be fitted:

$$Y = AK^\alpha L^\beta e^{\gamma_1 Dy_1} \ldots e^{\gamma_n Dy_n} \cdot e^{\varepsilon_1 D_{I1}} \ldots e^{\varepsilon_m D_{Im}} \qquad (3)$$

$$Y/L = A(K/L)^\alpha e^{\gamma Dy_1} \ldots e^{\gamma_n Dy_n} \cdot e^{\varepsilon_1 D_{I1}} \ldots e^{\varepsilon_m D_{Im}} \qquad (4)$$

Tables 7 and 8 differ only in the condition of $\alpha + \beta \gtrless 1$ (Table 7) or $\alpha + \beta = 1$ (Table 8). Some relevant results follow:

1) If only the dummy variables for industries are introduced in the pooled function, the α derived is 0.92494 without the restriction of $\alpha + \beta = 1$, and 0.95353 under the restriction of $\alpha + \beta = 1$. These are very close to the coefficient α derived from simple time-series functions of Table 2 (0.97566) and Table 3 (1.01521). Since the impact from the "industries" dummy is excluded here, the dummy of "years" (technical progress) is wholly represented in the value of α.

2) Looking at the results in which only the "years" dummy is introduced, $\alpha = 0.35740$ and $\beta = 0.57038$ without any restriction of $\alpha + \beta = 1$, and $\alpha = 0.3725$ under the restriction of $\alpha + \beta = 1$. However, from the cross-section functions of Table 5 ($\alpha + \beta \lessgtr 1$ assumed), the averages of α and β for the period of 1961–70 are $\alpha = 0.359$ and $\beta = 0.567$, mirroring the "years" dummy formulation.

Table 7. Production Function with the Dummy "Years" and "Industries"

$$Y = AK^\alpha L^\beta e^{\gamma_1 D_{y1}} \ldots e^{\gamma_n D_{yn}}, e^{s_1 D_{I1}} \ldots e^{s_m D_{Im}}$$

	Coefficient	t-ratio	Coefficient	t-ratio	Coefficient	t-ratio	Coefficient	t-ratio
Constant term	0.17227	—	0.21131	—	−0.83931	—	−1.23039	—
α	0.51486	(21.300)	0.35740	(17.712)	0.67248	(9.359)	0.92494	(50.879)
β	0.43579	(15.153)	0.57038	(25.369)	0.49935	(6.223)	0.31723	(4.843)
1961	—	—	0.02235	(0.750)	−0.00271	(−0.177)	—	—
1962	—	—	0.04500	(1.508)	0.00604	(0.367)	—	—
1963	—	—	0.09175	(3.063)	0.03106	(1.639)	—	—
1964	—	—	0.10789	(3.590)	0.03101	(1.466)	—	—
1965	—	—	0.11818	(3.926)	0.03728	(1.695)	—	—
1966	—	—	0.16178	(5.342)	0.06331	(2.527)	—	—
1967	—	—	0.20298	(6.635)	0.07865	(2.649)	—	—
1968	—	—	0.23988	(7.765)	0.09394	(2.791)	—	—
1969	—	—	0.29729	(9.501)	0.12862	(3.366)	—	—
1970	—	—	0.31970	(10.126)	0.13526	(3.278)	—	—
1971	—	—	0.31505	(9.913)	0.12368	(2.869)	—	—
Edible oil	—	—	—	—	0.12561	(4.013)	0.17461	(6.255)
Cotton spinning	—	—	—	—	−0.44465	(−5.800)	−0.46398	(−6.079)
Synthetic textiles	—	—	—	—	−0.32469	(−4.692)	−0.40743	(−4.079)
Paper & pulp	—	—	—	—	−0.35752	(−5.579)	−0.47182	(−8.718)
Chemicals	—	—	—	—	−0.25847	(−4.096)	−0.36135	(−6.585)
Drugs & medicines	—	—	—	—	0.06573	(1.320)	0.09106	(1.826)

$R^2 = 0.9248$ S. error $= 0.13385$ D.W. ratio $= 0.8515$

$R^2 = 0.9609$ S. error $= 0.09649$ D.W. ratio $= 1.6363$

$R^2 = 0.9907$ S. error $= 0.04706$ D.W. ratio $= 1.6138$

$R^2 = 0.9903$ S. error $= 0.04807$ D.W. ratio $= 1.4208$

Table 7 (*continued*)

	Coefficient	t-ratio	Coefficient	t-ratio	Coefficient	t-ratio
Glass	—	—	−0.05817	(−2.110)	−0.08572	(−3.236)
Cement	—	—	−0.27566	(−6.021)	−0.40134	(−14.044)
Petroleum refining	—	—	−0.15686	(−3.129)	−0.31000	(−12.086)
Blast furnace	—	—	−0.36085	(−3.777)	−0.50321	(−5.911)
Open & elect. furnace	—	—	−0.19948	(−6.065)	−0.24392	(−8.075)
Special steel	—	—	−0.22079	(−5.421)	−0.21887	(−5.341)
Non-ferrous metals	—	—	−0.22785	(−4.074)	−0.25267	(−4.569)
Electric wire & cable	—	—	−0.08232	(−1.902)	−0.06647	(−1.528)
Machine tools	—	—	0.03298	(0.813)	0.12897	(4.012)
Bearings	—	—	−0.08923	(−2.243)	−0.04041	(−1.053)
Automobile	—	—	−0.15494	(−2.125)	−0.20370	(−2.868)
Heavy electric equipment	—	—	−0.21100	(−2.330)	−0.20689	(−2.279)
Light electrical appliances	—	—	0.00994	(0.143)	0.08177	(1.201)
Optical Instruments	—	—	0.13821	(2.687)	0.28878	(8.956)

Table 8. Production Function with the Dummy "Years" and "Industries"

$$Y/L = A(K/L)^a \, e^{\gamma_1 D_{Y1}} \ldots e^{\gamma_n D_{Yn}} \cdot e^{\delta_1 D_{I1}} \ldots e^{\delta_m D_{Im}}$$

	Coefficient	t-ratio	Coefficient	t-ratio	Coefficient	t-ratio	Coefficient	t-ratio
Constant term	−0.05461	(21.357)	−0.11597	(17.566)	−0.16708	—	−0.32457	
α	0.52087	—	0.37251		0.61609	(8.789)	0.95353	(54.404)
1961			0.01905	(0.603)	0.00623	(0.409)		—
1962			0.04078	(1.289)	0.01800	(1.115)		—
1963			0.08559	(2.696)	0.04882	(2.689)		—
1964			0.09999	(3.141)	0.05371	(2.702)		—
1965			0.11069	(3.470)	0.05941	(2.848)		—
1966			0.15339	(4.781)	0.08871	(3.735)		—
1967			0.19262	(5.947)	0.11022	(3.946)		—
1968			0.22765	(6.966)	0.13113	(4.170)		—
1969			0.28369	(8.575)	0.17049	(4.767)		—
1970			0.30476	(9.134)	0.18117	(4.705)		—
1971			0.30060	(8.948)	0.16910	(4.163)		—
Edible oil					0.05837	(2.835)	0.08996	(4.406)
Cotton spinning					−0.24241	(8.812)	−0.14907	(−7.126)
Synthetic textiles					0.13731	(−7.005)	−0.14618	(−7.181)
Paper & pulp					−0.18954	(−7.909)	−0.25652	(−12.425)
Chemicals					−0.09156	(−4.127)	−0.14237	(−6.938)
Drugs & medicines					0.17988	(6.113)	0.28590	(13.561)

$R^2 = 0.6445$
S. error $= 0.13560$
D.W. ratio $= 0.940$

$R^2 = 0.7975$
S. error $= 0.10234$
D.W. ratio $= 1.741$

$R^2 = 0.9558$
S. error $= 0.04780$
D.W. ratio $= 1.516$

$R^2 = 0.9520$
S. error $= 0.04985$
D.W. ratio $= 1.233$

Table 8 (*continued*)

	Coef-ficient	t-ratio	Coef-ficient	t-ratio	Coef-ficient	t-ratio	Coef-ficient	t-ratio
Glass	—	—	—	—	−0.00258	(−0.132)	−0.00964	(−0.474)
Cement	—	—	—	—	−0.18608	(−5.558)	−0.31702	(−14.775)
Petroleum refining	—	—	—	—	−0.07451	(−1.800)	−0.25021	(−11.219)
Blast furnace	—	—	—	—	−0.09858	(−4.456)	−0.14873	(−7.250)
Open & elect. furnaces	—	—	—	—	−0.12516	(−6.265)	−0.14578	(−7.154)
Special steel	—	—	—	—	−0.12565	(−5.423)	−0.06552	(−3.182)
Non-ferrous metals	—	—	—	—	−0.08269	(−3.725)	−0.03178	(−1.549)
Electric wire & cable	—	—	—	—	0.01611	(0.620)	0.09871	(4.746)
Machine tools	—	—	—	—	0.06916	(1.770)	0.23216	(10.533)
Bearings	—	—	—	—	−0.01683	(−0.548)	0.09842	(4.640)
Automobile	—	—	—	—	0.04156	(1.908)	0.08814	(4.301)
Heavy electric equipment	—	—	—	—	0.02362	(0.651)	0.17096	(7.863)
Light electrical appliances	—	—	—	—	0.16085	(3.554)	0.35741	(15.698)
Optical instruments	—	—	—	—	0.15483	(2.983)	0.38634	(16.344)

Moreover, under the restriction of $\alpha + \beta = 1$, the twelve-year average of α in the cross-section functions was 0.373. This manifests almost perfect agreement with the result of the Table 8 case in which the "years" dummy is introduced.

It is a noteworthy finding that α and β in the function of Table 7 with a mere addition of the "years" dummy resembles with the parameters α and β in the simple cross-section function of Table 5, and that α and β derived in Table 7 with the inclusion of the "industries" dummy are very close to those derived from the simple time-series production function of Table 2.

3) From the pooled function without either "years" or "industries," $Y = AK^\alpha L^\beta$ yields $\alpha = 0.51486$; $\beta = 0.43579$, and $Y/L = A(K/L)^\alpha$ yields $\alpha = 0.52087$. However, if both "years" and "industries" dummy variables are included, $\alpha = 0.67248$; $\beta = 0.49935$ or $\alpha = 0.61609$ are derived from the above two functions, respectively. In other words, the value of α increases with the addition of both dummy variables.

4) The average share of capital in the value added for manufacturing is 56.7% in net terms excluding depreciation allowances, but 46.3% in gross terms including them. Therefore, the gross relative share of capital, 56.7%, is relatively close to the results ($\alpha = 0.515$ or $\alpha = 0.521$) computed without either dummy, but is considerably lower than the results ($\alpha = 0.672$ or $\alpha = 0.616$) derived with the two dummy variables included. However, the net relative share of capital is 46.3%, and this is much lower than either of the above two cases. Nevertheless, when compared to $\alpha = 0.359$ or 0.373 as based on the function with addition of the "years" dummy, both net and gross relative shares are greater.

Therefore, the problem of which α the actual capital share should be compared with remains. Generally, in a rapidly growing economy like that of postwar Japan, it may be plausible to assume that the actual relative share is higher than α computed from any production function. However, we have encountered difficulties, as explained above.

5) The coefficients of the "years" dummy in the pooled production function represent technical progress, so it is useful here to check their numerical values. In order to avoid any confusion that may arise, only the productivity function of the type $Y/L = A(K/L)^\alpha$ is taken up (Table 9). As Table 9 indicates, technology advance almost doubled in the case where only the "years" dummy was incorporated, while it increased by about 50% when both the "years" and "industries" dummy variables were taken into consideration. This divergence of technical progress presents another difficulty, but we postpone any discussion of this until after our studies based on the total factor productivity approach in the next section are completed.

Table 9. Technical Progress as Implied in Productivity Function with the Dummy
(Table 8 case)

	Level of technology		Rates of technical progress	
	"Years" dummy	"Years" plus "industries" dummy		
	(A)	(B)	(A)	(B)
1960	1.0000	1.0000	—%	—%
1961	1.0450	1.0145	4.50	1.45
1962	1.0984	1.0424	5.11	2.75
1963	1.2178	1.1190	10.87	7.35
1964	1.2589	1.1317	3.37	1.13
1965	1.2903	1.1466	2.49	6.98
1966	1.4236	1.2266	10.33	5.08
1967	1.5582	1.2889	9.45	4.93
1968	1.6891	1.3525	8.40	9.49
1969	1.9217	1.4808	13.77	2.49
1970	2.0173	1.5177	4.97	—2.75
1971	1.9980	1.4760	—0.96	3.60

6) Another check of the pooled productivity function requiring attention is the implication of the dummy "industries." One may assume the coefficient differential is just a reflection of the variation of technology level of various industries. However, the inter-industry differences in technology will be absorbed or offset in the inverse variation of inter-industry relative price structure in the competitive market. In terms of this, the inter-industry differences of Y should properly be explained by the inter-industry differences of K and L, leaving no scope for the part played by the technological gaps among industries. However, in the process of technological evolution, there certainly is room for insufficient adaptation of relative prices. The existence of cartels, oligopoly, patents, product discrimination, and other industry-specific factors may explain the inter-industry differential of the dummy variables. On the one hand, the dummy coefficients which show a positive sign in Table 8 are in the following industries: edible oil, drugs and medicines, machine tools, light electrical appliances, and optical instruments. In these industries, product discrimination is extremely important. Likewise, showing a distinctly negative coefficient are blast furnace steel, paper and pulp, cotton spinning, synthetic textiles, glass, cement, chemicals, etc. In these industries there is much less scope for product discrimination, and the degree of competitiveness seems to be greater.

In this sense, one cannot simply assume that the differences in the "industries" dummy are a reflection of interindustry technological differences. Rather, the dummy variables representing each industry may strongly reflect various market factors.

Total Factor Productivity Approach

Instead of measuring productivity in terms of labor or capital, recent efforts call for "total (factor) productivity" comparing output to composite factor input totals (with capital and labor combined in some way). This method was adopted by M. Abramovitz, J. W. Kendrick, R. M. Solows, and others.

There are two methods in this approach: one is to measure it directly in terms of $Y/(\bar{r}K + \bar{w}L)$, where r and $\bar{w}$ are the rate of return for capital and the real wage rate, respectively; and the second is to derive the accumulation of each year's $\Delta A/A$ from the equation $\Delta A/A = \Delta Y/Y - \alpha (\Delta K/K) - \beta(\Delta L/L)$, under the assumption of $\alpha + \beta = 1$. In the latter case, for α and β, the relative income distributive shares of capital and labor are often used. Rigorously, this assumes the prevalence of perfect competition.

In these cases, the portion unexplained by capital and labor is assumed to be technical progress. However, it is a matter of definition whether or not to treat all of the residual as technical progress. When all qualitative differences of productive factors, such as age composition, school career, sex, and work intensity for laborers; the differences in equipment purchases; and intangible investments (health, education, job training, research and development) are taken into account, then the residual may finally approach zero. However, our method is not as comprehensive, and such qualitative differences in factors and the effect of non-tangible factors are also included here simply as technical progress. Tables 10 and 11 are presented here, the former representing the total productivity approach ($Y/\bar{r}K + \bar{w}L$) and the latter derived by the residual method.

In computing $Y/(\bar{r}K + \bar{w}L)$, r and $\bar{w}$ in 1965 are used as the fixed weights for the series. Since the increase in K is much higher than that in L, and there is a rising trend in w, but not in r, the curvature of $\bar{r}K + \bar{w}L$ will be much steeper when the 1960 weight is applied than when the 1965 weight is used. In our tentative computation, when the 1960 weight is used, the 1971 index in manufacturing corporations as a whole will be 1.3999, while, as Table 10 shows, in the 1965-weight case it will be 1.6395. Since 1965 is almost in the middle of this period, the 1965 weight is used here so that any biases which may arise from the differences in the year will be minimized.

Table 10. Technology Level (Total Productivity Method)

	1960	1961	1962	1963	1964	1965	1966	1967	1968	1969	1970	1971	Annual avg. increase (%)
Flour milling	1.0000	1.0989	1.1771	1.2869	1.2956	1.3667	1.4024	1.2932	1.3812	1.5038	1.6363	1.5709	4.19
Edible oil	1.0000	0.7993	0.8138	1.0931	1.0359	1.0492	0.9247	0.8167	0.9961	1.2845	1.5541	1.0832	0.73
Cotton spinning	1.0000	0.9685	0.9428	0.9946	1.1128	1.1254	1.1445	1.1991	1.3382	1.4691	1.5555	1.6244	4.51
Synthetic textiles	1.0000	1.0851	1.1333	1.3320	1.2960	1.2687	1.5256	1.8375	1.9561	2.1609	2.1668	2.0903	6.93
Paper and pulp	1.0000	1.0301	1.0288	1.2459	1.2709	1.2742	1.3556	1.3911	1.4330	1.4730	1.5408	1.5358	3.98
Chemicals	1.0000	1.1234	1.2665	1.3228	1.4719	1.5778	1.6007	1.6676	1.7745	1.8706	1.8534	1.7993	5.48
Drugs & medicines	1.0000	1.1250	1.2308	1.2829	1.3251	1.2994	1.3621	1.4995	1.6272	1.8021	1.8779	1.8020	5.50
Glass	1.0000	1.0032	1.0419	1.1538	1.5249	1.4596	1.5728	1.6307	1.6930	1.7730	1.7951	1.8069	5.53
Cement	1.0000	0.9808	1.1695	1.1252	1.0218	1.0804	1.2819	1.3748	1.4040	1.3807	1.3063	1.3477	2.75
Petroleum refining	1.0000	0.8251	0.7857	0.8672	0.7259	0.9809	0.9853	0.9082	0.9334	1.0479	0.9856	0.8604	—1.36
Blast furnace	1.0000	1.0416	1.0158	1.1990	1.2723	1.2231	1.3234	1.3021	1.3196	1.4102	1.4003	1.3982	3.03
Open and electric furnaces	1.0000	0.9066	0.8489	1.1655	1.0735	0.9616	1.4725	1.3523	1.2509	1.6036	1.4349	1.1082	0.94
Special steel	1.0000	1.0808	1.1450	1.1799	1.2069	1.1557	1.4007	1.6067	1.6800	1.8951	1.8595	1.6620	4.73
Non-ferrous metals	1.0000	1.1418	1.3095	1.3956	1.4449	1.4990	1.3170	1.5067	1.4352	1.6110	1.3999	1.7047	4.97
Electric wire & cable	1.0000	0.9920	0.9826	1.0849	1.1375	1.1329	1.0588	1.1379	1.0694	0.9956	1.0706	1.2521	2.07
Machine tools	1.0000	1.2432	1.1979	1.1525	1.0806	0.9465	1.0348	1.3179	1.4559	1.5699	1.6805	1.5315	3.95
Bearings	1.0000	1.1048	1.1957	1.2608	1.3809	1.4261	1.5317	1.1860	2.0110	2.1522	2.2945	2.0724	6.85
Automobiles	1.0000	1.1268	1.2118	1.2813	1.2561	1.3021	1.3014	1.3361	1.3313	1.3768	1.2918	1.3172	2.54
Heavy electric equipment	1.0000	1.0855	1.1092	1.1051	1.1106	1.1179	1.2577	1.3772	1.5268	1.7020	1.8541	1.9509	6.27
Light electrical appliances	1.0000	1.0881	1.2048	1.2928	1.3812	1.4341	1.7049	1.9013	2.0832	2.3197	2.4271	2.5431	8.86
Optical instruments	1.0000	1.1355	1.2235	1.3359	1.4014	1.5415	1.9357	2.2200	2.3986	2.7749	2.9793	2.7834	9.75
Total	1.0000	1.0625	1.0964	1.1972	1.2329	1.2466	1.3495	1.4282	1.4965	1.6187	1.6345	1.6395	4.60

Not: Computed from the equation $U/(\bar{r}K + \bar{w}L)$, where $\bar{r}$ and $\bar{w}$ are the 1965 figures, assumed constant for 1960–71.

Table 11. Technology Level (Residual Method)

	1960	1961	1962	1963	1964	1965	1966	1967	1968	1969	1970	1971	Annual avg. increase (%)
Flour milling	1.0000	1.0943	1.1607	1.2705	1.2723	1.3449	1.3838	1.2753	1.3834	1.5278	1.6971	1.6579	4.70
Edible oil	1.0000	0.7791	0.7851	1.0820	1.0120	1.0256	0.9069	0.8288	1.0935	1.4184	1.6973	1.1991	1.66
Cotton spinning	1.0000	0.9543	0.9182	0.9656	1.0845	1.0960	1.1120	1.1663	1.3074	1.4414	1.5411	1.6340	4.57
Synthetic textiles	1.0000	1.0657	1.0967	1.2922	1.2409	1.2088	1.4559	1.7686	1.8966	2.1210	1.1617	2.1288	7.11
Paper and pulp	1.0000	1.0223	1.0134	1.2222	1.2458	1.2463	1.3299	1.3677	1.4224	1.4870	1.5661	1.5893	4.30
Chemicals	1.0000	1.1145	1.2501	1.2911	1.4388	1.5456	1.5677	1.6492	1.7842	1.9317	1.9555	1.9291	6.15
Drugs & medicines	1.0000	1.1268	1.2396	1.2830	1.3239	1.2964	1.3648	1.5175	1.6711	1.8959	1.9952	1.9126	6.07
Glass	1.0000	0.9905	1.0345	1.1446	1.5482	1.4818	1.6029	1.6755	1.7678	1.8885	1.9117	1.9346	6.18
Cement	1.0000	0.9577	1.1243	1.0555	0.9536	1.0014	1.1982	1.2816	1.3093	1.2987	1.2310	1.2789	2.26
Petroleum refining	1.0000	0.8015	0.7497	0.8376	0.6841	0.9342	0.9412	0.8662	0.8949	1.0282	0.9817	0.8484	-1.48
Blast furnace	1.0000	1.0289	1.0037	1.1738	1.2352	1.1823	1.2867	1.2656	1.2931	1.4144	1.4123	1.4195	3.24
Open and electric furnace	1.0000	0.8799	0.8323	1.1387	1.0345	0.9052	1.4345	1.2862	1.1614	1.5461	1.3743	1.0849	0.74
Special steel	1.0000	1.0565	1.1186	1.1143	1.1271	1.0759	1.3044	1.5003	1.5644	1.7873	1.7730	1.5895	4.30
Non-ferrous metals	1.0000	1.1173	1.2482	1.3139	1.3596	1.4062	1.2559	1.4401	1.3747	1.5879	1.3918	1.8070	5.53
Electric wire & cable	1.0000	0.9749	0.9689	1.0684	1.1236	1.1189	1.0447	1.1412	1.0815	1.0211	1.0761	1.3239	2.58
Machine tools	1.0000	1.1558	1.0772	1.0127	0.9497	0.8494	0.9207	1.1885	1.3103	1.3931	1.4908	1.3641	2.86
Bearings	1.0000	1.0693	1.1211	1.1636	1.2485	1.2850	1.3815	1.6847	1.8953	2.0651	2.2489	2.0413	6.70
Automobiles	1.0000	1.1254	1.2121	1.2866	1.2498	1.2970	1.2967	1.3483	1.3583	1.4488	1.3955	1.4736	3.59
Heavy electric equipment	1.0000	1.0921	1.1124	1.1103	1.1176	1.1254	1.2687	1.4070	1.5906	1.8263	2.0356	2.1724	7.31
Light electrical appliances	1.0000	1.0873	1.1903	1.2823	1.3654	1.4154	1.7153	1.9470	2.1721	2.4983	2.7059	2.8802	10.09
Optical instruments	1.0000	1.1358	1.2152	1.3367	1.4081	1.5392	1.9526	2.2657	2.4741	2.9452	3.2409	3.0134	10.55
Total	1.0000	1.0516	1.0767	1.1715	1.2038	1.2155	1.3209	1.4110	1.4952	1.6558	1.7008	1.7379	5.15

However, in the residual method of Table 11, the increase rates for K and L in each year are first averaged with the weights of relative gross income distributive shares of capital and labor, and then the average is deducted from each year's $\Delta Y/Y$ ($\Delta A/A = \Delta Y/Y - \alpha\Delta K/K - \beta\Delta L/L$). In this sense, it is the link relative of the $\Delta A/A$ series, for which each year's figure depends upon the weights variable from year to year.

In Figure 2, the estimates of technical progress from Tables 10 and 11 are drawn, together with the two indexes shown in Table 9, designated as the A series in the productivity function with dummy variables of "years" or "years plus industries." In this chart, the very close movements of the A series estimated by the residual method and the total productivity index can be recognized except for 1970 and 1971. However, the two other series in Table 9 derived from the productivity function, with the dummy variable "years" or "years plus industries," indicate extremely divergent results (in 1971 the former is 1.9980 and the latter is 1.4760). The estimates by the total productivity and residual methods are located just in between, as Figure 2 shows.

When the function $Y = AK^\alpha L^\beta e^{\tau t}$ is computed, an extreme instability of the coefficient τ emerges. Seemingly, a similar instability of the coefficients attached to the "years" dummy can also be found in the above pooled function. Therefore, subsequent addition of the dummy "industries" considerably changed the coefficients.

In this sense, the results computed by the total productivity and residual methods seem to be much more reliable, and therefore further analysis will be based upon these results.

In terms of the average annual percentage rate of increase in total productivity indicated on the right side of Table 10, those industries with increases higher than 6% are optical instruments (9.75%), light electrical appliances (8.86%), synthetic textiles (6.93%), bearings (6.85%), and heavy electric equipment (6.27%). However, Figure 3 makes clear the fact that in general these industries with relatively higher rates of total productivity growth are located lower than the rising straight dotted lines in A and B. In other words, the percentage rates of increase in total input, capital, and labor in these industries is less than the general average, and the growth rate of capital input is less than that of output.

In Figure 3, not only the growth rates of capital but also of labor input are lower than their corresponding output growth rates in synthetic textiles, light electrical appliances, and optical instruments. However, in the case of heavy electric equipment, although the capital input growth rate is below the general average, its labor growth rate surpasses the general average tendency. But heavy electric equipment

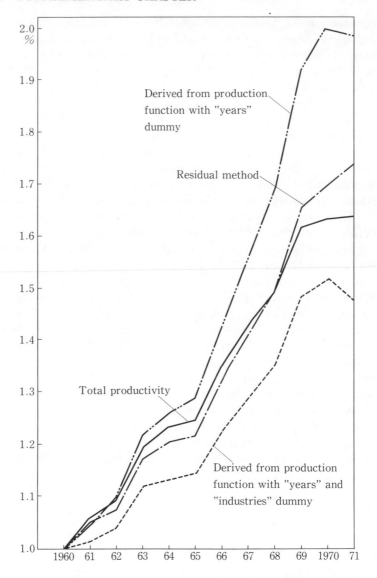

Figure 2. Alternative estimates of technical progress (manufacturing).

is relatively capital-intensive compared to light electrical appliances, so total productivity may have been more sensitive to capital growth than to labor growth. In the bearings industry, the capital input growth rate exceeded the general tendency indicated by the dotted line, but the labor input growth was below the general average line. Since the latter

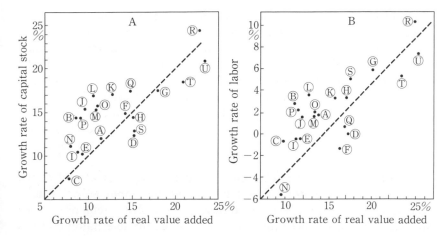

Figure 3. Inter-industry relations of *Y*, *K*, and *L* for 1960–71.

A— Flour milling	L— Open and electric furnaces
B— Edible oil	M— Special steel
C— Cotton spinning	N— Non-ferrous metals
D— Synthetic textiles	O— Electric wire and cable
E— Paper and pulp	P— Machine tools
F— Chemicals	Q— Bearings
G— Drugs and medicines	R— Automobiles
H— Glass	S— Heavy electric equipment
I— Cement	T— Light electrical appliances
J— Petroleum refining	U— Optical instruments
K— Blast furnace	

tendency surpassed the former, the total productivity growth showed a relatively high figure.

In those industries in which the total productivity growth was relatively lower, however—for example, edible oil (0.73%), petroleum oil (–1.36%), open and electric furnace steel (0.94%), electric wire and cable (2.07%), and automobiles (2.54%)—capital and labor input growth show a higher pace than the general tendency in other industries.

It should be noted that our observation merely relates to 1960–71, a period including the investment super-boom (1966–70), and therefore, when compared to the earlier investment stagnation period (1962–65), capital input growth may be overemphasized. Moreover, this phase still belonged to the period of high-pitched growth at 10% per annum. Consequently, the characteristics of the so-called "input-increasing phase" of prosperity emphasized by Joseph Shumpeter may have prevailed during this period. To put it differently, compared to the "output-increasing phase," the growth of capital input may have been accelerated, and therefore the technical progress computed as a residual may have been underestimated, particularly in petroleum refining, iron and steel, and electric wire and cable. However, in the estimate of capital stock, construction in process is excluded beforehand, with at least the uncompleted capital stock not included. Moreover, even if the fixed investment as a flow concept oscillated in an unstable way, capital equipment as a stock concept may have indicated a more moderate movement. Consequently, even if the above reservation must be kept in mind, we believe most of our analysis still holds.

Figure 4 indicates the relationship between the rates of technical progress (in terms of total productivity) and the output growth rates among industries. Except in six industries—petroleum refining, open and electric furnaces, blast furnace, electric wire and cable, automobiles, and edible oil—the industries examined scatter around the free-hand straight line, the slope of which (the ratio of technical progress to output growth) is shown by 0.4 vs. 1.0. Although the possibility of overcapacity may have existed in most of these industries, the automobile industry was an exception. The automobile industry was one of the most rapidly

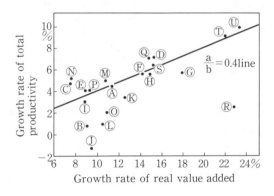

Figure 4. Technical progress and output growth by industry for 1960–71.

A—	Flour milling	L—	Open and electric furnaces
B—	Edible oil	M—	Special steel
C—	Cotton spinning	N—	Non-ferrous metals
D—	Synthetic textiles	O—	Electric wire and cable
E—	Paper and pulp	P—	Machine tools
F—	Chemicals	Q—	Bearings
G—	Drugs and medicines	R—	Automobiles
H—	Glass	S—	Heavy electric equipment
I—	Cement	T—	Light electrical appliances
J—	Petroleum refining	U—	Optical instruments
K—	Blast furnace		

growing industries: its annual growth rate was 22.8% in terms of output and 24.3% in terms of capital input. The 1970s saw further rapid technical advance in the introduction of industrial robots, etc., but in the 1960s no tremendous improvement in the production process or new specific equipment was introduced, as compared to the 1950s. However, the 1960s seem to have been a period of quantitative expansion in terms of output, domestic demand, and exports. If some technical improvements occurred in the 1960s, they had to be "embodied" in capital equipment.

In general, relative prices will tend to fall in those industries in which comparative labor productivities increase. This is true when the capital-output ratios are not very different among various industries, and therefore the changes in the unit capital costs will influence the unit total costs of all industries in the same ways. Actually, the capital-output ratio varies from industry to industry. Insofar as the concept of total (factor) productivity is prevalently used now, it is of some interest to explore to what extent an inter-industry correlation exists between the rates of change in total productivities and those of product prices.

Figure 5 indicates the negative relationship $P/P = 1.0796 - 0.4946$ $(\dot{A}/A)$. This means that about half of the inter-industry differences in increasing total productivity will be absorbed in relative price decreases. A low R^2 may cast doubt on this finding. However, it cannot be denied that variation in total productivity will cause alterations not only in relative prices but also in factor prices (e.g. wage rate) and excess profits among industries. It is not unusual, therefore, that the partial correlation is not high, but with price structure among industries flexible even in the medium term, the longer the period of our analysis, the more distinct an inverse correlation will be obtained between total productivity changes and price changes.

Elasticity of Substitution and CES Production Function

Since J. R. Hicks used the concept of the elasticity of substitution in his *Theory of Wages*, it has now become prevalent and has even been empirically verified. Simply, the elasticity of substitution is the relation of the percentage change in the factor proportions (e.g. capital-labor ratio K/L) which will arise due to the percentage change in the factor-price ratio (e.g. wage rate/rate of capital return w/r). If the elasticity of substitution is unity, an increase in w/r will cause an equi-proportional rise of K/L, and therefore the relative income distributive share wL/rK will remain constant. If the elasticity of substitution is beyond unity, the increase in K/L will be greater than that in w/r, and therefore wL/rK

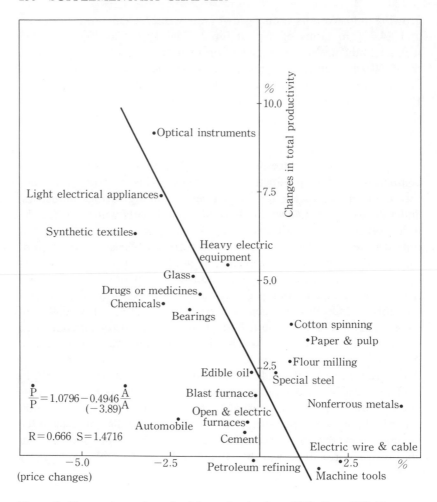

Figure 5. Changes in total productivity and price from 1960–62 to 1969–71.

will decrease. In the same way, when the elasticity of substitution is less than unity, wL/rK will increase.

The so-called CES production function (the production function in which a constant elasticity of substitution is implied) takes the following formula:

$$Y = [aK^{-\rho} + bL^{-\rho}]^{\frac{1}{-\rho}} \tag{5}$$

where a and b are the distributive parameters, and $\rho = (1 - \sigma)/\sigma$ or $\sigma = L/(1 + \rho)$ when ρ is the elasticity of substitution. Converting

(5) to the form $Y^{-\rho} = aK^{-\rho} + bL^{-\rho}$, and differentiating it by K, we obtain

$$(-\rho)Y^{-(1+\rho)}\frac{\partial Y}{\partial K} = (-\rho)aK^{-(1+\rho)}.$$

In this way, under perfect competition where equality between factor prices and the values of marginal productivities prevail, we derive

$$r = \frac{\partial Y}{\partial K} = a\left(\frac{Y}{K}\right)^{1+\rho} = a\left(\frac{Y}{K}\right)^{1/\sigma}$$

$$w = \frac{\partial Y}{\partial L} = b\left(\frac{Y}{L}\right)^{1+\rho} = b\left(\frac{Y}{L}\right)^{1/\sigma}$$

$$\frac{w}{r} = \frac{a}{b}\left(\frac{K}{L}\right)^{1/\sigma} \tag{6}$$

$$\frac{wL}{rK} = \frac{b}{a}\left(\frac{K}{L}\right)^{(1-\sigma)/\sigma}$$

In equation (6) explaining wL/K,

If $\sigma = 1$, then $(1-\sigma)/\sigma - 0$. $\therefore$ $wL/rK = $ constant,

If $\sigma = 0.8$, then $(1-\sigma)/\sigma = 0.25$. $\therefore$ wL/rK will rise,

If $\sigma = 1.2$, then $(1-\sigma)/\sigma = -0.167$. $\therefore$ wL/rK will decrease.

Bearing in mind the equations in (6), we can use any of the following equations for the estimation of the elasticity of substitution σ:

$$\log(Y/L) - -\sigma\log b + \sigma\log w$$

$$\log(Y/K) = -\sigma\log a + \sigma\log r \tag{7}$$

$$\log(K/L) = -\sigma\log(b/a) + \sigma\log(w/r).$$

In the case of the Cobb-Douglas function under perfect competition, the distributive share will be equal to $\alpha/(\alpha + \beta)$ or $\beta/(\alpha + \beta)$, and therefore unit elasticity of substitution is always implied. However, with CES production function, opportunities for other than unity are also implied insofar as the elasticity of substitution is constant. In this sense, the CES production function is understood as more general.

From the time-series data for 1960–71, the three regression equations $(w \rightarrow Y/L; r \rightarrow Y/K; w/r \rightarrow K/L)$ are estimated, and they are shown in Tables 12, 13, and 14, respectively. In manufacturing as a whole, the

Table 12. Elasticity of Substitution Estimated from Time Series (1)

$$\log\left(\frac{Y}{L}\right) = -\sigma \log \alpha + \sigma \log (w)$$

	Constant term	σ	t-ratio	R^2	Standard error	D. W. ratio	Labor share
Flour milling	0.30948	*0.81512	(27.583)	0.9857	0.01671	1.478	0.4172
Edible oil	0.33588	0.73931	(7.964)	0.8502	0.06625	1.712	0.3513
Cotton spinning	0.23714	*0.85759	(18.093)	0.9674	0.02542	1.553	0.5290
Synthetic textiles	0.43010	*0.93837	(22.778)	0.9792	0.03412	0.956	0.3481
Paper and pulp	0.34339	*0.90779	(27.476)	0.9856	0.01879	1.634	0.4186
Chemicals	0.38378	*1.11129	(34.950)	0.9911	0.02235	0.594	0.4515
Drugs and Medicines	0.39625	*0.83944	(20.854)	0.9753	0.02832	0.932	0.3373
Glass	0.35756	*0.98892	(20.232)	0.9738	0.3210	1.476	0.4349
Cement	0.44418	0.88343	(11.103)	0.9175	0.04571	1.285	0.3142
Petroleum refining	0.59107	0.97457	(11.496)	0.9226	0.04932	1.920	0.2475
Blast furnace	0.36824	*1.04108	(19.414)	0.9716	0.02860	2.041	0.4429
Open and electric furnaces	0.32953	0.94853	(7.008)	0.8139	0.07979	2.083	0.4494
Special steel	0.26140	*0.86797	(11.971)	0.9282	0.04820	1.365	0.4998
Non-ferrous metals	0.27286	*1.13899	(12.972)	0.9383	0.04394	1.509	0.5760
Electric wire and cable	0.30571	*0.83177	(15.578)	0.9565	0.02730	1.516	0.4290
Machine tools	0.24604	0.64834	(4.384)	0.6236	0.08286	0.742	0.4174
Bearings	0.33176	*1.00148	(29.951)	0.9879	0.02589	0.711	0.4664
Automobiles	0.42869	*0.77058	(19.240)	0.9711	0.02601	1.032	0.2778
Heavy electric equipment	0.27414	*0.79802	(18.256)	0.9680	0.02935	0.750	0.4534
Light electrical appliances	0.35676	*0.90272	(27.411)	0.9856	0.02901	1.040	0.4025
Optical instruments	0.22568	*1.03985	(37.033)	0.9920	0.02206	1.737	0.6067
Total	0.35515	*0.92891	(33.282)	0.9902	0.01765	1.454	0.4146

* indicates the value of σ, R^2 of which is highest in Tables 12–14.

elasticity of substitution is computed as 0.92891 in the "$w \rightarrow Y/L$" way, as 0.21908 in the "$r \rightarrow Y/K$" method, and as 0.86168 in the "$w/r \rightarrow K/L$" direction. One of the major reasons underlying such divergent results may be that when the explained variable is Y/K, its variation over time is extremely limited (i.e., its reciprocal K/Y in manufacturing was 2.6082 in 1960, but 2.6469 in 1971). In such a case, the extent of correlation will naturally be less, while in the cases where the explained variable is Y/L or K/L, the inter-temporal variations are considerably greater, so R^2 will tend to be higher.

The distributive parameters a, b, and b/a can be derived from $\sigma \log a$,

Table 13. Elasticity of Substitution Estimated from Time Series (2)

$$\log\left(\frac{Y}{K}\right) = -\sigma \log a + \sigma \log (r)$$

	Constant term	σ	t-ratio	R^2	Standard error	D. W. ratio	Capital share
Flour milling	−0.09345	0.39742	(6.487)	0.7888	0.01179	1.185	1.1785
Edible oil	0.01384	*0.50077	(12.116)	0.9298	0.02050	0.469	0.9383
Cotton spinning	−0.17367	0.39338	(2.400)	0.3020	0.02527	0.449	2.7363
Synthetic textiles	0.13924	0.91924	(8.531)	0.8671	0.02324	0.615	0.7056
Paper and pulp	−0.23887	0.43584	(5.814)	0.7489	0.00820	0.735	3.5324
Chemicals	−0.22026	0.38731	(3.589)	0.5193	0.01207	0.727	3.7042
Drugs and medicines	0.10377	0.58228	(1.868)	0.1845	0.02985	0.154	0.6634
Glass	0.06295	0.69474	(6.241)	0.7753	0.01986	0.847	0.8117
Cement	−0.20006	*0.55600	(17.391)	0.9648	0.00637	1.519	2.2899
Petroleum refining	−0.02747	*0.79358	(22.570)	0.9788	0.00791	1.340	1.0830
Blast furnace	0.06635	0.76528	(4.937)	0.6800	0.02076	1.129	0.8190
Open and electric furnaces	−0.10552	*0.50802	(8.251)	0.8591	0.02905	0.584	1.6135
Special steel	−0.20109	0.28750	(7.710)	0.8416	0.01246	1.833	5.0055
Non-ferrous metals	0.23688	0.84653	(2.975)	0.4165	0.05845	0.608	0.5250
Electric wire and cable	0.13624	0.72157	(8.051)	0.8350	0.02662	1.289	0.6474
Machine tools	0.02774	*0.31053	(6.908)	0.8094	0.02386	1.008	0.8141
Bearings	0.02534	0.52016	(16.460)	0.9608	0.00474	1.723	0.8939
Automobiles	−0.02249	0.53525	(14.199)	0.9480	0.00732	0.574	1.1016
Heavy electric equipment	0.20862	0.81509	(1.502)	0.1025	0.04888	0.262	0.5547
Light electrical appliances	0.25197	1.06496	(7.206)	0.8224	0.03032	0.870	0.5800
Optical instruments	0.28332	0.65342	(6.727)	0.8009	0.02422	1.352	0.3685
Total	−0.27010	0.21908	(3.098)	0.4388	0.00517	0.468	17.096

* indicates the value of σ, R^2 of which is highest in Tables 12–14.

$\sigma \log b$, and $\sigma \log (b/a)$, respectively, and these are also listed in Tables 12–14. However, in the case of Table 13, where R^2 is low, $a = 17.096$, an extremely abnormal figure, is obtained in manufacturing. In Table 12, where the explained variable is Y/L, b (labor's relative share) is estimated as 0.4146. This suggests that the results in Table 13 are unrealistic. Since the computed labor income share in Table 12 is 0.4146, the capital income share is 0.5854 ($= 1 − 0.4146$). The difference between this 0.5854 and the capital income share in Table 14, 0.6253, is not considerable.

The elasticity of substitution can also be computed from cross-section data year by year for 1960–71. Tables 15 and 16 compute this by applying two formulas: $\log (Y/L) = -\sigma \log b + \sigma \log (w)$ and $\log (Y/K) = -\sigma \log a + \sigma \log (r)$. There are three points to be noticed, as compared to the results derived from time-series data.

1) The elasticity of substitution computed from cross-section data is close to unity (for example, the twelve-year average of σ is 1.1536 (Table 15) or 0.9930 (Table 16). These values are a bit higher than those derived from time-series data (0.92891 or 0.86168 in Tables 12 and 14). This may reflect the fact that in the time-series function, the causal relation from factor proportion variation to factor price changes seems to be more important than the reversed causation, particularly in the process of technology transfer from abroad. However, in the case of the cross-section, the causational relationship between factor price changes and factor proportion variation may have been established over a long span of time.

2) The relative income share for labor, derived from the regression equations, is generally higher in the cross-section than in the time-series case. For instance, the 12-year average labor's share computed in the $w \rightarrow Y/L$ direction in Table 12 (time-series case) is 0.4146, whereas in Table 15 (cross-section case) it is 0.4913, a bit higher.

3) In the case of time series, the regression equation ($r \rightarrow Y/K$) is not usually statistically significant, but in the cross-section case R^2 is higher in the direction of $r \rightarrow Y/K$ rather than of $w \rightarrow Y/L$. This means that the inter-industry variation of Y/K is greater than that of Y/L. Nevertheless, the time-series variation of Y/K is so small. In addition, the fact that the inter-industry variation of r is greater than that of w may affect the statistical results.

We have tested some other formulas presented by T. C. Liu, G. H. Hildebrand, and Ryuzo Sato, but with varying results, so in this English version other such explorations are omitted. Our major impression is that the elasticity of substitution which is statistically significant is not generally different from unity. In the 21 segments of manufacturing, 14 industries show elasticities of substitution ranging from 0.82 to 1.14, while 7 show elasticities of less than 0.79. However, on the whole, the elasticity of substitution seems close to unity in manufacturing.

Seemingly, the CES function is more general than the Cobb-Douglas and other functions. However, in the computation of a, b, and σ, the distributive parameters a and b are a kind of actual averaged relative shares of factor incomes. They differ considerably from the elasticity coefficients α and β computed by the Cobb-Doublas function. In the Cobb-Douglas function, the parameters α and β are computed, whether or not it be equal to the actual distributive share. However, in the CES

Table 14. Elasticity of Substitution Estimated from Time Series (3)

$$\log\left(\frac{K}{L}\right) = -\sigma \log(b/a) + \sigma \log(w/\gamma)$$

	Constant term	w/r	t-ratio	R^2	Standard error	D. W. ratio	Capital share	Labor share
Flour milling	0.21628	0.59032	(19.761)	0.9725	0.02538	1.559	0.6729	0.3271
Edible oil	0.30586	0.54398	(7.832)	0.8458	0.07312	1.530	0.7849	0.2151
Cotton spinning	0.12105	0.67379	(9.597)	0.8923	0.04157	1.400	0.6020	0.3980
Synthetic textiles	0.33121	0.83138	(11.772)	0.9260	0.04914	0.839	0.7145	0.2855
Paper and pulp	0.23527	0.82378	(17.361)	0.9647	0.02995	1.563	0.6587	0.3413
Chemicals	0.01983	1.17638	(17.517)	0.9653	0.04471	0.565	0.5907	0.4903
Drugs and medicines	0.25293	0.69730	(11.714)	0.9253	0.04113	0.866	0.6975	0.3025
Glass	0.15957	0.91418	(9.417)	0.8885	0.05630	1.379	0.5991	0.4009
Cement	0.44304	0.77931	(8.827)	0.8749	0.06200	1.182	0.7873	0.2127
Petroleum refining	0.54246	0.89548	(10.170)	0.9030	0.06195	1.774	0.8014	0.1986
Blast furnace	0.10337	1.02700	(12.579)	0.9346	0.05213	1.990	0.5577	0.4423
Open and electric furnaces	0.27684	0.69027	(4.866)	0.6734	0.13071	1.560	0.7157	0.2843
Special steel	0.15428	0.65812	(6.642)	0.7967	0.08892	1.261	0.6318	0.3682
Non-ferrous metals	−0.19006	1.15706	(7.305)	0.8264	0.10332	1.364	0.4066	0.5934
Electric wire and cable	0.13366	0.77993	(11.805)	0.9264	0.05217	1.392	0.5974	0.4026
Machine tools	0.13894	0.39790	(3.289)	0.4716	0.11802	0.693	0.6908	0.3092
Bearings	0.06929	0.96443	(15.418)	0.9556	0.04837	0.699	0.5413	0.4587
Automobiles	0.36616	0.70310	(18.235)	0.9679	0.03161	1.082	0.7684	0.2316
Heavy electric equipment	0.13714	0.55896	(7.667)	0.8401	0.04678	0.683	0.6376	0.3624
Light electrical appliances	0.13934	0.76444	(12.452)	0.9334	0.04469	1.028	0.6034	0.3966
Optical instruments	−0.19572	1.06763	(10.605)	0.9102	0.05934	1.690	0.3960	0.6040
Total	0.19172	0.86168	(19.447)	0.9717	0.02948	1.386	0.6253	0.3747

Table 15. Elasticity of Substitution Estimated from Cross-Section (1)

$$\log\left(\frac{Y}{L}\right) = -\sigma \log a + \sigma \log (w)$$

	Constant term	w	t-ratio	R^2	Standard error	D. W. ratio	Labor share b
1960	0.44721	1.15424	(5.781)	0.6185	0.1042	1.768	0.4098
1961	0.38187	1.01455	(5.848)	0.6240	0.0879	1.730	0.4203
1962	0.34084	0.95169	(4.888)	0.5337	0.1005	1.678	0.4384
1963	0.39002	1.00740	(5.957)	0.6329	0.0948	1.879	0.4334
1964	0.38030	1.12534	(7.446)	0.7313	0.0785	1.526	0.4593
1965	0.36852	1.28724	(5.897)	0.6281	0.1053	1.715	0.5173
1966	0.38130	1.31777	(6.866)	0.6976	0.0933	1.701	0.5136
1967	0.36399	1.09458	(5.826)	0.6222	0.0923	1.231	0.4650
1968	0.35227	1.08030	(6.013)	0.6374	0.0890	1.257	0.4720
1969	0.35022	1.20653	(7.293)	0.7230	0.0787	1.507	0.5125
1970	0.28815	1.37822	(7.543)	0.7365	0.0795	1.440	0.6179
1971	0.24068	1.22485	(5.380)	0.5829	0.0898	1.185	0.6361

Table 16. Elasticity of Substitution Estimated from Cross-Section (2)

$$\log\left(\frac{Y}{K}\right) = -\sigma \log a + \sigma \log (r)$$

	Constant term	r	t-ratio	R^2	Standard error	D. W. ratio	Capital share a
1960	0.22051	0.96243	(10.353)	0.8415	0.07912	1.420	0.5900
1961	0.21661	0.94867	(12.981)	0.8933	0.06847	1.493	0.5911
1962	0.20918	0.90244	(10.788)	0.8523	0.08031	1.344	0.5864
1963	0.24978	0.99896	(12.480)	0.8856	0.06857	1.735	0.5623
1964	0.28160	1.03595	(14.714)	0.9151	0.06238	1.449	0.5348
1965	0.25549	0.94032	(8.396)	0.7765	0.10138	1.444	0.5349
1966	0.29061	1.03327	(10.147)	0.8360	0.08506	1.696	0.5233
1967	0.28015	1.03208	(13.007)	0.8937	0.07238	1.183	0.5353
1968	0.27396	1.01570	(14.627)	0.9141	0.06739	1.176	0.5374
1969	0.27381	1.04099	(17.576)	0.9390	0.05715	1.742	0.5457
1970	0.28735	1.02986	(17.411)	0.9379	0.06137	1.627	0.5260
1971	0.31217	0.97544	(11.462)	0.8670	0.09175	1.195	0.4786

function, the distributive parameters are just a replica of the actual shares, assuming perfect competition. Starting from the actual shares, the relationship between the percentage changes of factor proportion and those of factor prices is inductively quantified. The numerical values may vary due to differences in market structure, industry, size of firm, and the developmental stage. However, the elasticity of substitution is a mere *ex post facto* empirical formulation of a quantifiable relationship. The CES function has a high generality in its formal structure, but its logical structure is simply an empirical reflection of actual phenomena, and therefore may not present any new theory of income distribution.

Consequently, the merit of our study, if any, may exist in the exploration of the interrelationships between cross-section and time-series production in the process of rapid technical progress, rather than in the computation of the recent more sophisticated forms.

INDEX